WHITE SAILS BECAME ME:
MEMOIRS OF A SEAFARING HERITAGE

WHITE SAILS BECAME ME: MEMOIRS OF A SEAFARING HERITAGE

A MODERN-DAY RENAISSANCE MAN TAKES YOU ON A JOURNEY LIVING MORE ADVENTURE THAN MOST PEOPLE DARE TO DREAM

by

Nicholas F. Starace II

Bascom Hill Publishing Group
Minneapolis, MN

Bascom Hill Publishing Group

212 3rd Avenue North, Suite 290

Minneapolis, MN 55401

612.455.2293

www.bascomhillpublishing.com

ISBN - 978-1-935098-48-5

ISBN - 1-935098-48-9

LCCN - 2010935521

Editing by Sarah Cypher of The Three Penny Editor

Photographic editing and arrangements by Dorine M. Starace

Photo credits where applicable appear in photo captions

Back cover sketch from National Maritime Historical Society magazine, *Sea History*

Some images from Wikipedia, the free encyclopedia

Cover replica of *Racing Home - The Cutty Sark* by Felix Rosenstiel's

Widow & Son Limited, London

For more information about this book and the author,

visit http://www.whitesailsbecameme.com

Cover Design by Alan Pranke

Typeset by Sophie Chi

Printed in the United States of America

Signature Book Printing, www.sbpbooks.com

DEDICATION

This book is dedicated first to the memory of my son Nicholas III, who never had a chance at a full life, but in the twenty-six years he was with us demonstrated how much he had to offer. I wish he was dedicating a book of his to me, instead of the other way around, but fate had other plans.

And to the *grandest* people in my life—this book is dedicated to Grandfather Michael who, very early in my life, cast the mold for what my life would become. To the three lads who bring joy into my life every day of their lives: grandsons Benjamin, Brian, and Nicholas IV.

Lastly, to my daughter Dorine and son Michael, who have filled my life with great pride in their character and achievements.

TABLE OF CONTENTS

FOREWORD

The sea has sparked the imagination of mankind like no other feature of our planet. Mountains we can climb. Deserts we can traverse. But the sea is unconquerable, incomprehensible and omnipotent. Yet the great salty deep is also mystically attractive. We can sit for hours watching the onrushing waves. The ever changing seascape complements our thinking processes. There is great pleasure in reading a book by the shore. And from Homer to Herman Melville great writers have known that nothing engages a reader like the epic struggle between man and this mighty primordial element.

Nick Starace has presented us with the story of his life interwoven with his interaction with the sea. From his childhood days fishing with his father off the coast of Long Island, to his seagoing days and currently as a licensed U.S. Coast Guard Captain, Nick has recounted the extraordinary life of a sailor with briny blood in his veins and a character as straight as the masthead. Nick's education at the United States Merchant Marine Academy, his service as an officer on the legendary liner, the SS *United States*, along with naval action in the Taiwan Straits during the Quemoy artillery barrage and years building leviathan supertankers around the world have provided grist for many a fine yarn. But there is more to this book. The author has given us an insightful, running commentary on the events which transpired in the macrocosm during his lifetime.

Memoirs are among my favorites in the world of *belles lettres*. It is a joy to read the story of life's adventures in the words of the one who lived them. From the perspective of a historian, an autobiography is a primary source. It is evidence without the inherent distortion of hearsay. At various times in my life I have devoured the books which great men and women have written about themselves. Almost every writer on historical subjects has an ax to grind. When we read autobiography we don't have to puzzle about the writer's subjectivity.

Alas, in our time the memoirs of statesmen have been largely debased. Ghost writers have usurped the voices of the principal actors on the world's stage. Thus when we read the autobiography of a contemporary political figure we are taking in nothing more that an authorized biography. We look in vain for the personal touch, the unexpected insight. Furthermore, today's state memoirs are crafted with consummate political correctness and complete avoidance of fundamental controversy. Their historical significance is often nil. For this reason the serious student of today's autobiography looks to the writings of keen observers, regardless of their immediacy to the sources of power in society. The *Diaries of Samuel Pepys* and the wonderful *Education of Henry Adams* are great, early exemplars of brilliant personal accounts penned by sensitive witnesses to history. It is to this group of observant memoirists that Nick Starace belongs. He has lived through the halcyon days of America's nationhood and into the era of faceless globalization where our national identity has been effaced in a universal marketplace for oligarchs. Nick Starace's social, political and economic analyses are always interesting and well reasoned. They form a delightful point of departure for generalized discussion. Were I a professor of Contemporary American Studies, Nick Starace's autobiography would be an important part of my syllabus for the senior colloquium.

I have known Nick Starace for a quarter of a century. We share a passion for fine automobiles and other things mechanical, as well as an undying affection for ships, those saucy conveyances which have allowed us and our ancestors to traverse the great waters. Nick is a deep thinker and it has been a pleasure to converse with him about the meaning of things. I have been glad to count him as a friend. In reading Nick Starace's fine volume I have come to know many personal details of his life which he had not shared with me before. Becoming acquainted with the details of his diverse experiences I was struck with a sense of inevitability that he should offer me the honor of writing this foreword. Many of his experiences have paralleled my own to an extent that I never knew. When I finished reading Nick's manuscript I felt a heightened sense of kinship to this extraordinary man.

My parents knew Nick Starace. My mother, in particular, was a person of impeccable breeding and great discernment. She was the daughter of a Swiss mechanical engineer and a Russian noblewoman. She was brought up in China from 1923 until 1938. I vividly remember her comment to the effect that Nick is a consummate American. "He is a perfect gentleman; completely at ease in any company. Yet for all I know he might be descended from either Virginia plantation owners or steerage immigrants.

That is the essence of being an American." She took Nick's persona as a supreme testimonial to our democratic educational system that had forged our national character, self assured, but never overbearing. Nick is a former naval officer, international executive and world traveler. In every guise his country can be proud of him as an interpersonal ambassador. Nick's affection for the distant lands where he has worked and lived, as well as for those which he has only visited, reflects his own open and friendly spirit. My mother could not have shared Nick's love of Japan. She could not overcome the knowledge that the Japanese had used the same exquisite skill with which they vivisect a carp when they would interrogate a Chinese civilian or an American prisoner during the Second World War. But it is good that terrible memories should be put to rest in the interest of universal amity.

A great book improves its readers, expanding horizons and deepening understanding. Nick Starace's memoir tells us a great deal about America and the world in the second half of the twentieth century and beyond. When our protagonist begins his narrative before World War II the United States of America was a nation possessed of a democratic ideal yet firmly anchored in European culture. With an ideological foundation established by the framers of the Constitution we assimilated the best and the brightest individuals that the Old World had to offer along with a healthy infusion of African and indigenous American stock. The product of this evolutionary process was the strongest, most industrious and most innovative nation state on the surface of the planet.

Alas, in the course of the second half of the twentieth century, America seems to have lost her bearings. A healthy and unified nation state has been replaced by a political entity, which is merely an economic system rooted in cosmopolitan globalization. A hearty people have degenerated into a mass of cogs trapped and exploited in an oligarchic marketplace. One is tempted to opine that America as a nation, as a culture, as a component of western civilization, has ceased to exist.

But Nick Starace gives us hope for the future and consequently the strength to soldier on into the new millennium. Nick's life fraught with challenges, obstacles, tragedy and triumph teaches us that we as individuals and as a society can persevere and carve out a positive future. Nick learns from his experiences and confirms the validity of the fundamental verities on which America was built.

It has been an unmitigated pleasure to have known Nick Starace. It is enlightening to read his book. I am deeply honored to have been asked to write the foreword to this important memoir of a great man with real class.

John Kuhn Bleimaier
"Falkenhorst"
Hopewell, New Jersey, USA

ACKNOWLEDGEMENTS

In writing this book I had two objectives in mind. First to give my three grandsons an idea of what Granddad did with his life, and in so doing instill in them values that would become a beacon. The other was to leave behind a bit of family history for future generations to appreciate and preserve.

With those objectives in mind, I quickly learned that writing a book makes you realize how much help you've had along the walkway of life. You realize that very little of what you have been able to achieve would have been possible without the love, support, and encouragement of so many people. Here then is the cast of characters who played that role in the drama of my life.

I could never have written this book without my Grandfather Michael, whose example of hard work, family values, and humility are still vivid and have remained an inspiration to me all of my life. He died too soon to realize that it was his breath that filled the sails of my life. His seafaring soul and influence are at the very core of this book.

A special thanks to my mother and father for believing in me. By example they showed me that the only things more important than family are the values they instill in you. I came to learn that those values meant family togetherness, a strong work ethic, and a respect for law and order. The advice was to do the best you can, don't dwell on the negative, and be happy with what you have. Those lessons served me well in life and in writing this book.

To my sister Anne Goldman, brother Tony Camuto and their spouses Murray and Mary, whose lives set a standard that I tried to emulate, but could never quite measure up to. Many of my achievements can be traced to their influence. Anne helped me get through the most difficult time in my life when I lost my son Nicholas III. Her love, compassion, and advice made an otherwise unbearable path navigable. A special thanks to Tony, who was my literary springboard, the first person to read the manuscript from stem to stern. His endorsement gave me the confidence I needed to go "full ahead." He made several constructive suggestions, as did Anne on the sections of the manuscript that she read.

I also want to thank my daughter Dorine, for her early editing efforts and for frequently jumping in to help sort out my computer software glitches. Most important was her considerable effort in doing all of the photographic work. I couldn't have finished this book without her.

I would like to mention the many others who shared their valuable time and commented on different aspects of this book. I'm thinking now of my son Michael, aunts Katie Starace and Rita Starace, niece Patricia Camuto, nephews David Goldman and Christopher Camuto, cousins Constance Borgo, Cecelia Mahnken, Jim O. Starace, James (JP) Starace, and Alice and Nicholas Scutari for their support and/or literary contributions. And I am grateful to have friends like Frank Apicella, Bob Boorujy, Vice Admiral John D. Bulkeley (deceased), John M. Burke, Bob Carney, Millie

Catanzaro, Lenny Catanzaro (deceased), Jim Dull, Max Freedman, Susan Gibbs, Jessica Godofsky, Mary Therese Hankinson, Bob Hensley, Allan Jenks, Celine Judet-Pena, Tom Mellina, Rick Monaco, Tony Naturale, Joe Nunziato, Rob Palmer, Dr. Michael Parziale, Ramona Pitera, Chara Rodriguera (Calderone), Dr. Donald H. Slocum, and George Wilson, who all gave me encouragement and/or comments.

To fellow-authors Bob Carney (*Lost at Sea*), Sarah Cypher (*The Editor's Lexicon: Essential Writing for Novelists*), Tony Naturale (*You'll Never Believe It* and *Let's Talk Fitness),* and Grange (Lady Haig) Rutan, (*Death of a Bebop Wife*), for their input and inspiration in writing this book. What they accomplished gave me enough motivation to say, *Yes, I could do this.* To my dear and long-time friend John K. Bleimaier, Esquire, whose extraordinary literary talent and intellect are matched only by the passion we share for our Mercedes-Benz automobiles. John wrote the Foreword to this book because he is well positioned to introduce me and the book itself. To my friend, former New Jersey Governor Brendan T. Byrne for his encouragement and stalwart advice that we are never too old to take on new challenges. He proves it every time we work out at the fitness center. To Drs. Ada and Gene Kane whose artistic and professorial endeavors are a beacon to all their friends and associates.

To the members of the Ship Model Society of New Jersey—Tom Ruggiero, Ed Hegstetter, Al Geigel, Ken Schuetz, Dr. H. Steven Fletcher, and Don Otis, to mention a few—whose camaraderie and unique skills have inspired so much of what this book is all about. I have seen the world from ship-decks and quaysides, but it took the miniature version—model ships—for me to see my family and the path my life would take. Grandfather Michael was a boat-builder, seaman, and ship caulker. When he came to this country he brought an unusual passion that he would pass on to me: model-shipbuilding. More than just a hobby, it is a passion that binds club members together. It inspires us to share our ideas and talent.

A portion of this book is devoted to the many men and women who have served our country in the military during peace and war. They have inspired so much of what this book is all about. I talk about their spirit, which is undeniable. I talk too about their dedication, which is beyond reproach. Yet, notwithstanding the risks of military service, these wonderful young people keep coming forward to serve. They serve out of a sense of duty. For their willingness to make sacrifices and walk in harm's way, I salute them. I am honored to use this book as a way expressing my gratitude to all veterans for their unwavering dedication. Life's greatest gift *is* to give, and they prove it every day they serve.

I am deeply grateful to my former wife Ronnie, who put up with my neurotic antics and short temper for over thirty years and in spite of me raised three wonderful children. In the process she, as much as anyone, gave my story moral substance and decency.

I mustn't forget my father-in-law Michael O'Hare for his enthusiastic support. He believed in me and was interested in everything going on in my life. He was always in my corner no matter the battle. He died long before I finished writing this book and would have been proud of it not for its literary merit, but because of my having written it.

I was blessed to have Sarah Cypher, a freelance editor, writer, and writing teacher perform most of the editing. In addition, her suggestions on reorganizing sections of the book were invaluable, as were her critiques. In the end, however, her most valuable contribution was guidance on where sections of the manuscript needed further development. She brought out the best in the manuscript, and the final results made the nights of burning the midnight oil well worth it.

Alas, to my beloved Kings Point—what can I say? It is not only the foundation on which I built a career, but the bricks-and-mortar that embodied my life. To this day it is the single-most important instrument in the achievement of lifelong goals. Someday, the course of my final voyage will steer me back to Kings Point, and my ashes will be spread at her shoreline. I will rest peacefully under the fluttering and weaving sea gulls, the twinkling lights and stars, the foghorn's drone and the buoy gongs. It is where I belong! There, a benevolent son will rush to her shores, echoing a lasting tribute and thank you.

Lastly and most important, my faith in God and country enabled the American dream for my family and me and gave me the strength and wisdom to write this tale.

My sincere apologies and appreciation to those of you I may have overlooked. Mea culpa!

PREFACE

This book began when I stepped aboard the first ship I was ever assigned to, the SS *Exford*, in Jersey City, New Jersey in 1954.

The old ship had seen better days, and I hoped I wouldn't see the end of my better days while serving aboard the rusting black leviathan. She looked as foreboding as something out of a Jack London novel. I wondered if she would hold up in the wintry North Atlantic, an ocean notorious for its angry sea and violent storms. By the end of the second trans-Atlantic crossing heading eastbound to Europe, we had our answer.

We hit a hurricane so severe that the old gal was barely able to make steerageway, doing at best a pitiful two to three knots. When the bow dipped below the thirty-foot waves, the vessel would shudder, creak, and groan as if she were about to break in half. The monster waves pounding her decks made it easy to believe that after any one of them, she would not rise again. The howling, whetted winds propelled sea spray and whistled through the cargo rigging and around the superstructure, creating eerie, frightening sounds I had never heard before. To make matters worse—a lot worse—every time the vessel heeled thirty to thirty-five degrees to one side, I held my breath, prayed, and wondered if she would capsize or come back. Each time she came back, I went through the same agony when she heeled to the other side. That went on, and on, and on.

To the experienced mariner—surprise!—this was routine stuff. But for a green kid it was like crossing swords with the devil. Was I destined to lose? Our captain was an elderly Estonian gentleman who had immigrated to the United States as a lad, and thereafter spent his entire life, luckily for us, at sea. Thanks to his experienced and steady hand, we would make it through. There was never any doubt in his mind that we would make it. By the end of the voyage I was not discouraged or scared off by the experience; oddly enough, it whet my appetite for more. That appetite would be satisfied as I went on to several similar experiences in the Pacific and Atlantic Oceans having learned to take typhoons and hurricanes in stride. I had overcome my fear of the sea-devil.

By the end of that first voyage, I had embarked on a lifetime adventure that I believed would be worth documenting. And so for the first time in my life I started to keep a diary. For many years thereafter I would jot down notes every time I experienced something noteworthy. Every so many years, I would stash the notes into what would become volumes of manila folders. I was intimidated by the daunting task of writing a book because of the scope of the work, and my vulnerability. I always thought that getting up on a stage or in front of a camera was the ultimate in laying yourself bare. However, it does not compare to putting your life story in a book. So I kept putting it off until March 2005.

I had just returned from a historic tour of Iwo Jima, commemorating the sixtieth anniversary of the battle.

A college classmate, Max Freedman, suggested I write a story of my trip and submit it for publication in the school's quarterly magazine. So ended a half-century of delay. From my point of view, one thing has become abundantly clear; writing a book is like reading a very good book—you can't put it down. And so it was with me. Once I started writing, each paragraph was like a brush stroke in a painting, and I never stopped or looked back until the painting was complete.

And once I finished writing the book, I couldn't resist the temptation to stand back and assess my life. I asked myself if I had really achieved my goals. Had I satisfied my philosophy of life? Had my life made a positive difference in anyone else's life? Had I earned the right to be an American, and to deserve the fruits of the American dream? I had no excuses because I had been given every opportunity by friends, family, God and country to grow and prosper. I can truthfully say that without exception I achieved everything I set out to do. But my philosophy of life is that we are put here to salvage our souls, and that ultimately the road to that salvation will be measured not by how much we do for ourselves, but how much we do for others. I'm still working at it and will continue to do so, and I'll have to work especially hard because I have a date with a son waiting for me in heaven, who I surely do not want to disappoint. I'm sorry to say that thus far I haven't quite measured up to making a substantial difference in the lives of many people. Simply put, I'm not sure I possess that innate ability to inspire others. Now, in the twilight of my years, I doubt I'll come out ahead on this count.

I have always acted in the best interests of *my* America. My sentiments can best be summed up in the old quotation, "My country, right or wrong." Wisconsin Senator Carl

Schurz said it in 1872, and his words have often been misconstrued; he meant that America, when right, should be kept right, when wrong, it should be put right. Still, in almost any context it seems to be politically incorrect, and invites narrow, biased viewpoints. Critics would probably say we need to be more objective about who we are, and what needs to be changed about our country. Yet, right or wrong, it continues to permeate my innermost spirit, just as lessons learned from the catechism have stayed with me lo these many years. Some thoughts get so ingrained they stay with you forever. Take for example the Pledge of Allegiance. When I recite it, it is still an oath. I am serious when I say I think my life has indeed been worthy of the American dream, and that in some small, humble way I have helped make that dream become a reality for others.

The two voyages on the SS *Exford* were the beginning of a lifestyle that would bear witness to a world that would change many times over. As a mariner and businessman I traveled it extensively, and saw it first as a poor man and then, through diligence and hard work, as a wealthy man. I would see the Berlin Wall collapse, and China and India become an integral part of the global supply chain. I would hear *globalization* become a household word. I would learn from history how modern warfare evolved from its World War I origins through to the Gulf Wars. I would see its latest incarnation come into its maturity, one more insidious than anything before it. It struck without warning, and was indiscriminate. Heretofore, my perspective of the geopolitical climate had always been viewed from land and sea. Now we look to the skies, and I would see its deadly effects firsthand.

These voyages into history would take on even broader meaning. There were fewer and fewer of us left who had knowledge of family history. The old-timers were passing on, and so it became one of my objectives in writing this book to leave behind a bit of family history for younger generations to appreciate and preserve. The other objective was to give my grandkids an idea of what Granddad did with his life, and in so doing instill in them the values that become a beacon. Financial gain was never an objective, but there was a sincere desire to rise above tragedy and to hopefully make a positive difference in the lives of others.

Here then, is the story of an immigrant family, my family. We came to this country after it finally emerged from the shadows of a dreadful civil war, and saw its transformation from a national powerhouse to an international superpower; a superpower that would dominate the twentieth century. See how I took a seafaring passion and tradition, and turned it into a successful career, hobby, and lifestyle. Share the tragedies that befell my family, and how we survived by virtue of a strong determination to fulfill our destiny in America. In fulfilling that destiny we have labored in its shipyards, learned in its classrooms, toiled in its shops, prayed in its churches, sailed under its flag, and fought and died in its wars. For that, I, Nick Starace, owe it everything.

1

TERRORISM IN THE SKIES

I am sure that never was a people, who had more reason to acknowledge a Divine interposition in their affairs, than those of the United States; and I should be pained to believe that they have forgotten that agency, which was so often manifested during our Revolution, or that they failed to consider the omnipotence of that God who is alone able to protect them.

—George Washington

Many years later, American investigators established Mohammed Rashed's movements leading up to the bombing of Pan Am Flight 830, the flight I boarded on August 11, 1982, with my wife, Ronnie. Rashed had boarded that same plane with his wife and child the day before, and flew from Baghdad to Tokyo. On the Hong Kong–Tokyo leg of the journey, Rashed, a member of a radical Palestinian nationalist group called The 15th of May, took out a handheld bag and wedged it underneath his seat, 47-K.

The weight of a subsequent passenger sitting down would activate a time-delayed pressure switch that would then detonate his bomb.

The flight originated in Baghdad, stopped in Singapore, Hong Kong, and then in Tokyo for approximately three hours before heading to Honolulu. In Tokyo, Rashed and his family deplaned and booked a flight back to Baghdad. On our leg of its journey, the plane, a 747, carried 267 passengers and a crew of 15. Most of the passengers were Japanese nationals traveling to Hawaii for their honeymoon.

I was working in Taiwan on a temporary business assignment when my wife and I decided to take a one-week vacation to Beijing and Shanghai. We had joined Flight 830 in Hong Kong. Even though my stomach was still talking back to me after a bad plate of teriyaki chicken the night before, we were looking forward to a two-day layover in Hawaii before heading home.

I traveled a lot for work in those days. "Travel" meant living abroad for anywhere from a few months to a few years, and during this assignment Ronnie and I decided it would be in our children's best interests for her to remain at home. I worked for a major oil company, putting my years in the navy and the merchant marine to good use. The ocean was in my blood, and in the blood of my forefathers. I grew up with a love of ships, and when I found a job that would allow me to work in the maritime industry, I felt a deep connection not only to my own dreams, but to my grandfather—he was a boat-builder and seaman in Italy—and even to American history at large. We are a nation of people who sailed from afar, and we built our wealth and our strength on the high seas. So it was not with a little irony, as I took my own place in the lineup of history, that my work was about ships, but I spent much of my time in an airplane.

History is made up of individual lives, individual concerns—and so it was with my personal drama. I commuted home every couple of months, but the long periods abroad had created stress in my marriage, on top of stress at work. Ronnie and I hoped that a layover in Hawaii and my week at home would relieve some of the tension between us. I believed at the time that I'd remember this trip as a turning point—something that would show us whether our future held hope or divorce. There was indeed a lot at stake when we boarded that airplane, but not in the way we imagined.

At approximately 9:00 a.m., as we answered the last call for beverages, Rashed's plastic explosive detonated in the right rear of the main passenger compartment under the seat of a sixteen-year-old boy, Toru Ozawa, who was traveling with his parents from Japan. The bomb blew a hole about 12 by 36 inches in the floor between the cabin and the cargo hold. The fuselage ruptured, and an instant later, flash fire, lots of smoke, and flying shrapnel ripped through the air.

Ronnie and I, sitting in row 4 of the first class section experienced the initial blast as a deafening explosion that rocked the plane in the air. The cabin cockpit rapidly filled with acrid blue smoke so thick that the emergency oxygen masks dangling in front of our faces were barely visible. The giant plane dipped into a screaming forty-five-degree dive. We grabbed each other's hands and armrests and held on for dear life. It was Hail Mary time. And when that time comes, your life really does flash before your eyes.

I also kept thinking of what it would be like trapped inside the plane as it hit the water. The fuselage of the plane would make its submarine-like crash dive to death. If we survived the first impact, it would be agonizing, clawing at the window next to us, unable to break it, as the water level slowly rose and covered the wreckage. That was not how I had expected to die at sea—I thought more in terms of Admiral Farragut's line, "Damn the torpedoes ... Full speed ahead!"

The rapid loss of air pressure caused the plane to drop immediately from an altitude of 26,000 feet to 10,000 feet. The cabin was full of flying utensils, books, pens, and cups. Passengers screamed and yelled. Then, the captain's voice came over the intercom, reassuring passengers that the plane was under control and due to land within minutes.

After the plane leveled off at about 5,000 feet, things began to return to normal. We were now making a controlled descent into Honolulu from 140 miles out. I must give credit to the crew, who performed brilliantly in assisting passengers and trying to calm their fears. They brought a couple of passengers forward and seated them in our section of the plane, where there were a few vacancies. The first passenger had blood on her shoulders and was in shock, unable to relay anything coherent. However, the second passenger, whose hair was almost completely singed away, began to tell us of the hell the passengers in the aft cabin had experienced. There was hysteria, dangling oxygen masks, fire, and dense smoke. They felt certain we were going to plunge into the sea. He said there was an odor in the smoke, "Kind of like the smell of a shotgun blast." It was from him that we learned someone was dead.

Miraculously, the pilot was able to land the plane safely at Honolulu Airport at around 9:30 a.m., about twenty minutes after the explosion. A battery of emergency equipment awaited us on the ground—fire trucks, ambulances, police cars, and every other kind of emergency equipment imaginable.

Oddly, as we disembarked from the plane, it dawned on me that in all the confusion I had left two bottles of liquor in the overhead compartment. I dashed back on board and retrieved the two bottles. As I was about to leave the aircraft again, it occurred to me to have a firsthand look at the scene around row 47. I thought the crew or other officials on board by this time might stop me. However, as I walked aft through the right aisle unhindered, there lying in the aisle in full view were the bloody remains of the poor young man who had been killed in the explosion. There was blood all over the seat and some of his intestines were splattered around the seating area. Passengers who had vomited from the sight made it a grisly, foul-smelling scene.

As it turned out, fifteen people on either side of him suffered shrapnel injuries. The boy was killed from the explosion, which propelled him into the aisle, blew a hole in his abdomen, tore off a leg, and mutilated the rest of his body. His parents had watched him bleed to death. Later his father, Shigetsugu Ozawa, confessed that "at the time my honest emotion was to wish the plane would crash into the ocean, as I had lost the will to live since my son was no longer alive." My wife and I could not begin to imagine such heartache, not until we lost our son Nicky six years later.

Feeling queasy, I made a quick exit from the plane and rejoined my wife in the lounge. After we disembarked, police, FBI agents, and airline staff interviewed the passengers and crew. All baggage was thoroughly searched. Trained dogs were brought in to check for possible bombs aboard the plane and in the luggage. During an impromptu news conference later that day an FBI spokesman said they thought the incident was caused by an explosive device rather than a malfunction in the aircraft. How times have changed! In this day and age everyone would have already jumped to the conclusion that the cause was a terrorist bomb, which it was.

When we got to the hotel we quickly called home to assure everyone that we were safe. It was a good thing we did, because by that time news and TV reports had alerted the world to this: the first terrorist air-bombing.

†

Two days later we were faced with the prospect of flying again, this time to the mainland. We were edgy, but the astronomical odds of another incident of this nature occurring again within such a short period gave us the courage to get back on board another Pan Am flight leaving Honolulu. After all, what other practical alternative did we have? We never heard another word about the incident from Pan Am, the FBI, or any of the other authorities since the day of the bombing. Moreover, no individual or group claimed responsibility for the bombing. It took years of other terrorist bombings and investigation before the United States Justice Department fingered Mohammed Rashed as the courier who planted the bomb. He was to stand trial before an American court for many terrorist acts against American passenger planes in the 1980s, including an identical bomb on another Pan Am plane in August 1982, which was discovered in Rio de Janeiro and defused without injury.

When terrorists supported by Iran and Syria had bombed the Marine barracks in Beirut in October 1983, the Iraq-based, Jordanian-born Rashed had already tried to kill more than a thousand people by planting as many as fifteen high-powered bombs on American airplanes and in Western embassies. In a 1998 hearing in Washington, he was formally indicted with murder, attempted murder, sabotage, and a number of other crimes in connection with the Pan Am bombings. He was charged with placing the bomb under Toru Ozawa's seat.

He pleaded guilty in the District of Columbia on December 17, 2002, following a U.S. Appeals Court challenge that upheld the charges in the indictment. On March 24, 2006, almost a quarter of a century after that terrible morning, Mohammed Rashed was finally sentenced for the crime in federal court. The 59-year-old Palestinian had been in U.S. custody for eight years. When he is released in 2013 and deported, he will have spent approximately twenty-five years in custody. The U.S. court judge also imposed restitution of $116,525 to be paid to the parents of Toru Ozawa. Cold comfort indeed.

†

This first terrorist air-bombing proved to be a turning point in my life, if not in our marriage. I have traveled far and wide and have seen the world many times over. From my travels and readings I am well aware of how military conflict has changed since the founding of this country and the role my family has played during half of its history. That background gave me a respect for the right of every person to pursue a better life, and reinforced the years I had spent in service of my country onboard her ships. But what changed was subtle. I realized there was little that even a multi-billion dollar, nuclear-powered aircraft carrier could do to protect us against our new enemy: terrorism. During my chapter in history's long voyage, our technical wizardry has created a way of life in America, and on 9/11, has also been used as a terrible weapon against us.

I try to see the present as my grandfather would have seen it from his position in history. American civilians have been called upon to make the kind of sacrifices never before envisaged. Yes, there would still be conflict on the battlefield, but we would become familiar with a new kind of warfare after 9/11. We would feel threatened at home and abroad. New and strict "homeland security" measures would inhibit privileges we had always taken for granted. There was apprehension and suspicion towards immigrants, and even long-time resident foreigners. Ethnicity was the new buzzword. So were technology, political correctness, transparency, modernization, and globalization. As the sole remaining superpower economically and militarily, America was expected to provide global leadership in stabilizing all this madness, and did.

As a parent and grandparent, my reaction is the obvious: I wonder, "What kind of a world am I leaving behind for them?" My fears are considerably different and more alarming than those my parents and grandfather had for me. I think they were always confident they were leaving behind a better world than the one they found. I also think that my grandfather had every confidence that with each succeeding generation, the American dream would become more than a cliché—it would become a reality for his family. He knew there was no "free lunch," but he expected every one of us to be given the opportunity to earn it, and with hard work, even relish some of the extra goodies. Perhaps for the first time in our history, we have to ask ourselves if we are willing to make the sacrifices that are necessary to assure the greatness of succeeding generations. Given the decline in recent years of U.S. economic prosperity, perhaps we also have to ask ourselves if the dream is in jeopardy. There are those who think it is, but I firmly believe there is still no other country in the world that affords more opportunity and freedom.

Even as I look back over five generations of Staraces and their families in this country, I see a persistent belief in the spirit and values that drew our ancestors across oceans. The dream may seem tougher to realize, but it will survive as long as we pursue it. At the same time there is always a sense of pride in our roots and a willingness to return to those roots to better understand them. I therefore remain steadfast and optimistic in my belief that my kids, and their kids, and their kids will bear witness to a better world. It is the simple faith that there is goodness in human nature, and that it will eventually embrace us all. Without that kind of faith, we are all doomed.

That day at 26,000 feet, sitting next to my wife somewhere far above Hawaii, I glimpsed something of the intersection between the personal and the historical. Perhaps from this tragedy, I began to see a way into the book I conceived so many years before on the decks of the SS *Exford*.

2

BROOKLYN ROADS

The world will little note, nor long remember what we say here today, but it can never forget what they did here.

—President Lincoln's Gettysburg Address, November 19, 1863

Born to a working-class culture, I was a child of the Great Depression, who was raised in the South Brooklyn (later called Greenwood Heights) and Red Hook sections of the borough, in a tenement straight out of Dickens. That's not a boast, just a fact. We lived in three rooms, and my "room" was a corner of the living room wherein my bed was a convertible sofa. As a kid I was awakened from my naps by the rumble of the subway trains outside the window. In the wee hours of the morning the gray, long-tailed critters would tiptoe into the kitchen and make short work of garbage tidbits. The door lock was certainly not jimmy-proof, and one time thieves got in pretty easily and took a few pieces of jewelry including the first watch I ever owned. They even had the gall to eat some of our food.

We had no backyard with a garden, sandbox, or swings, but we still had lots of fun playing sidewalk games and stickball in the street. The *Daily News* cost two cents. Nearly every boy read comic books and made model airplanes. TV was just coming of age, and we only had a radio. I can still remember listening to my favorite program, *The Lone Ranger*, and Brooklyn Dodger baseball games. People from Brooklyn, especially the kids of that era, vividly remember Mayor Fiorello La Guardia reading the comic strips to us over the airwaves when New York newspapers went on strike. We also remember the little old ladies dressed in mourning black collecting horse manure from the street to fertilize their gardens. Memories linger of an innocent kid who, just before leaving the restaurant, took Mom's tip off the table because he thought she left it there by mistake. When they got home, he proudly gave the money back to her fully expecting a pat on the head. Instead, he heard a moan and then caught hell for his juvenile faux pas.

As a young lad I would frequently ride my rickety old bicycle down to the Gowanus Canal in Brooklyn, and sit on the pier at the foot of 31st Street near my home, watching the merchant ships coming and going. The ship whistles cried of faraway places. For most people there is something almost mystical about ships and the sea, and it was so for me, conjuring up images of white sails in the sunset. I vowed I would someday go to sea in one of those ships; that was my dream, and it would dictate my entire life.

†

I will always remember the sound of my mother weeping at night as she lay in bed. My dear brother Tony, who was almost too young to serve in World War II, enlisted in the U.S. Navy at the age of seventeen, the ink on his high school diploma not yet dry. He served aboard a navy destroyer helping to stave off Grand Admiral Karl Doenitz's hoard of German U-boats in the North Atlantic. His ship was involved in two kills.

I was too young to understand my mother's tears, but later as a parent I would recognize the anguish of anyone whose son or daughter is sent in harm's way. Nor will I forget a prevalent war poster of the day, showing a dead sailor in navy blue, lying on his back, washed up on a beach. Its caption: A CARELESS WORD ... A NEEDLESS LOSS. It was intended to warn people of what could happen by talking too much about ship movements. I don't remember where we were going, but my mother and I were taking a subway ride. As we walked along the platform she suddenly burst into tears at the sight of that poster, for reasons that even a boy could understand. The poster was vivid and cruel, and being displayed at a time when U-boats were sinking American ships in sight of our East Coast.

Tony returned home safely. Many years later in reminiscing about the war with his loving wife Mary, he wrote this tender piece that beautifully captures the thoughts of a war veteran rejoicing to have made it through.

AT SEA, 1944

I lie on my mattress in the
Well of a 36 inch searchlight
On a destroyer slowly leading
A convoy towards the Mediterranean

The mid-Atlantic is relatively calm
The sky cloudless
Most on board are below decks
Hopeful that submarines are not near.
I awake from a semi-slumber
And turn my gaze skyward
The sight that I see
This broad expanse of brilliant light
Across the sky
Awakens and excites my senses
Causes me to gasp
Wraps me in a spell
The awesome view
Stirs feelings of wonderment and
Yearnings for answers to questions

What is this unfathomed deep?
What is existence all about?
The sight reduces my concept of self
To the tiniest of specks imaginable
I am in another dimension.
Skies over my native Brooklyn
Never revealed such wonder or
Gave rise to such feelings
The hope that the enemy is not near
Is shattered by the harsh sounds

Blaring from the speaker system
The call to general quarters
Battle stations
My reverie is over
The spell broken by stern reality
I make my way to my battle station
Hoping there will be other nights
When I can be wrapped in the spell
Of this wondrous sight
The Milky Way

—Anthony Camuto

Tony wasn't our only veteran. My mother had three cousins—Sal, Joe, and Pete Blumetti—who served in the navy, army, and Marine Corps respectively during World War II. Sal and Joe served throughout the war and survived, but Pete never made it. He had served in the South Pacific facing a very tough Japanese adversary. After a year or so, he contracted malaria and had to be sent back to the United States. He was in and out of military hospitals for years, but could not be cured. Finally, in 1947, two years after the war was over, he died at home. His mother, Aunt Dora, remained in silent depression until her dying day and was never quite the same woman. She cried herself to sleep every night, not being able to cope with the reality of losing him.

†

One of the things Mom often did to take the family's mind off the war was to visit Coney Island. Nearly everybody reading this will have heard of Coney Island, but few will have heard of one of its main attractions, Luna Park.

The amusement park had spectacular rides, freak shows, animal acts, restaurants, food stalls, a monkey theater, concession stands, Japanese gardens, Venetian canals, the world's largest ballroom, and yes, even an imaginary trip to the moon. Unveiled May 16, 1903, it was an unmatched playground opposite the beach. Thousands of lights illuminated the entire park like an early Disneyland. Most Sundays during the summer my mother would take me to Coney Island for a day of swimming at the beach, and the visits to Luna Park were a special treat. For a city-kid like me it was an absolute wonderland. On August 12, 1944, the park disappeared as it had debuted, in a blaze of glory.

While we were in the park an electrical fire started in a ride called the Dragon's Gorge. At first we didn't see the flames, but smoke billowed into the sky. The remarkable thing was how rapidly it spread. The place went up like a matchbox. Most notable was the roller-coaster ride, an old dilapidated structure made entirely of wood. It was soon a towering inferno, and its heat so intense that we had to protect our faces. There were frightening screams and then panic. Parents holding children in their arms started to scramble towards the exits pushing and shoving as they went. The thickening smoke caused a mad exodus, which in turn caused some people to be trampled. My mother somehow remained calm, holding my hand for dear life. It was difficult to breathe normally.

By the time we got to the street, the fire department and police were on the scene. Ambulances administered treatment for smoke inhalation and care for the injured. I remember briefly seeing Mayor Fiorello La Guardia, who'd rushed to the scene from City Hall. The Little Flower, as he was affectionately known, was invariably at the scene of emergencies. We later learned that while all of this was going on approximately 750,000 people stood watching the ten-alarm blaze from the beach. Nearly everything in the park was destroyed in the fire and Coney Island lost its main attraction forever. After Mom and I were fully recovered we glumly returned home the way we came, by train. Years later when we talked about the fire she said, "We were lucky to get away with our lives that day."

Many years later, I was destined to be intimately involved with another tragic fire that would claim sixteen lives.

†

When World War II ended everybody embraced the opportunity to reflect and rejoice. Hopefully this would be the beginning of the lasting peace for which everybody hoped and prayed. The worst was certainly over. Soon there would be no more shortages. No more drives for tin, copper, and other scarce materials. Tires worn thin to the core could soon be replaced. No more shortages of sugar and other commodities. My father could throw away his gas rationing stamps, as could my mother her meat rationing stamps. The relentless promotion and sale of bonds was over, too. The air raid wardens could put aside their paraphernalia. Sure, some of the victory gardens continued, but more as a hobby than necessity. Now was a time to celebrate, and one of the ways people did that was with block parties. Nearly every block had somebody in the military. Soon after their return, a block party was arranged and people poured out on to the street enjoying food, drink, and the exhilaration of PEACE. Of course, it all culminated in—what else?—a parade. For a change we kids could run wild, and did. But there was sadness too, especially for the Gold Star Mothers. Families with sons or daughters in the military would hang a small flag in the window with a star on the flag for each one in the service. The stars were blue unless a loved one was lost in the war. Then the blue star flag was replaced with a gold star flag.

My recollection of the block parties after the war is vague, but the same scenes would be repeated not ten years later. A church procession came through my block during the Korean War. Eleanor, a Gold Star mother, lost her son Vinnie, a Marine. He was a couple of years older than me, but we were friendly from our stickball days. As the color guard passed by and dipped the flags in her honor, she fell to her knees on the cold ground. She wept uncontrollably, repeatedly murmuring, “Forgive me, Vinnie, forgive me.”

Her tears gave me my first inkling to the reality of war. As a youngster I saw war as a faraway adventure filled with heroes and glory. It seemed so exciting in the movies and war games we played in the street. During World War II, I used to think it was a pity that I was too young to join my brother in that epic drama. With the Korean War, however, I was beginning to realize its grim actuality, but was still too young to join the fray. The Korean War did not get the same degree of support from the American people as World War II, and received far less attention. In addition, Americans were not called upon to make anywhere near the sacrifice they made for World War II. This time there were no air raid threats, nor was there any rationing. But advances in military technology and tactics made the conflict as violent and bloody as anything before it, with the exception of World War II. Also came the awareness of a world that would be fighting with itself for the rest of my life. In my travels I would witness the remains of its most devastating clashes.

†

During my childhood days in the '40s and '50s we did more than just play Ring-a-Levio and Kick the Can. We rooted, fanatically, for the Brooklyn Dodgers. They played at Ebbets Field, which was considered hallowed ground by me and two million other nuts who looked upon "Dem Bums" not just as a baseball team, but as family. My childhood revolved around them. To the fans who loved them, they were much more than the local baseball team. Every swing of Gil Hodges' bat could change the course of my day.

Baseball in Brooklyn was social. Television was new in those days, but you didn't have to own one to see the games. People would actually gather around storefronts or go to the home of one of the "rich" kids on the block, where there was a television. People would gather on the street corners, on the stoops and in homes to talk and argue baseball. Betting on the games was commonplace. Who you rooted for sort of defined who you were; you tended to ally with other Dodgers fans while keeping at arm's length from the Giants and Yankees fans—but you knew everybody in the neighborhood, and it was all friendly.

In those days, subway rides were a mere five cents. And believe it or not, many star players took the subway to get home after the game. Really. You could also attend a World Series game by just going out to the park the day of the game to buy a ticket. Admittedly, it was only a bleacher seat and you had to get to the park to stand, or sit, or sleep, in line at 4:00 a.m., but that's what my buddies and I did to see game six of the 1949 World Series between the Dodgers and the New York Yankees. The Bronx Bombers lived up to their nickname that day by bombing us 11–5. For a ticket price of $1.25, it was well worth it.

Ebbets Field. It wasn't just a ballpark. It was a cathedral, my place of worship. I remember vividly the first time I saw

Jackie Robinson play there. It was a night game. The home uniforms were a bright white silk with blue trim. The players were white. The lights were brilliant white. In all of that I shall never forget the sight of those hawser-like muscular black arms extending out from the sleeves. The new color jolted my consciousness, and changed baseball forever. His exploits on the field were in one word, electrifying. In later years I was able to get his autograph waiting outside the ballpark, which is something kids always did after a game. I still have that autograph, along with many others.

I also recall a miraculous catch by little-known outfielder Al Gionfriddo on Joe DiMaggio's long drive in game six of the 1947 World Series. The Yankee Clipper came to the plate in the sixth inning with two men on and the Dodgers leading 8–5. He was the potential tying run. He hit the first pitch to deep left field to Gionfriddo, who raced toward the bullpen railing with his back facing the field. He turned, leaped, stuck out his glove and made the catch just to the left of the 415-foot marker in front of a low metal gate. It's been said the catch was one of the greatest in baseball history and eventually led to his lasting celebrity. It has also been said it was the only time the majestic Joe DiMaggio ever showed any emotion on the ball field. In disbelief as he rounded second base, DiMaggio shook his head and kicked at the dirt. The Dodgers held on, winning the game 8–6 to force a seventh game that the Yankees won.

There was no greater thrill for me than to play football in this baseball shrine. I was a member of the high school varsity team as a running back, and we were scheduled to play three of our home games there. There I was sitting in the Brooklyn Dodger locker room on a seat in front of the locker of one of my idols, Gil Hodges. As the time approached to go out onto the playing field, butterflies gathered in my stomach, not because of the game we were about to play, but because of the excitement of actually being on *that* field. As we approached through the Dodger dugout, I sat on the bench for a few minutes looking out on the hallowed ground. How many times had I sat in the stands looking onto these benches, dreaming of the impossible, and here it was, come to life. The only people missing now were the Dodgers themselves. We had a pretty awful team in my senior year, and we lost all three of the games we played at Ebbets Field. But who cared?

No discussion of Brooklyn Dodger baseball would be complete without mentioning what is arguably the most unforgettable moment in all American sport. In mid-August the Dodgers were thirteen-and-a-half games ahead of the Giants in the 1951 pennant race. No one, and I mean no one, thought the Giants had the slightest chance of winning the pennant. But then it happened. The Giants went on a late-season tear, winning thirty-seven of their final forty-four games thereby forcing a three-game playoff with the Dodgers. They split the first two games in typical war-like fashion. In game three at the Polo Grounds, the Dodgers were leading 4–1 going into the bottom of the ninth. The Giants scored a run, and then the Flying Scot, Bobby Thomson, stepped to the plate to face Dodgers relief pitcher Ralph Branca. Thomson ran the count to one ball and one strike. He then hit the "Shot Heard Round the World," a three-run walk-off home run that gave the Giants a 5–4 victory and the National League pennant. Seeing the ball disappear over the fence, Thomson jumped crazily around the bases before disappearing into the mob of jubilant teammates that had gathered at home plate.

I remember where I was as if it were yesterday. It was October 3, 1951, around four o'clock. Our high school football team practiced every weekday after school at the Red Hook ball fields. We were suited up and ready to go out on the field, but were glued to the radio. Our coach kept pushing us to get a move-on, but we begged him for a few more minutes so we could hear the end of the game. He obliged, and we were stunned as we heard the Giants announcer Russ Hodges screaming, "THE GIANTS WIN THE PENNANT! THE GIANTS WIN THE PENNANT! THE GIANTS WIN THE PENNANT! THE GIANTS WIN THE PENNANT!" My close friend Arnie and I walked out of the locker room sort of numb, and proceeded to do our usual pre-practice two laps around the field. We didn't weep. We didn't sob. We just cried. This was tantamount to my life coming to an end—that's just how I felt. It would become the darkest memory in my childhood.

Speaking of Ralph Branca harkens me back to a time roughly twenty-five years after his infamous pitch to the Flying Scot. It was the mid '70s and we were living in Harrison, New York, in the heart of plush Westchester County. Soon after moving in we learned that of all people, Ralph Branca was living with his family in a home approximately one mile north of us. Not surprising, because we later found out there were a lot of sports notables living in Harrison. Pete Rozelle, who was the commissioner of the National Football League at the time, lived about a half-mile away. Our daughter Dorine, who was attending Catholic parochial school, would ride the school bus with one of the daughters of Wellington Mara. At the time Mara was president of the NFL's New York Giants and co-owner with his brother Jack. The Maras owned a magnificent eight-bedroom home about two miles from us, and it was through our daughters that we got to know each other. Long after we left, Joe Torre and his family lived in Harrison while he was manager of the New York Yankees.

It is no wonder we were devastated to learn in 1957 that our beloved Bums would be moving to Los Angeles the following year. Unfortunately, team owner "Judas" O'Malley was discouraged by dwindling attendance and lured to Los Angeles by the promise of bigger crowds, a fancier stadium, and more money. He simply didn't have the emotional ties to the team that most Dodgers fans did. But baseball is big business and big business is about money; there's no room for emotion or loyalty. In fairness to O'Malley I should mention the other culprit in this affair, the all-powerful Robert Moses who was the head of several New York public works commissions. Their dispute focused on not being able to agree on a location for a new ballpark. Had Moses been more supportive of O'Malley's planned location and less focused on his own agenda, the club's move to Los Angeles might never have taken place. For most people, fifty years would be sufficient time to forget the Dodgers were ever in Brooklyn or that they ever left. But I know because I was one of the poor kids it happened to. I couldn't get over it then. I still haven't gotten over it, and I guess it's fair to say I never will. The final game was September 24, 1957, before approximately 6,000 heartsick, nostalgic fans. I was heartbroken. These had been happy hours during happy times. World War II was over and the Greatest Generation was well on its way to taking us to the greatest period of prosperity the country had ever known.

3

SHIPS OFF THE OLD BLOCK

We hold these truths to be self-evident; that all men are created equal and independent, that from that equal creation they derive rights inherent and inalienable, among which are the preservation of life, and liberty, and the pursuit of happiness.

—Thomas Jefferson

My grandfather, whom I affectionately called Poppie, had a great influence on me. Clearly, it is to him that I owe this passion I have for all things nautical, which has been the shaping force in my personal and professional life. His passion for ships was an anchor across generations.

There are times when I think I am more my grandfather's son than my father's. My aunts reminded me that as a boy I would sit for hours watching him build period sailing ship models, which he put together not from kits or drawings, but from memory. Except for the rigging lines, everything, and I mean everything, was handcrafted. My introduction to that world started quite early in my life, and my grandfather's fascination with ships rubbed off; at least the passion, if not the talent.

Family folklore has it that he jumped ship while serving as a seaman on an Italian-flag merchant vessel, to carve out his new life in America. For most of his life in this country he worked as a ship-caulker in Brooklyn shipyards, always close to the water and the thing he loved most—ships. As a boy, my father worked with him for a few years and was thus christened into the maritime world for which we were destined. My grandparents were from very humble beginnings. Humility was considered a great virtue and implicit in everything they did and said. It made a huge impression on me, such that it is the single-most admirable trait I look for in people, and I have often wished I could have been a better disciple of it. Ever so attractive, it is a trait I will come back to time and time again in this book. (In the French language the word—humilité—sounds almost divine. And folks, I heard that remark about French humility.)

He, like so many European immigrants before him and since, had the courage, fortitude, and vision to leave familiar surroundings to carve out a new life in the New World. To this day I cannot begin to imagine the kind of courage required to take such a daring step. The sacrifices he had to make were huge. He didn't know it then, but he would soon find out that, yes, there could be prosperity, but only through initiative, skill, and hard work.

Together, he, my grandmother, and later his second wife, had fourteen children, two of whom died at an early age. They went on to raise eight sons and four daughters. My father, Nicholas, was the second-eldest. They were dirt poor, but managed to get through two world wars and the

Great Depression without going on relief, as welfare was called in those days. They had too much pride and dignity for that. All they asked for was opportunity. In return they gave their family values, a strong work ethic, and their culture. They also gave their sons and grandsons, who fought in defense of this country in two world wars and the Korean War.

He never said so, but we knew that down deep he felt conflicted over the fact that three of his sons, Sal, Pete, and Joe, joined the military to fight against an enemy that included a Fascist Italy. (It is mere coincidence that they have the same first names as the Blumetti relatives mentioned earlier.) His loyalty, however, remained with America, of which he was so proud.

†

I was around twelve years old when I started working in my father's plumbing shop in South Brooklyn. You might even say I was raised in a plumbing shop since I spent so much time there, especially as my mother, who was a dressmaker, held down a full time job. (That notwithstanding, she rarely missed putting three meals a day on the table, seven days a week.) Frankly, I felt deprived having to work every day after school and even Saturday, while the other kids were out playing. My father would rationalize it by saying hard work and struggle build character.

Together they taught me the niceties of good manners. One example in particular became frustrating for me over the ensuing years. That had to do with the belief that a man on a train or a bus should give up his seat for a woman. My problem is that it got so ingrained, no amount of modern day reasoning can erase it. Yeah, I know, I'm a dinosaur, and that my type has undergone mass extinction largely because of the feminist movement circa 1975—but what can I say? I am what I am. Trouble is, in today's world I am almost embarrassed to offer my seat. God forbid, she might insist that I keep it. Then I would feel very uncomfortable, maybe even guilty for the rest of the journey and want to scream out loud, "Please lady, take the damn seat!"

Those were humble beginnings during which I met "Damon Runyon characters" that in themselves could be the subject of another book, and learned the plumbing trade in the course of the next eight years. The work was hard, and not without some risks—especially if one got a bit careless. On one such occasion my father was working on one end of his bench soldering something, while I was fiddling with something at the other end of the shop. Next to him was his ever-present bottle of Coca-Cola. In the same vicinity he had a bottle of muriatic acid, which was used as a cleansing agent for soldering. While focused on the soldering at hand, he reached over to take a drink from the Coke bottle that he thought he saw out the corner of his eye. Instead, he picked up the acid bottle. After he took one sip I knew something had gone terribly wrong from the awful screams that came echoing across the shop. Rinsing with water didn't help much to alleviate the burning, so it was off to the hospital. He suffered pretty bad burns, but there was no permanent damage. This was perhaps my first lesson in safety, with many to follow.

My father was in fact the most hard working and industrious person I ever knew. I never saw him with his feet up, reading or watching TV. That simply was not his style. The guy never stopped moving, always on the go doing something no matter how trivial or important it was. Relaxation was not in his vocabulary. To be candid, he was also a hard taskmaster who was too demanding of the people around him. He expected the most they could give and the best they could give, but in a manner that did not always endear him to others. One thing he expected above everything else was personal responsibility. To be responsible meant being answerable and accountable for your actions and meeting your obligations and duties without being pushed. Never one to mince words, here was a no-nonsense, no-BS guy who gave no quarter and asked for none. At times ill-tempered, and fearless too, he would never let anybody or any situation get the better of him. He had exceptional mechanical skills that I inherited and passed on to my children; and come to think of it, a lot of what I have just said pretty much sums up the profile of yours truly, except that my father was not a control freak.

Dad was not a very social person, maybe because of his bluntness, which came across to some as curt. Or maybe it was because he had some quirky, even morbid notions. I don't know what prompted him, but he used to say, "Death is around the corner." I am infinitely curious about death, but not to the point of musing aloud. He also used to say half-jokingly that after people were married for many, many years they began to look like each other. I don't know where he got that idea, but my mother would quiver every time he said it, and many years later, I'd see the same apprehension in the eyes of my wife.

†

My father would take me on his boat when I was four years old and tie me to it at dockside while he puttered around. Neither of us could swim a stroke. In 1938, toward the end of the boating season, most of the boat owners at the marina were scurrying around their boats making the usual preparations before haul-out. The location was the old Ben Macree Yacht Club in the Bensonhurst section of Brooklyn. My father had given the marina a target date by which he wanted his boat, *Dolores,* hauled out before winter. She was a sleek thirty-four-foot Elco Cabin Cruiser named for my mother. There was, however, a serious problem that added a sense of dire urgency to the marina's activity. The Great Hurricane of 1938, sometimes referred to as The Long Island Express (which stands as one of the worst disasters in North American history), was about to hit.

This was truly a yachtsman's worst nightmare. According to one account,[1] "The storm was tracked as it moved west from Africa to the Bahamas Islands. [The National Weather Service] knew it was a very powerful storm as it had reached category 5 strength [155-plus mph winds] on September 19, but it was believed that the hurricane would curve out to sea before reaching the Northeast." Unfortunately, that erroneous bit of relief spelled doom for most of the boats in the marina. It gave management enough leeway, or so they thought, to relax the pace at which they were hauling out boats. The account goes on, "Instead of curving out to sea, the storm moved due north and accelerated in forward speed to 70 mph. In the history of hurricanes, this is the fasted known forward speed ever recorded." The hurricane hit eastern Long Island on September 21 "with wind speeds that exceeded 180 mph! ... Few on eastern Long Island's south shore had a chance when the storm surge hit. ... Waves between 30 and 50 feet pounded the coastline with millions of tons of sea water, sweeping entire homes and

[1]www2.sunysuffolk.edu/mandias/38hurricane/weather_history_38.html

families into the sea [killing 682 people]. ... The hurricane produced storm tides 14 to 18 feet across most of the Long Island and Connecticut coast." That was the scene at the Ben Macree Yacht Club as *Dolores* tugged at her mooring like a bulldog on a leash, awash in gigantic waves that would eventually pound her to pieces.

The haul-out equipment at Ben Macree was primitive compared to the traveling lifts currently in use. Today a boat can be hauled and blocked in less than an hour. In 1938 it took closer to three hours. There were simply too many boats to haul to avoid disaster. When the storm hit, more than half the boats were still waterborne, most tied to anchored moorings. *Dolores* was one of them, and didn't stand a chance. She broke her mooring and, helpless as a child, drifted aimlessly towards a nearby jetty whose jagged boulders gouged her hull time and time again. She disintegrated, and slipped into the sea crying out for help that would never come. One desperate boat owner ventured out to his boat to do what he could to save his cherished cruiser, *Better Days,* and was never heard from again. Even some of the boats that had been hauled out were destroyed as they sat on their blocks.

A day or two later, while standing on the shore near the marina, my parents watched pieces of debris from every type and size boat wash ashore. There was planking, masts, cabin siding, floorboards, life jackets, and even pillows bobbing up and down. My mother said it was the only time she ever saw my father cry.

My grandfather said to him, "Will you cry as much for me when I go?"

I don't know if he did, but it was the only time *I* ever saw him cry.

†

At the age of fourteen I went to New York City by myself to attend my very first boat show, a tradition I would maintain almost every year since. I brought home dozens of brochures and drooled over them for hours, picking out the boat I dreamed of buying with all its wonderful gadgets.

One of my early favorites was the forty-foot Matthews Sedan Cruiser, a luxurious yacht for the day. To show you what *early* meant, the boat was wooden-hulled. However, the time for that dream to come true was a long way off. In the meantime, I settled for a used, dilapidated sixteen-foot rowboat, badly in need of repair and overgrown with seaweed. A boyhood friend and I bought it for the princely sum of $10. I was so conscientious about it that I even took a piloting and small boat handling course given by the United States Power Squadron to prepare myself for my very first command. Nut that I am, I even kept the graduation certificate—and yes, I still have it. Unfortunately, that boat was the first *she* to break my heart. After working on it for three months and just before getting ready to launch, it was stolen. I was devastated. To give you an idea of how passionate I was about that little boat, I kept the purchase receipt and have treasured it to this day, like a death certificate of a long-lost loved one.

†

There's a notorious sandbar in Brooklyn between Sheepshead Bay and the Gerritsen Beach Canal Bridge. This was Dad's first season with his thirty-two-foot cabin cruiser *Dolores II.* Unlike her predecessor, she was usually in a heap of trouble, which she would soon share with me, big time.

This was before the days of depth-finders on small boats. Moreover, Dad was not familiar with the waters. We had a sure-fire combination for disaster, and en route to Sheepshead Bay, he erroneously navigated over the sand bar. He needed three feet of water, but there were only two available at the time. With a CRUNCH, we were stuck in the mud. When the tide went out fully, we were high and dry. Being a single-screw (one propeller) boat, she simply heeled over and rested on her side. We had little choice other than to get out and walk around the sandbar for several hours, waiting for the tide to come in. When it did, we floated off the sandbar and went merrily on our way, bearing a lesson—never go anywhere with your boat unless you have carefully reviewed the charts for your voyage and destination.

This was the first of *Dolores II*'s black-sheep adventures. When we got her, she had seen her better days and damn near ended ours—twice. One fine day we were cruising up the Narrows in New York Harbor, headed for the New Jersey side of the Statue of Liberty to do some crabbing. Lo and behold the engine conked out in the middle of the deep-water channel. Dad and his friend frantically started to work over the engine to get it restarted. No luck. Then our luck turned even worse. A five hundred-foot freighter was barreling south in the channel on her way out to sea. I should point out that a large vessel has virtually no room to maneuver in a narrow channel. In other words, it could not safely change course. When the ship's captain started to blow the ship's whistle, we knew we were in deep trouble. He couldn't change course and we were powerless. As the ship's huge bow got closer and closer we prepared to jump overboard with our life jackets on, even though my father couldn't swim and there was still the risk of getting drawn into the ship's propeller.

With the ship approximately two hundred feet away, it looked certain it was going to ram us. As it got even closer, a ray of hope emerged: we were a bit off-center from the ship's course. One hundred feet now, and we're ready to jump, but held on, thinking maybe there was still hope. It would have been all over then, except for the fact that the crest of the ship's bow-wave pushed us out of the way. As the ship drew even with us, we could almost touch its side-shell plating. As the side rail glided past, high above, several of the crew leaned over and waved their fists. You can imagine what they were calling us. The three of us breathed a sigh of relief, still not realizing how close we had come to death.

So went my first brush with the other side at the tender age of fifteen. We drifted aimlessly for a while before sighting a U.S. Coast Guard vessel that eventually came alongside to take us in tow. The ship had probably advised them of our situation, and the only lasting misfortune that day was that we had to buy our crabs for dinner.

†

One year later, I was very focused on dating, but high school football and fraternity activities had taken a back seat to boating, and I knew the direction my life would be taking. It was during this time that I'd experience my second brush with death.

We were looking forward to a beautiful evening for a fishing cruise as my father, Cousin John, and I scurried around *Dolores II* checking to ensure everything was battened down for the open sea. As we sailed away from the Shell Bank Yacht Club in Brooklyn's Gerritsen Beach Channel, the sky was an ominous gray, and a stiff breeze was blowing. Our estimated time to the Ambrose Light area, where we planned to fish for the pugnacious bluefish, was approximately two hours. As we cleared the bay and headed out for open waters, the dismal day was getting squeezed under a low sky, and the surface of the sea was streaked with zigzagging white rays; the waves were climbing higher. Never had I seen the sea so rough here. Soon the Rockaway Jetty was visible on our port side; you could tell by its distinguishing profile—jagged boulders that reached toward the sky, seeming to ask for rescue from the punishing sea. The waves unfurled violently around them.

I decided to go below to fetch more foul-weather gear, and at that instant I heard a loud squealing noise followed by severe hull vibrations. The boat was shivering. I immediately dashed forward in the cabin to look out the forward port. The anchor was gone! It had been lashed down on the open fore-deck, and apparently the heavy weather had worked it loose, causing it to fall overboard and take with it two hundred feet of line, the end of which was attached to the boat. In nautical circles the end of an anchor line attached to the vessel is referred to as the "bitter end."

Fortunately, that's not how things turned out, but we were coming close.

I dashed up on deck only to see the sea's wrath leaving nothing untouched. Waves smashed against the hull and deck. Dad tried to maneuver in the direction of the anchor to retrieve it. Instead, the engine went dead. John was on the fore-deck trying to haul in the anchor without much success. I had to move carefully. I kept telling myself that I must not be thrown overboard. We were approximately one thousand feet from the jetty; and the heavy seas and wind drove our powerless craft even closer. My fear was mounting. Dad worked on the engine, because without it, there was no way to head back toward the anchor and lift it on board, or even cut it loose. Even this would be difficult—working on an open foredeck lifting a forty-pound anchor in tumultuous seas is risky at best. Back aft, I held on to my lifeline. The jetty was less than one hundred feet away. I had the impression that a single wave would be enough to crush us like a nut under an elephant's foot. No radiotelephone available and no help in sight. Who else would have gone out in this weather?

Our first contact with the jetty was a glancing blow—the stern hit a boulder. Water gushed into the cabin, sending a cascade of galley equipment, books, and bottles across the floorboards. The boat rolled and pitched helplessly, and at the next contact, the steel rudder shuddered over sharp barnacles on the rocks. The boat lunged sideways. I was flattened against the side of the open cockpit and inadvertently let go of the lifeline. Then with one quick motion I was projected helter-skelter across the cockpit to the other side. At that moment I believed it was the end. I was on my way to join the legions that have perished the same way. However, in the great maritime novels, death seemed somehow more adventurous. In a flashing instant I thought of my family, friends, my beloved Brooklyn Dodgers, and all those I might never see again.

Then I felt a line hit my shoulder and saw my father at the other end frantically motioning and yelling for me to grab it. Each wave unfurled in spouting foam, reaching higher than the cabin mast. I was flung across the boat again. This time I almost landed in the sea, but somehow grabbed the lifeline and clutched it tight. Next thing I knew I was lying on the deck, cold and trembling. My father's face was ghost-pale.

We were surrounded by the repetitive, lashing sea. How I loathed it in that moment. I suddenly hated everything that used to give me so much pleasure—the sea I used to love.

My father asked me to go below and let him know how much flooding we had. The cabin was in shambles, and I cringed at the sight. Books on the bunk, scattered broken glass, a pack of cigarettes and a ketchup bottle bobbing up and down. Floorboards were floating at my ankles. We were of course still taking on water as a result of the stern damage. The clock still worked; it was 10:35 p.m. I relayed the cabin condition to my father. The heavy seas were making it virtually impossible for John to haul in the anchor. After a large gulp of cold coffee, I couldn't believe the music in my ears. The engine was running again. Dad's desperate efforts paid off and we were once again underway.

We slowly moved away from the dreaded jetty in the direction of the anchor. A few minutes ago we were in hell, but now there was hope of getting out of this mess safely. Our only chance was to cut the anchor loose, head straight for the nearest land and beach the boat. In cutting the anchor line we fully realized that should we lose power again, we would be at the full mercy of the sea. It was a chance we had to take.

After a look at the charts we decided to head for nearby Breezy Point, which had quiet sandy beaches, safe for swimmers and fools like us who dare in too close with a boat. By going aground there, we could make temporary repairs, get help and return to our homeport. It was my turn to man the hand bilge-pump. Without it, we would have already sunk. I was on the verge of exhaustion, but this was no time to give up.

The sea was relatively calm now and so were we. I was on deck and thought I saw a blinking navigational light. What a relief. And was that a buoy gong? Was I dreaming all this? Yes, that's it—any minute I was going to wake up to the smell of bacon and eggs. But no. That navigational light was getting brighter. By God it was not an illusion. Visibility was poor, but the depth soundings told us land was definitely near. Water depth twenty feet ... fifteen feet ... ten feet. We waited anxiously for the soft impact of the boat meshing with the sandy beach.

We fell forward slightly as the keel ploughed its way through the sand. The boat stubbornly pushed ahead for another eight to ten feet, digging its way onto the beach before coming to a complete stop. When we stopped the engine there was a deafening silence and a dead calm, as though the entire world had come to a standstill. The time was nearly 2:00 a.m. Dazed, bewildered, and fatigued we looked at each other, grateful to be alive with *Dolores II* still beneath our feet. I was lulled to sleep by a gentle breeze under a soft sky. The gallant lady, sitting on her keel, swayed as gently as seaweed in the tide. With regret, I thought of all those lovely bluefish that got away. Where were they now? Safe indeed from our impotent hooks.

The three *Dolores II* incidents, the latter two paired with death, showed me a new side of my father. Faced with danger he remained cool and collected, and didn't lose hold of his knowledge or common sense. Moreover, his concern for safety was directed at John and me, even at the expense of his own. It also demonstrated that my father had confidence in me and my ability to handle responsibility. I wasn't a kid anymore. I came away from our boating excursions convinced that we were indeed "ships off the old block." When it came to boating we were certainly on the same wavelength—and even though I wasn't all that keen on fishing, we went because of his interest in the sport of it. And of course we shared baseball interests and went to games together. That notwithstanding, our relationship was becoming increasingly strained.

We were at loggerheads over my career path. In preparing for high school we squabbled about the type of school I should attend; anxious to get started on a maritime career I wanted to attend a maritime trade school. Fortunately my parents insisted on an academic school to prepare for college. For that I shall be eternally grateful because it put my life on the right track, and got me my eventual admittance to the United States Merchant Marine Academy at Kings Point, New York. Nevertheless, the career issue would soon come to a head.

Dad was never supportive of my aspirations to follow a maritime career. His dream for me was to be a doctor, and he constantly pushed me in that direction. He wallowed in a "my son the doctor" syndrome. He was in awe of doctors because they helped him considerably in his lifetime. When people asked me, "What do you want to be when you grow up?" he would invariably answer for me, "A doctor." The brainwashing went on for so many years that I began to answer the question with what he wanted to hear, never really meaning it. I simply did not have the vocation for it, no more than I had it for, say, the priesthood.

Meanwhile, in the 1950s, South Brooklyn and Red Hook were not where the future doctors of America were growing up. There were plenty of scary incidents, and you learned survival. You had to, because sometimes trouble happened when you least expected it—like the day several guys from our football team got chased by a gang of ten guys with bats, or the night when five guys cornered my friend Steve and me as we walked our girlfriends home. As our groups passed each other, one of the guys said, "You girls could use new friends." Tough guy Steve blurted out, "They don't need any new friends." Before we knew it, the five of them had the two of us pinned against a fence. In the next instant we heard an all-too-familiar sound of switchblades clicking open. The glistening steel in the light of a nearby lamppost was unmistakable, too. For young thugs, it was the weapon of choice—on stage, on the screen, and on the real-life streets.

We scuffled, kicked and got cut, but fought our way out of that one. They chased us for a bit, but fortunately for this Nick—we got out of there in the nick of time. There were enough thugs to keep you on your toes, but the person I remember most is Red Bounty. I had just started my freshman year at high school. It was in science class that we first met. We even sat next to one another in the front row. He was two years older than everyone else in our class—a sixteen-year-old freshman aching to quit, and even at that young age he had developed a reputation for being a nasty guy who liked to hurt people. He'd found the right venue in the Tigers, one of the more notorious Brooklyn gangs of the day. We developed a casual relationship; he suggested on a couple of occasions that I meet with some of his friends to "join the club."

Given my vulnerability at that time in my life, I remain especially grateful to my family who gave me the values that got me past temptation. Values then primarily meant family togetherness, a strong work ethic, and a respect for law and order. The advice was always to do your best, don't dwell on the negative, and try to be happy with what you have. I might have been fighting with my dad most of the time in those days, but somehow the values went deeper. So, being somewhat of a loner, I declined Red's offer.

After that he pretty much kept to himself. He was nearly always in trouble, and when he wasn't in trouble, he was looking for it. He found it one evening in a gang fight with the Tigers' archrival gang, the South Brooklyn Boys. The "D's" were at it again—that's to say the Donkeys and the Dagos, as they were called. One summer evening they had it out in the park. This was all white-boy stuff, no blacks or Latinos. Red pulled out a gun and pumped two bullets into a kid's stomach. Poor kid died that evening in the hospital. The next morning the school was a beehive of gossip and chatter about a rumble in the park. Nobody had the real story until a day or two later when we saw Red Bounty's picture on the very front page of the *Daily News*. The headline read GANG KILLING IN PROSPECT PARK. His photo took up the lower half of the page. There he was in court standing in front of a judge, as big as life, and from the expression on his face was enjoying every minute of it. We never heard about him again. He probably ended up in jail or dead at an early age, and years later, when I saw *West Side Story*, I felt I could somehow relate.

That night when my father came home with the same newspaper, he said, "Nicky, do you see this? I want you to stay away from guys like this in school. They'll only get you in a lot of trouble." In his later years my father used to like to say, "Youth is wasted on the young." In Bounty's case, he was dead right.

Little did he know how close to trouble I had come. Nor did he fully realize how I continued to drift away from his visions of my future. By this time I had a very clear vision of what I wanted to do with my life. The more he expressed disapproval, the more determined I became to be my own man. My impulse was to politely suggest to him to get off my case. However, I was so intimidated by him that I would skirt further confrontation while doggedly steering my own course. There was never any doubt in my mind that my father loved me, but he was strong-willed, and for the first time in my life I had to challenge him on an issue more critical to me than to him. For the first time in our turbulent relationship I was determined that he would not dominate me.

Another high school incident involved a guy in English Composition class, who was a fairly good student, but a gang-type all the way. You could easily tell from his walk, and his mannerisms. One day while we were listening to a classmate give a book report in front of the class, the guy casually leaned over and said to me, "Nick, I have something to show you." As he reached into his pants I said to myself, *This is the last guy who I would have thought was gay.* What he actually came up with was closer to my expectations: a .38 caliber handgun. He was so proud of that gun; he kept turning it over in his hands very gently. And he made very sure to demonstrate to me that it was indeed loaded—that was important to him—and he let me know in no uncertain terms that he was an elevated member of the infamous Tigers and a disciple of the notorious Red Bounty.

†

Like most teenagers I had an avid interest in cars. By the time I was seventeen I had a driver's permit that enabled me to drive provided there was a licensed driver in the car with me. However, I had bigger ambitions. I wanted to take some of my friends for a spin, even go out on a date. I had my own key, but not the registration. That's a chance I was willing to take. The challenge was how I would get the car away without my father knowing. I devised a dumb scheme whereby I would take the car during a time when I knew he was going to be off somewhere else for a while. The first time it worked out fine—three of us drove to an amusement park for a couple of hours before heading back. When we did get back, I was even able to park in the same spot. Cars were so sparse you could actually find parking with ease.

Things went so well I planned another outing, this time with my girlfriend Ronnie and high school chums Lenny and Millie. I don't even remember where we went, but we were gone longer than planned. When we got back, the original parking spot was gone, so I took the nearest one. That was a bad omen. When I got home and opened the door I was shocked to see my father sitting there, with a glare on his face that struck fear in me. I could feel myself go numb. His first words were, "Where have you been?"

There was no point in denying it, so I simply fessed up.

He gave me a verbal lashing and then a good old-fashioned thrashing, which was par for the course in those days. And by thrashing, I don't mean a spanking. Quite apart from the thrashing I sensed an underlying tension that stemmed from our ongoing earlier career-path feud. I couldn't help but feel that with each whack he was getting even, and at the same time getting it out of his system. Yet through it all I have to admit that according to his way of thinking he was always acting in my best interest.

†

Finally, as I got well into my teens I got up enough gumption and made it clear to my father that my career path was going to take a different direction. My mother was caught between a rock and a hard spot, but I knew, and so did my father, that she was on my side. Nevertheless, he kept hoping and pushing me. Right after I graduated from high school I failed the entrance examination for the United States Merchant Marine Academy. I didn't have the grades for med school, so if my dreams failed, I would have probably ended up stepping into his plumbing business. I took the examination again six months later and was accepted.

He was very upset with that. For a while we were actually estranged over it. Caring for me as he did, he was hurt, even shocked, by the estrangement. Through his hard exterior I could see a man struggling to find a way to resolve critical issues with a son who had finally broken out of his subservient shell.

In those six months I worked at a bank and went to night school cramming mathematics courses. By then I was nearly nineteen years old and driving legally. To make driving even more enticing, my father had purchased a new Cadillac Coupe de Ville. He would let me use the Caddie, and besides being on eggshells with him, I was always very careful not to ruin a good thing.

One night Ronnie and I went to one of those passion pits of the 1950s, a drive-in movie, with our good buddies Lenny and Millie. There we were, all comfy and cozy with the popcorn and omni-present speaker hanging from the front left window. A back window was open slightly to let the steam out. For those of you who have never been to a drive-in movie, let me explain that there was usually a mad rush to get out of the place at the end of the movie. If you didn't move quickly you could get stuck for an hour or more. So there I was, Mr. Smarty Pants, getting ready to bolt out of the place five minutes before the movie ended.

At just the right moment I started the car, revved the engine, put it in gear and we were off with a BANG. The bang was the shattering of the left window, which was ripped out, chrome frame and all, because this simpleton simply forgot to remove the speaker. It even startled Lenny and Millie, who had been too busy making out in the back seat to pay any attention to the movie. I jumped out of the car, put the speaker back on its rack and began to assess the damage. Shattered glass everywhere. No injuries, but I was still devastated. How was I going to explain this one? Ronnie tried to console me, but I still had to face the music when I got home.

My first thought was to not go home that night. I didn't dare suggest to Ronnie that her folks let me sleep over that night, because her father would have thrown me clear out the window, and they lived on the fourth floor.

When I got home my parents were asleep so I decided to let it go until the morning. I didn't get a bit of sleep that night. Next morning I heard my mother rummaging with breakfast. When my father got out of the bathroom I broke the news to him. The dejected look on his face told the story of a parent asking himself where he had gone wrong. After all, no sooner had he lost the career path battle, than he was faced with a behavioral problem that was difficult to rationalize, especially since I was a guy who was usually pretty well behaved.

Maybe it helped that I had a tear in my eye. I was genuinely sorry, and I was scared. He was of course upset, but took it rather well. After all, it was an accident, albeit a stupid one. I think that giving it to him straight with no deceit made all the difference. This time there was no thrashing. Perhaps he came to realize that physical abuse doesn't solve behavioral issues. In fact, there was no punishment at all; he even let me use the car again. In the remaining five years of his life we never had further confrontations. I would go so far as to say they were the best years of our relationship. With my mother's encouragement, there was even forgiveness on both sides. That was a stark turning point in our relationship, and it made me very happy because I did not want him to go to his grave with either of us holding on to any animosity. We said what needed to be said, and that conversation is best left between just the two of us.

4

ACTA NON VERBA

The aim of education must be the training of independent acting and thinking individuals who, however, see in the service to the community their highest life achievement.

—Dr. Albert Einstein

Deeds Not Words. That is the motto of the United States Merchant Marine Academy located at Kings Point, New York, of which I am a proud graduate, class of 1957. Most people refer to it simply as Kings Point. Its scenic eighty-two-acre waterfront campus is located on the north shore of Long Island, New York, twenty miles east of New York City.

The Long Island Sound is an idyllic location for a maritime school. From the Academy looking out on the sound, you can see a panorama of every marine activity imaginable: the sailboats heeling under full sail, the tugboats laboring with their stubborn loads, the streamlined yachts flaunting their luxury, the awkward rhythm of sea gulls fluttering and weaving about overhead, the occasional schools of fish breaking water, and, at the gray dawn of morning, the waves breaking against the windswept shoreline. The salty haze tickles your nostrils. At night, the horizon is sprinkled with the twinkling lights of the Throgs Neck Bridge, and the flashing green light of Stepping Stones Lighthouse, and the stars give the place an almost mystical feeling. You hear a never-ending sequence of belching steam whistles, foghorns, and buoy gongs. It's all there—from harsh winters to soft summers—as unmistakable as a calling.

The place itself almost could serve as a test of your vocation. If it whets your appetite, you are ready for the acid test of going to sea. If it turns you off, best call it quits right then and there. I had passed the preliminaries well before entering the Academy, and I was ready for the acid test that would soon come.

†

The Academy was opened and dedicated in 1943, and accredited in 1949 as a degree-granting institution. In 1956, Congress enacted a law making it a permanent institution. In 1963, Kings Point was used as the site for the training of the ship's officers for the first nuclear powered merchant ship, the NS *Savannah.* In 1965, the Academy created the dual license program, which gave graduates the opportunity to earn both deck and engineering licenses. In 1974, Kings Point was the first of the five federal academies to admit women. Eight such women became the first female graduates of any federal academy in 1978. And in 2006, the Academy was honored to host President George W. Bush as the first President of the United States as its commencement speaker.

All graduates receive bachelor of science degrees (in my case, marine engineering), U.S. Coast Guard merchant marine licenses as a third mate or third engineer, or both. In addition, graduates are commissioned as ensigns in the U.S. Naval Reserve. Since its inception the USMMA has been of service to the nation in peace and war. Its proud record and the outstanding service of all those who call themselves Kings Pointers truly reflect the Academy's motto, *Acta Non Verba.* Those three words have been the guiding light by which I have lived my life.[2]

I have known many young people who struggled to find their way. Trying to decide on a trade school or college was an enormous challenge; trying to decide on a career path was an even greater challenge. Some go into adulthood still not knowing what they want to do with their lives. Many fall into jobs and lifestyles somewhat randomly. Unfortunately, they settle rather than choose and sometimes suffer disappointment in the process. Not me. It is said that some people are born with a silver spoon in their mouths. I was born with an anchor in mine.

Gaining admittance was *the* turning point in my life. Driven by a strong passion for all things nautical, it was the only college I had any interest in attending. I was foolish enough not to apply to others colleges—with no back-up schools, it was Kings Point or nothing. My daily existence was going to be all about discipline, goal-orientation, and leadership. Here, I thought, was an institution where the rich relationship between America and the sea would come together for me. Here is where I could study engineering. Here is where notable personalities and maritime events would be celebrated going back to the days of Christopher Columbus and Amerigo Vespucci. Here is where it would

[2]The book In Peace and War, by Jeffrey L. Cruikshank and Chloe G. Kline, is an illuminating read for anyone with an interest in Kings Point or the U.S. maritime industry.

all come together in a vision that would become *my* lighthouse.

Notwithstanding all that enthusiasm and determination, I failed the entrance examination first time out. I simply had not worked hard enough in high school. Not to be deterred, I worked as hard as I ever have to prepare for the next admission exam. Any success I have had in my life has been through drive, determination, and hard work. It paid off; I was accepted.

In those days, besides passing a physical examination that would qualify the applicant for a naval reserve commission, admission was based on a competitive academic entrance examination with a quota accepted from each state. These days a congressional nomination from the applicant's representative or senator is also required. Competition was keen, and scores on the entrance exam had to be high to gain admission.

Once accepted, however, it soon became evident that it was easier to get in than to stay in. Being a federal military academy, life changed quickly once you walked through the door. Besides carrying a full academic load for the Bachelor of Science degree, the military aspect of academy life took its toll on one's time and attention, especially during the first year. Practicing close order drills and life boat drills, taking fire fighting class, marching to and from class, fulfilling mess hall duties, being down for lights out at 10:00 p.m., and up for reveille at 6:00 a.m., readying for white glove room inspections, facing extra duty and loss of liberty for infractions, at times seemed like a full time job in itself. Class was in session most of the day with a precious two hours of free time allowed in the afternoon. After that it was evening mess and mandatory study time till 9:30 p.m.

You'd get a half-hour of free time until lights out, except for plebes (freshmen) who were at the mercy of upperclassmen during that period. School was in session nearly eleven months of the year—no spring breaks here. No overnight liberty for plebes, either, as they might get contaminated with too much civilian or family contact. Sure there was plenty of grumbling, but the stock answer from the faculty was, "This is not a party school"—and it wasn't.

Academic failure was not tolerated. Fail two subjects and you automatically got set back to the next class. Fail again and you were out the door, no questions asked and no summer school make-up.

Attrition in this demanding environment was steep. In my class, only two out of three were still standing at graduation. Some got set back, some dropped out, and many didn't even make it through the plebe year. However, it was (as intended) a good test of how quickly you could develop a sufficient sense of determination and personal discipline to survive. Survival, in turn, generated a great sense of personal accomplishment and the beginnings of that great, satisfying feeling one gets from being able to say *I can do this*. That feeling grows as you survive more obstacles. It's the sense of self confidence that carries over in later life. Thinking back, it was a pretty good system.

†

During the sophomore year a cadet-midshipman spends the entire year at sea training aboard U.S.-flagged merchant vessels. In today's curriculum, midshipmen spend six months at sea during their sophomore year and six months at sea during their junior year. The "sea year" is a maturing experience: Wide-eyed, green kids sail off as working members of an oceangoing ship to learn their trades and see the world. This unique approach to training a cadet for a sea-going career gave me the opportunity to serve on three ships that took me to Morocco, England, Republic of South Africa, Germany, Namibia, Italy (including Sicily), France, and Mozambique. And that was just the beginning of a career and lifestyle that would eventually take me to the four corners of the earth, visiting over eighty countries and places ranging from Tahiti to Buenos Aires; from the Taj Mahal to Loch Ness; from Iwo Jima to Bali; from Hiroshima to the Great Wall of China; from Saudi Arabia to Moscow; from Berchtesgaden (Hitler's mountain retreat) to Sydney, and from Valley of the Kings in Luxor, Egypt, to my favorite location, the city of Florence and its surrounding Tuscany Hills.

It is my favorite because it is infused with centuries of art, style, culture, and scenic beauty all wrapped up in one region. The rich olive groves, steep rows of vegetation, landmark cypress-lined roads, and ancient stone churches tucked into the hillsides are but a taste of the scenery and lifestyle. Here's a modest endorsement from none other than Albert Einstein who is quoted as saying, "The ordinary Italian uses words and expressions of a high level of thought and cultural content. The people of northern Italy are the most civilized people I have ever met. The happy months of my sojourn in Italy are my most beautiful memories."

†

During my sea year, our first voyage was across the North Atlantic aboard the cargo freighter SS *Exford.* I was nineteen and had never been outside New York except to visit relatives in Jersey City, New Jersey. I was in awe of the ocean's vastness, a far cry from the local rivers, bays, and canals to which I was accustomed. It was certainly a far cry from the slime and stench of Brooklyn's answer to Venice, the Gowanus Canal. My world had been made up of candy stores, crowded city streets, the rattle of subway trains, school yards, pool halls, and corner hangouts. Now we spent days, even weeks, at sea without seeing anything but sea and sky and the occasional marine life. I found great comfort going out on deck in the early morning and leaning over the rail with a cup of tea in hand—I became convinced that nothing captures the beauty of the sea like the sun coming up on the horizon. Strange, but I found comfort too in the vast enormity of the sea. In my bones I knew it was the most powerful force on earth, demanding great respect.

To go out on deck at night was eerily maddening. I had never known darkness to be so dark, the silence to be so silent. You couldn't see the hand in front of your face. Except for the rush of the sea cresting past the ship's hull, there was utter stillness. My body instinctively got in sync with the vessel's rolling and pitching, but I shivered at the thought of falling overboard at night. Would it be cold? How long would I last before being lost to the sea bottom miles below? Or would sharks get me long before I reached the sea bottom? I couldn't shake those crazy thoughts.

Remember that bow scene in the movie *Titanic,* with DiCaprio and Winslet perched like eagles atop the bow railing? I loved going to the forward-most part of the vessel, and looking down at the ship's bow cutting through the water, sending out large bow waves, and a spume that almost reached the anchors nestled in their hawse pipes. I was always mesmerized by it, convinced that, yes, I had found what I was looking for. I was indeed on the right course to my destiny.

During one of my excursions to the bow it dawned on me that my grandparents and mother had made a similar crossing in some of the same shipping lanes. Overlapping lanes, indeed, but our thought processes must have been running different courses. My thoughts were of hope, education, ambition, and the likelihood of returning home to a bright future. Theirs must have been one of fear, uncertainty, and anxiety, but they must have borne hope for the future, too. What unfolded for our generations is very much a part of what this book is all about.

Upon arrival at our first foreign port, my classmate and dear friend Joe Nunziato and I were awakened by the noisy rattling of the anchor and anchor chain whistling through the hawse pipe before hitting the water. The vessel shuddered, and then prepared to anchor for the night. We scampered up to the top bunk in our cabin to look out the porthole to see the twinkling lights of Casablanca. Just think, from Brooklyn to Casablanca in one fell swoop. The next morning after the vessel docked, Joe and I were as excited as a couple of kids going to their first circus, and were the first crew members to go ashore. We didn't find Rick's Café Americain of *Casablanca* fame, but we let our imaginations run wild. We were as green as the water that pounded us at sea, and it must have showed.

†

The second merchant ship I was assigned to was a cargo freighter named the SS *African Moon*. She routinely plowed her way on a seventeen-day run from New York to Cape Town, then around the Cape of Good Hope and north to ports along the southeast coast of Africa.

Our last northbound port of call was Beira, the second largest city in Mozambique (550,000 people as of 2006).

Mozambique is now an independent nation, but while I was there it was still a Portuguese colony, and ruled with an iron fist. Public hangings were still carried out. In fact, we learned there would be a public hanging in the main square a couple of days after we arrived. At first, we thought it was a joke, but a few of us decided to go anyway. It was no joke, nor was it as I had imagined from movies. Even though the area around the hanging platform was crowded, we managed to get within one hundred feet of it. I shuddered when they placed the hood over his head—it was really going to happen. We didn't know why the prisoner was going to be hanged, but the crowd was not sympathetic with his plight; when the trap door suddenly opened with a bang and he fell to his death, there was a smattering of yells and applause. There was even scattered chanting. The grizzly deed was done with proficiency, and to my surprise completely void of any emotion from the officials *and* the condemned. The image of his struggling legs and twitching feet is something I will carry to my grave.

It was during our stay in Beira that I jumped at the chance to go on safari, albeit a camera safari. Only the guide was armed. The Captain was kind enough to give me the time off; in those days cargo handling was not as mechanized as it is today, so a vessel could spend as much as a week in port handling cargo. There were five of us, plus the guide. The safari took us to the Gorongoza Mountain and National Park, which is situated northwest of Beira near the border of Zimbabwe. At the time it was one of Africa's most bountiful natural game reserves. It has since fallen into disarray and the government is working to restore the park to its former glory—according to the latest data it comprises nearly three million acres of open plain, bush, swamp, and waterways of all sorts and sizes. Believe me, this was no zoo.

Our guide was a Mozambique native who was fluent in English. He was our teacher and our guardian, and would, by the end of the safari, become our friend. We were told up front that his was not going to be a comfy, handholding safari. We should not expect fine linens or hot water. For our own safety we were not to do anything without his guidance. Our transportation was an expedition vehicle with a roof hatch and a window seat for each of us. Roads were often bumpy and river crossings numerous. There were a few instances where bad roads and flooding necessitated detours. At the end of each day we had a briefing to help us prepare for the next day of game viewing. Each night we would layover in one of the tented bush camps. In the chill of the evenings we relaxed and compared notes around a campfire, listening to the unfamiliar, haunting sounds of the African night.

Somebody in our group asked the guide if we would see snakes. He said it was very doubtful, as they are timid creatures that attack only if threatened. He further commented that snakes hanging from tree branches to attack people are strictly Hollywood fiction. Besides there was plenty of prey for them to forage so they didn't need us, thankfully.

Our days were steeped in natural beauty. Wildlife spread across what seemed like a never-ending sea of open plain, and the plain teemed with wildlife—lions, elephants, zebras, leopards, hyenas, wildebeest, hippos, cheetahs, giraffes, African buffalos, and antelopes of all shapes and sizes. Even the grotesque warthog. There also seemed to be an infinite variety of bird life, not least of which were the commonly known flamingo, starlings, and pelicans.

An incredible diversity of the flora blended so beautifully with some of the finest birding that I had ever seen. God, I thought, nature does a magnificent job. The only animal I wished to see and didn't was the tiger. Back then, they were limited to the Asiatic plains, and today, the majority of the world's tigers now live in captivity.

Against that backdrop our days were filled with guided game drives and walking safaris. We had our scariest outing the first day on foot. We came across a herd of bull elephants and I guess we got too close; they spooked. One jumbo came directly at us, and we ran for dear life back to our vehicle—and just in time to avoid being stomped on. I had seen these creatures in the zoo, but it was nothing compared to what I saw out there. The massive brutes give the word jumbo new meaning. After we were back in the vehicle, we stayed there for a while to do more elephant watching. Before long we had a ringside seat to elephant wrestling. A few of the elephants were going at it, more in a playful than hostile way.

That night the guide told us we would have to get up at 4:00 a.m. to possibly witness a lion kill. The next morning, rising with the African sun, I looked out on the vast plain and it took my breath away. It was a sight, smell, and sound like no other I had ever experienced or ever will again. The serenity and colors of the wilderness are truly something to behold, especially for a kid from Brooklyn. After breakfast we set out in our vehicle and drove for about a half hour. The guide stopped intermittently to scan the plains with his binoculars. Finally he spotted what he thought was a lion that had just made a kill on one of their favorite prey, the zebra. He drove quickly to the scene, whereupon we found the carcass of a freshly killed zebra. We were feeling sorry for the zebra, but our guide was quick to remind us that not every chase ends in a kill and that predators including the lion must work hard for a meal. The carcass was already half eaten, and was a mess of gore. The pity of it was that we had chased the big cat away from her breakfast (the lioness does all of the hunting), but the guide speculated that she was probably off in the distance somewhere watching us, and that she and the rest of the pride would return to the feast after we left. Rather timid, I thought, for the king of the beasts, but the iron monster we were riding was probably intimidating. In any event, we didn't stick around long enough to find out.

After lunch we drove to a pride resting area to get a close-up view of the big cats. We began to feel a bit uneasy. Seeing lions at the zoo is one thing, but seeing them in the wild is quite something else. As we approached a group of six or eight lions, they seemed relaxed. We were so close it seemed that you could reach out and touch them. The cubs were the best part—playfully jumping on and crawling over mama in the same way you would expect of a housecat. The guide cautioned us to remain in the vehicle at all times with the windows up, lest a lion might decide we were tastier than a zebra.

Speaking of cubs reminds me of a subject that has always intrigued me and that has to do with lions killing their young. Yes, I know what you are thinking—what parent hasn't had the urge?

When a new male takes over leadership of a pride they are often confronted by the cubs of the males they defeated. These guys have no time to spare protecting the offspring of their predecessors because their own time with the pride will probably be limited. In fact, successful males that takeover a pride have about two years before another younger, stronger coalition will replace them. Females will not normally mate again until their cubs are at least eighteen months old; therefore, males kill all the young cubs in their pride in order to bring the females back to mating readiness. The females resist the infanticide until their efforts seem hopeless, and then give themselves up to the new ruler for copulation.

Killing all the cubs also helps to enforce their dominance over other members of the pride. In addition, it eliminates the chance of any rivalry against offspring the new male might later father. So you see there is logic to what might otherwise seem like utter madness. Older cubs and sub-adults stand a chance, however, because they can often escape from infanticidal males. These cubs are evicted and must fend for themselves, although occasionally their mothers will leave with them and remain apart from the pride until the cubs reach independence. I also learned that one of the primary reasons female lions live in groups is to protect their young against infanticidal males. Males are 1.5 times larger than females so a female alone is powerless, but females in groups can succeed in keeping males away from cubs.

The next day we drove for a while and then set out on foot for a lengthy walk. An encounter with wildlife on foot is an unforgettable experience. You become tentative about every step you take, and suspicious about everything lurking around you. More to the point—you are downright scared. The guide invited us to join him in search of animals and birds in their natural habitat. He even threw in a free lesson on the art of tracking. Later on we got a chance to see a hippopotamus, but did not dare to get real close. We were told they are one of the most dangerous animals in Africa and when provoked will charge with alarming speed for their size. On the way back to the camp we saw a variety of animal herds, but no other kill.

On the penultimate day of our safari we had another anxious moment when a swarm of hyenas chased our vehicle. We were driving off the plain approaching a bush area when two dozen or so hyenas starting circling around our vehicle. They would charge, back off, charge again and back off repeatedly, while at the same time jumping up and down letting out those devilish screams and barks. The guide indicated we were in no real danger; it was just the nature of these nasty little creatures to play out their aggressiveness.

†

During the trans-Atlantic crossing aboard the SS *African Moon,* I had begun stargazing in earnest. It seemed as though you could take in the entire universe without obstruction. The African night ignited the same feelings for me. Its haunting sounds and stillness were conducive to lying out, gazing up at the stars, feeling as though you could run your fingers through them. During my childhood I could never appreciate the grandeur of the universe, because of the prosaic confines of the concrete canyons in which I existed. But here, on the rolling deck of the SS *African Moon,* and on the African plain, my spirit and imagination ran wild. Even now, whenever I stargaze, it always makes me wonder about the boundaries of our universe and where it all ends. If you dwell on that thought long enough it can drive you stark raving mad.

Think about it for a minute. What is at the end of the universe, if it really does end? The very thought that there is perhaps no ending is the part that is mind-boggling.

You might suggest that at the end of the universe there are boundaries, no matter whether the universe is flat, or like a sphere, or whatever. Then you ask yourself what is beyond that? Could it be nothingness? But then, what is nothingness? The thought of a never-ending universe without boundaries begs more questions. How can the universe go on, and on, and on, and on without ending? If we look to Albert Einstein for enlightenment, he is quoted as saying, "the discovery and use of scientific reasoning by Galileo Galilei (1564-1642), was one of the most important achievements in the history of human thought and marks the real beginning of astronomy and physics." Yet, as far as I could determine even Galilei's astrological revelations shed little light on the "end of the universe" question. So I still rack my brain with this hypothetical question: If I were in a space vehicle traveling a thousand miles an hour and traveled into space FOREVER, how can it be that I would not come to the end. Doesn't that blow your mind?

But enough stargazing. Back on earth, on the final day of our safari we passed through a native village. There was a local market, but not much from which to choose. There was no one hounding us to see or buy anything. That convinced us that we were really out in the bush. Although we were not restricted from taking photos I felt uneasy about it, almost as if we were invading their privacy. The villagers were on guard and somewhat suspicious. They certainly weren't about to entertain us in any way—except for one incident in the village, which may have been staged. We watched an excited male ostrich with his awkward gait move gingerly toward a female. He mounted her in what seemed like a wild kingdom moment. You should have seen these two—he flopped from side to side on top of her, falling on and off, while feathers flew everywhere. He was so gangly and uncoordinated that I don't think it could have been much fun for either one of them.

The other thing that really struck me was the meagerness with which people lived their lives. Even the children weren't playful, which further suggests the hardship and rigors of life in the wild. They just stared at us. Here was a place and a people existing much the same way their ancestors have lived for centuries. There were no motor vehicles of any kind; the locals used boats or donkeys for transportation. With homes made of wood and cow dung, there was no plumbing, appliances, or even radios, not to mention television. That has stayed with me for a long, long time—especially when I'm griping about not getting my newspaper delivery, or traffic jams, or the price of gasoline.

The safari adventure, even a camera safari, is like stock trading; not for the faint of heart. An open mindset is essential. The rewards of a trek through a virtually untouched game reserve are worth the hassle, and yes, even the risks. Speaking of risks, I should mention that not once did the guide have to draw his weapon. Cheers, Bwana.

The trip to South Africa was eventful for a couple of other reasons. We docked in Durban, a city on the east coast. Vernon, the ship's second assistant engineer learned from the agent who came aboard that his cousin was aboard a ship docked nearby. As he prepared to go over and visit his cousin he asked me if I'd like to join him. I gladly accepted the chance to perhaps meet a fellow cadet aboard the ship and witness the inner workings of another vessel. As we approached the vessel on foot we could see a lot of commotion with police vehicles and ambulances standing by. When we approached the gangway to board the vessel we were stopped by the police and told no one would be allowed to board as one of the crew members had just died in an accident. We hung around for approximately thirty minutes making inquires as to what happened. Finally, we learned from one of the crewmembers that the guy who was killed was in fact Vernon's cousin. He had been in a bosun's chair lowering himself inside the ship‘s smoke stack to inspect emergency repairs that had been made by shipyard workers. (A boatswain's chair, commonly referred to as a bosun's chair, is a self-tending seat used to suspend a person from a line in order to perform work aloft.) The details were not yet known, but speculation was that either the chair slipped and fell with him in it, or he fell from the chair. In either case the result was same. He fell approximately sixty feet into the cold boiler and was killed instantly from multiple bone and skull fractures. After an hour or so, stretcher-bearers brought his mangled body off the vessel into an ambulance. Vernon was in a state of shock. For all of us it was a sad ending to an otherwise happy voyage. It was also a stark reminder of the importance of safety awareness so often drummed into us during our training at Kings Point.

During this voyage I had my first homosexual encounter, which occurred in Cape Town. I had spent a very pleasant day sightseeing. The city had so much to offer, and I am sure still does. It was late afternoon and I was getting ready to head back to the ship. Problem was that I was desperately lost, and it began to rain heavily, which only made matters worse. The more I searched the more I went around in circles. Before taking a taxi that I couldn't afford back to the ship, I decided to ask one more person for help. The guy I asked seemed to know his way around the city and was willing to help. He said his car was parked nearby and that he would drive me back to the ship. After we got in the car he made no effort to start it. Instead he just wanted to talk, mostly about how lonely and depressed he was feeling over the loss of a friend. Typical of my naiveté at the time, I had no idea where he was going with the chatter until I felt his hand on my knee. When I bolted he became apologetic realizing it wasn't going to happen. We parted company with no hard feelings (no pun intended). I exited the car pronto and did what I should have done in the first place—hailed a taxi.

†

Upon our return to New York I discovered that National Geographic was doing a story about the United States Merchant Marine Academy. *Kings Point: Maker of Mariners* focused on academy history, its unique training program, and the call that "binds Kings Pointers in the brotherhood of the sea." Not all graduates serve that calling for a lifetime, but few escape the bond that invariably occurs between the school and its graduates, and between graduates. We are a close group, proud of each other and our maritime heritage. In my experience most graduates lend their support to, and maintain a close association with, the Academy for the rest of their lives. That bonding does not occur at all colleges. For example, I received a master's degree in engineering from Stevens Institute of Technology in Hoboken, New Jersey. I walked out the door after graduation and have not set foot in the place since, nor have I kept in touch with any of the graduates or donated a dime to the school. Not to be critical, but I think that's typical of many college graduates.

My classmate George Wilson, who got stuck as my first roommate, describes the bond this way.

> To understand this bonding, it must be remembered that the combination of academic and military life was basically a 24/7, 365-day way of life. You lived, ate, went to class, had successes and screwed up with a very close-knit group. A group with diverse backgrounds, but now all with the same aspirations and stresses in trying to achieve those aspirations (sometimes just survival). A good study in group dynamics indeed. In the end, this kind of life fostered very close bonds. Some 50 years later, we still count our classmates as close friends and a group of us still attempt to get together as often as we can. The large class turnout at the recent 50th reunion attests to that fact. Not many schools can boast that kind of loyalty.

The National Geographic story says it all: "Words of one of the school songs well sum up the faith with which they face the voyage of life:

Heave ho!
My lads, heave ho!
Let the sea roll high and low.
We can cross any ocean, sail any river,
Give us the goods and we'll deliver."

Unbeknownst to me, arrangements had been made for me to be interviewed for the story. The writer, a guy by the name of Nathaniel T. Kenney, wanted very much to make an impromptu visit on board one of the ships carrying cadets. It had been explained to him by the academy staff that during the sea year cadets are scattered over the oceans. The world is the sophomore's campus, and he travels across it on three, maybe four different American-flag merchant ships. In some cases a cadet may log as many fifty-thousand miles or more. Typically a vessel will carry one deck and one engine cadet. On the day the writer came on board the SS *African Moon*, the deck cadet Hal Kruse was ashore, but I was on board standing watch. The writer was accompanied by Commander C. Sandberg, the assistant head of the engineering department. At the time we were unloading baled hides and frozen lobster tails from Cape Town. The chief engineer summoned me to his room to meet our guests. I already knew Commander Sandberg, for whom I had great respect as a professional and as a gentleman. They asked me to go back to fetch my sea project, which each cadet is expected to work on during his hours off watch. As I left, Mr. Kenney commented, "This was a wide-eyed plebe last year?" (The commentary is taken from the article.)

"Yes," said Commander Sandberg. "They mature fast at sea. It's a wonderful system."

When I returned with my sea project they leafed through it reviewing each task I had been assigned. Mr. Kenney said he was impressed with the way I had described and sketched the ship's refrigeration system that kept the vessel's lobster tail cargo frozen.

"Starace, the chief likes you and wants you to sign on for another trip," said Commander Sandberg. I replied that although I liked the SS *African Moon* and everybody in her, I wanted a tanker next for experience.

"OK, I'll try to set it up," he said.

Mr. Kenney then asked me to go out on deck with him. In his article, he described our meeting this way.

> Later, Starace and I stood alone on deck watching the busy tugs scurrying about their affairs and the quarreling gulls wheeling above the masts. He told me of whales spouting in the windy South Atlantic, of raising lonely St. Helena in the dawn, and of the white mists blanketing Table Top Mountain behind Cape Town. He had had an education, all right.

As fate would have it, the SS *African Moon* docked at a pier at the foot of 33rd street in Brooklyn. On arrival, as the ship maneuvered through the canal preparing to tie up, I positioned myself on deck to take it all in. When I saw the very spot at 31st Street where I used to sit watching the big ships coming and going, a lump formed in my throat. The kid had finally realized his dream, coming home to where it all began. That's part nostalgia and part reality.

†

For most of us, settling into the classroom was quite an adjustment from the sea year. During our junior year we were coming down the home stretch into final exams. It became quite apparent from the grades already posted that I needed an A in thermodynamics to come out number one in the class. It was considered to be the toughest course by far and was worth the most credits. I studied for that exam like I had never studied for anything before or since. Going into it I was confident. Coming out of it I was even more confident. On the day of reckoning the instructor, Lieutenant Commander Sid O. Carlson, started handing out our exam papers with the marks scribbled in red on the top page. When he got to my paper he said to the class, "This is the first time in all the years I have been teaching this course that anyone has ever handed in a perfect final exam. Congratulations, Starace."

I didn't walk up to the front of the room to get it; I flew. I thought getting a perfect score on the final exam would mean an A for the course and therefore the highest grade point average for the year.

When the final grades were posted, I saw next to my name, "Thermodynamics—B." Notwithstanding Carlson's reputation for being a tough marker, I was flabbergasted. When I talked with him about it, his rationale was that I was a B student going into the finals. He felt to get an A, a student had to be an A student throughout the course. Consequently, I finished third in the class. It was certainly a disappointment, but there was something positive to take away. After all, like everyone else I would be facing more disappointments in life, most of them a lot more serious than this one. The important thing was to learn from the experience, rise above it and move on. Getting top scholastic honors in the class would not have meant I was the brightest guy in the class, either. It would have simply meant that I was willing to work as hard or harder than anyone else. That has always been one of my greatest strengths.

Years later I saw Lieutenant Commander Carlson at an industry conference. As we approached each other and his hand reached out to receive my handshake, he said facetiously, "Don't tell me. I remember."

†

I arrived at the next crossroads in my life during my final year at the Academy. Classmate Hal Kruse convinced me to take the examination to enter flight school at the Naval Air Station in Pensacola, Florida. Known as the "Cradle of

Naval Aviation" and home of the Blue Angels, Pensacola serves as the flight-training center for every naval flight officer and enlisted air crewman. Hal's rationale was that jet aviation was the wave of the future and that it would afford us an exciting and glamorous career. It would certainly be a far cry from our days aboard the SS *African Moon*, when for relaxation we read poetry to each other from a classroom book of verse. Edgar Allen Poe's, "Annabel Lee," was *the* favorite—I can still recite it from memory. This is when my love of poetry crystallized. I agreed to take the exam not because I was especially motivated to fly jets, but because it was a way we could stay together; we had become very good friends on the football team, and this would be a sort of buddy system gesture.

Off we went to Floyd Bennett Field in Brooklyn to take the exam. I didn't tell my parents about it, thinking they would probably not like the idea. I'd deal with that later if I had to. The examination was extremely rigorous and lasted all day. One of the more demanding aspects was the simulated flight cockpit wherein your reflexes were tested against aerial combat situations. The maze of instruments on the control panel were so complicated it made me realize the contraption didn't even have a steering wheel. Your psychological make-up was evaluated too; the occupation required mental toughness. I was sure I failed.

But two weeks later when I received the acceptance letter I damn near jumped out of my skin. By this time, Hal had gotten me pumped up about the idea. With the letter in hand, I ran to his room two buildings away. I rushed into his room yelling, "Hal, I got in, I got in!" As soon as I saw the dejected look on his face, I knew he had not. He handed me his "We regret to inform you ..." letter. It said they found he had a slight heart murmur. So slight that it had not been detected during his physical examination to get into the Academy. When he asked me what I was going to do, I didn't have to think twice about it. He wasn't going, so I wasn't, either.

If he had been admitted to Pensacola, I would have stayed in the navy and gone on to fly fighter jets off carrier decks. The timing was such that I would have been ripe for early Vietnam duty. Later, I would have maybe had a naval flight career or a career as a commercial pilot. All this, based on somebody else's hopes. I have always looked at myself very honestly, but at the time I guess I lacked the maturity to know better. Were it not for a few imperfect tissues in Hal Kruse's heart, I would have been separated from my passion.

5

FROM HERE TO INFINITY

Show me a good loser and I will show you a loser.

—Vince Lombardi, NFL head football coach

In my last year at the Academy I was jolted by the death of my grandfather. Memories of him are still quite vivid. When my father called to tell me of his death I was devastated by the realization that I would never see him again. For the first time in my young life I lost someone for whom I cared deeply.

Almost up until the time he died at the age of 86, he would come to visit us. He would take the subway on his own. When we hugged I remember how his tough beard felt like sandpaper across my face. He would arrive in the one suit that he owned, always clean and neat. The hat was slightly crumpled. The white shirt was nicely ironed, and the tie was evenly pressed, although a bit spotted. The fingers of his left hand were terribly disfigured from the missed blows of his caulking mallet; such is the occupational hazard of a ship caulker. He had never been in a hospital or even a dental chair. He would tell you it was because of the wine he so fondly consumed in moderation all of his life. My warmest Christmas memories are those spent around him. To see the glow in his eyes and the smile on his face with his entire brood of children, grandchildren, and great grandchildren around him is something that has stayed with me all these many years. So has the love of Aunt Katie, who is the last living member of his fourteen sons and daughters. She makes me proud to be of the same bloodline.

At his funeral my parents insisted that I be there in my Kings Point full dress uniform. As the priest said my grandfather's last rites that morning, I looked again at the sky and thought of my hours lying on the foredeck, looking up at the night sky. I flashed back to a time when I would sit next to him in the basement watching him weave his ship-modeling magic, cutting and stitching the white sails to perfection. The seeds of my life and what I would become were sown in the basement of that two-family home in Bensonhurst. Later on, so many times I wondered about the sky over his passage to America, and what lay on the other side—of the ocean, and of the sky itself. We're told that for a small fraction of a second the universe was an infinitely dense and hot fireball. For as long as I can remember, I have wondered, as I did on the SS *African Moon*, if the universe is as infinite in time as it is in space. What is beyond the edge? Where do heaven, hell, and everything in between fit into this colossus? Only the answers to those questions might temper the enormous curiosity I have always had about death and the hereafter.

I believe that amid all of this, God knows everything right down to the fall of the tiniest sparrow. He knows my grandfather. He cares about our smallest problems, our biggest hurts, and our every joy. To my mind there is only one explanation to the boundlessness of space: the answer is beyond human comprehension. Infinity is unfathomable. Thus whatever the shape of the universe and the galaxies beyond, there is nothing called a boundary and hence nothing called the edge or end of it all. That answer does not begin to satisfy the utter madness I feel when I think about the universe, or about history, or about my grandfather—not then at his funeral, and not today, as I still sometimes lie on the foredeck of my yacht on a clear evening, gently rocking, staring into a star-drenched sky.

After my grandfather died, Christmas was never quite the same. But the family still spent time together as often as we could at BBQs, holidays, and any other excuse we can come up with. For such a large family, the pride we share in each other is in itself a success story—the American dream come true, even though life changed for all of us who were close to my grandfather.

I know he was proud of me for following in his footsteps. Like him, I was a MARINER at heart who loved the smell of the sea air as much as life itself.

6

LADY IN WAITING

For the moon never beams without
bringing me dreams
Of the beautiful Annabel Lee,
And the stars never rise but
I feel the bright eyes
Of the beautiful Annabel Lee.

—Edgar Allen Poe, from "Annabel Lee"

February 1957 was one of the most momentous periods in my life. In a flash, I graduated from Kings Point, got married, and got my first seagoing job. Ronnie and I were married two days after graduation. It was not a military wedding, but instead was performed in her local parish with all the pomp and ceremony that goes with a Catholic rite. She looked stunning with her red hair flowing from under her white veil. I was a mere accessory on her arm in my dress blue uniform. For Ronnie, who was raised with strong Christian values, nothing could have been more appropriate. We started our married life as do most couples, with hopes and aspirations for a long and happy life together. After a one-week honeymoon in Miami, which included a two-day trip to naughty and kitschy Havana just before Castro took over, we settled into a modest three-room apartment in the Bay Ridge section of Brooklyn. We were about to embark on a thirty-four-year journey that would take us to the four corners of the world while raising three lovely children, and to the utter despair of losing one of them.

†

After graduating from Kings Point in 1957 I was doing what I was trained to do—sail American-flag merchant ships. In accepting the job I came to realize that I was extending a seafaring tradition that went back to both of my grandfathers, who had sailed in the Italian merchant marine. They witnessed a major transition in seafaring—sail to steam power. When they, as boy sailors, looked to the sky they saw white sail—I saw what I would become. My first seagoing job was on the SS *United States* serving as one of its engineering officers. The technical director from United States Lines, Nick Bachko, a Kings Point graduate himself, came to the Academy looking to hire two deck officers and two engineering officers. After he interviewed a group of us, I was lucky enough to get one of the engineering slots. Recruited right off campus, I could not have asked for a better steppingstone into my career.

On her maiden voyage, July 3, 1952, the SS *United States* passed Bishop's Rock off the coast of England, three days, ten hours and forty minutes after her New York departure, thus shaving ten hours from the record the *Queen Mary* had held since 1938. At an average speed of 35.59 knots she had won the greatest race in history, taking the Blue Riband

and Hales Trophy for being the fastest ocean liner ever. During sea trials she hit a maximum speed of 43 knots on one leg of her speed runs. There is evidence to suggest she could go faster, but she has never been run "flat out."

She was widely considered to be an engineering marvel, the most technologically advanced liner of her day. Advanced materials made her virtually fireproof—the butcher's block and piano were the only wood used in her construction. With extensive watertight compartments, along with the fireproof materials, she was the safest vessel ever built, and state-of-the-art throughout. In 1999, those credentials earned her a place on the National Register of Historic Places.

Notwithstanding the fondness many people had for ocean travel, jet travel laid waste to the passenger liner era. As a result, in 1969 the Big "U" was put out of service, but has fortunately avoided the scrap heap. To this day she is a lady in waiting, an endangered species with time and tide eating away at her innards at a pier in Philadelphia, Pennsylvania. There she rests, looking more like a bedraggled tramp steamer than the crown jewel of the U.S. Merchant Marine that she once was. Sentimental fool that I am, if I were to walk aboard the great lady today I think I could intuitively find my old cabin—or what's left of it.

Over the years several revival plans have been made to bring her back to some form of service. Conversion to a cruise ship, floating hotel and conference center, or museum are but a few ideas. I think reactivation to cruise service is unlikely because it is not economically viable compared to building a new vessel. Conversion to a stationary facility is probably a more realistic goal, and even that is doubtful without local or federal government financial support. A one-hour documentary film, *SS United States: Lady in Waiting*, aired on public television stations nationwide in May 2008. Two years in the making, it highlighted the vessel's illustrious career and will help "bring our nation's flagship back into the spotlight of historical significance she so richly deserves." Hopefully, the film will provide added impetus to ongoing efforts by the SS United States Conservancy to preserve and revitalize the vessel. The world premiere of the film was held on board the *Queen Mary* in Long Beach, California. As a former crew member, I supported the Conservancy in the making of the film by offering film I had taken while serving onboard, authentic paraphernalia from the vessel, and personal anecdotes. I was interviewed during the making of the film and appear in it. I also had the good fortune to attend the gala premiere May 3, 2008, in Long Beach.

†

My first day on board I was overwhelmed; there was so much to learn and do. Two engine rooms, four sets of main propulsion steam turbines, and eight boilers—it all seemed so expansive and complicated. Certainly nothing like I had seen in my sea year. While the work wasn't tiring, the level of responsibility I was given on day-one of my job intimidated me. I was no stranger to ships, but I wasn't quite sure I was prepared for what was expected of me.

The executive chief engineer gave me a walk-through of the engine room. The hissing of high-pressure steam, the high-pitched whine of the turbines, and the intense heat from the boilers created an atmosphere worthy of an inferno, or so I thought at first. I asked myself, *What have I let myself in for?* The fact that I was new didn't help matters. But a Kings Point education was in my bones. I quickly gained knowledge and confidence, and took on more and more responsibility. Ultimately, the experience taught me what it means to step up to the kind of challenges I would be facing the rest of my life.

On board the SS *United States* I was part of the best institution of its kind in the world. I worked on the best ship of its kind, designed and built by the best professionals, working alongside the best marine engineers in the business. I still have the pay stub from my very first trip—a whopping $424.61 before taxes, for eighteen days' work with some overtime. That was big money in those days, certainly more than I had ever dreamed of making.

She was pristine from stem to stern. To give you an idea of just how fastidious the owner and crew were about her upkeep and appearance, a "smoke watch" would be posted every time she entered or left New York Harbor, where she drew so much attention. On those days, the order of the day was NO BLACK SMOKE. Oil-fired steam boilers that are properly maintained and operated should emit only a light haze. Nothing was to mar the majestic presence of this great lady as she made her way into and out of port along the Hudson River. A watch-stander was therefore posted on the stack deck to immediately report any black smoke to the engine room. The concern was not for environmental reasons, as there wasn't the environmental sensitivity then as there is now. It was primarily a matter of good operating practice, and at U.S. Lines we prided ourselves on the professional manner in which we ran our ships. If there was black smoke emanating from one or both of her two stacks, we would soon hear about it from the U.S. Lines head office, as the vessel was always observed as she steamed past the office en route to and from her mid-town berth. To be honest I cannot remember if we ever got a reprimand, but the threat kept us on our toes.

Movie stars and politicians graced her decks on a regular basis. I played my first round of golf in Southampton, England, during one of our calls there, and I met Bob Hope during a stopover. He told me that his fondness for ocean travel prompted him to make many trans-Atlantic crossings on the "Big U," as she was affectionately known. His trusty golf clubs close at hand, he quipped, "Golf is my profession. Show business is just to pay the greens fees." (No, he did not invite me to play a round of golf.) For many of us he is remembered mostly for his work with the USO in entertaining our troops overseas. Within a show business career that spanned approximately eighty years, his USO career lasted half a century, during which he headlined approximately sixty tours. I'm sure he is still at it, delighting the service guys on the front lines of the hereafter.

Another frequent passenger was the beautiful Rita Hayworth, known to film-goers as "The Love Goddess." The sight of her sunbathing on the aft deck was enough to convince me of her legendary beauty. Whenever former crew members and aficionados of the great ship get together, they tell sea stories. A favorite is the one about the toilet seat in Ms. Hayworth's cabin. During one of her trips, the chief engineer was so bewitched by her beauty that he wanted to have something to remember her by. As chief engineer, he had a master key to all the cabins. He entered her room while she was out and removed the toilet seat—a mystery that went unresolved until 1990 at a reunion of SS *United States* crew members held at Kings Point, when the old devil admitted to the larceny at age eighty-eight. He also admitted to having key rings made from it, and passing them out to the crew so they could all have something that was *close* to Rita Hayworth. I'm curious if the story ever got back to her.

7

THE NAVY OF MY YOUTH

There is no surer sign of decay in a country than to see the rites of religion held in contempt.

—Niccolò Machiavelli (1469–1527)

To broaden my experience, U.S. Lines occasionally transferred me to other types of vessels. On one such occasion I was sailing to Europe aboard the cargo vessel SS *American Planter*. During the voyage the ship received an urgent message from the U.S. Lines head office saying that my draft board was hot on my heels, and that I was about to become a private in the U.S. Army. The obvious choice was for me to activate my ensign's commission in the navy, but would there be enough time given the fact that the ship was not due back in the United States for another three weeks?

Ronnie went to the head office to explain my situation to the management and hopefully get me an extension. Together they were able to plead my case to the draft board, which finally acquiesced and gave me enough time to get back as scheduled, without me having to fly home from Europe. Given the cost of my education, serving in the army as a private would have been a waste of taxpayers' money. As soon as the ship tied up in New York, off I went to the nearest naval recruiting office and became a commissioned officer with the rank of ensign virtually overnight. And so started my naval career.

†

With my entrance into the U.S. Navy I was extending another family tradition that went back to World War I. My military deeds pale in comparison to those of the men and women on both sides of my family who gave so much to our country in time of war. Their story must be told, and should always remain part of the family legacy.

Uncle Tony, the oldest son of my paternal grandparents, answered the call to fight in World War I shortly after the United States entered war on April 6, 1917. He shipped out to France the same year, where, as part of an infantry battalion, he experienced trench warfare at its ugliest until the end of the war on November 11, 1918. (At this writing there is only one surviving doughboy from that war, at age 107.) What a pity that nearly a century after the war to end all wars was over, we are still at it. We never heard him discuss the war except to say how he used to dread the thought of possibly falling victim to poison gas, which became one of the most feared and vividly remembered horrors of the war. He would also reflect on how at night he and others in his company would frequently exchange light repartee with German troops in the opposing trenches, only to be faced with how to best kill each other the very next day. He was such a gentle, soft-spoken man that it was difficult for us to understand how he could be trained to harm anything, much less kill someone.

It's a question the human race has been asking itself since the beginning of time. What drives average people to take a life or sacrifice their own in armed conflict? What motivates them to put their lives at risk in storming a beachhead, or parachuting from a plane, or manning a ship in submarine-infested waters? Initially the motivation might be patriotism, indoctrination, glory, or peer pressure. But once in the battle arena, there is a strong argument that soldiers fight to protect and help the soldier at their side. The bonds they form in combat is something civilians cannot be expected to understand.

Unfortunately, it would be all too soon before Uncle Tony's son, my cousin Michael, and three of his seven brothers, Sal, Pete and Joe, would go off to World War II. All of them served in the military until the end of the war. My father was lucky—he was too old for the second war and too young for the first.

Uncle Pete, a modest and kind man, served with the U.S. Army in the South Pacific for nearly four years and was in the thick of the fighting from the beginning. His unit was brought in to relieve battle-weary Marine units during the Battle of Guadalcanal. He never spoke a word about the war until years later. At a family gathering we were sitting around the kitchen table (where else?) having a few drinks when, without prompting from anyone, he started to talk. Then he started to weep, and for the first time I heard him relate some of his wartime experiences.

I asked, "What's wrong, Unc?" He confessed that he had "killed hundreds" of the enemy as part of a machine gun squad repelling waves of Japanese Banzai (Long Live) suicide attacks. As he spoke, a photo of him came flashing back to me. Funny how you remember those things. It was a shot of him that my father kept in his wallet and liked to proudly show. On an island somewhere in the South Pacific, Uncle Pete was sitting on sand bags that surrounded his machine gun nest, his clothes tattered and torn. That photo made what he was telling me real. He also talked about the horrors of the flamethrower used by soldiers to kill and dislodge the enemy. He was letting it all out for the first time, and it must have felt good to at least talk about it after all these years. I listened and offered what feeble solace I could. He wept some more, finally forced a bit of a smile and we had another drink. I'm sure he took whatever was left of those bitter memories to his grave, and hopefully, some piece of mind.

Next to go to war in my generation was my cousin Tom Starace, who served in the Marine Corps during the Korean War. Like Uncle Pete, he never talked about the war, but of all his many achievements, I think there was nothing he was prouder of than being a Marine right up to the day he died. When you visited his home the one thing he was quick to show you were his decorations, honors, and awards, as well as photos of himself in his Marine dress uniform. He was quick to point out that once a Marine, always a Marine; you are never an ex-Marine.

Not to be forgotten are all the women in our family who stayed behind playing a vital role in the workplace and in the home. It was largely due to their work, support, letters, love, and faithfulness that victory on the battlefield was possible. Without their sacrifices and that of millions of other women just like them, the wars could not have been won.

Recalling my brother, he served his time in the navy when I was still playing stickball in South Brooklyn. Now I was embarking on a similar path, and he was proud of me. However, I was still a bit too inexperienced to recognize the grim reality of war. He had witnessed it firsthand, and is the first to revile war as a way of settling international disputes.

We had a small dinner party at home a couple of days before I shipped out. With the exception of my mother, everybody was in a festive mood. She tried to hide it, but I knew she was uneasy. Having gone through the trauma of my brother serving in the navy during World War II, she realized that even in peacetime there are risks in military service—subsequent ship operations in the Straits of Taiwan proved her right. After a while I began to feel guilty about putting her through that. Rather than risk a tearful scene at the airport, we said all our goodbyes at the party. My father gave me a hug and a handshake, and told me, "Show 'em what you're made of."

Ronnie drove me to the airport, and there, alone among the river of travelers, we said a quiet and tender farewell.

†

After ten weeks of further officer training at the Treasure Island Naval Base, San Francisco, I reported to the USS *Tolovana* (AO-64) in Sasebo, Japan, as a brand new ensign. I was a bit overwhelmed by what life in the navy might bring, and for that reason it was with great relief that I spotted the smiling face of classmate Bill Eckert at the top of the gangway as I reported aboard ship. He had reported for duty six months earlier, and came out specifically to greet me, and to show me the ropes.

We would remain lifelong friends (he eventually died of cancer in 2005). Back in the day, one of our inside jokes was the particular interest we took in pointing out the ship's vermin to each other. It had plenty of roaches and to a lesser extent rats on board, but on two occasions we were startled by some snakes—one a four-footer, and the other about three. They probably got on board with stores and provisions we had loaded at one of the ports of call, and knowing nothing about snakes, and liking them even less, I simply cordoned off the area and called the local authorities to deal with them.

Our ship's homeport was Long Beach, California. A typical deployment was six months operating with the Seventh Fleet in the Pacific, and six months in and around the homeport involved with training, upkeep, and periodic overhauls. Most of navy life is training, training, and more training, especially in peacetime. You train for war hoping it will never come, and history has shown that training is a major factor in the final outcome of any war. The better-trained side usually comes out on top—but at a high price, as I would find out on several occasions during my naval tenure.

The USS *Tolovana* was a large tanker, referred to in the U.S. Navy as a fleet oiler. Its function was to refuel other naval vessels at sea, *while underway*. This is a very tricky and difficult operation requiring a great deal of seamanship and coordination on the part of all hands. Aircraft carriers are especially challenging because of the protruding flight deck. Picture it—two vessels, an oiler as the guide ship, and let's say a carrier as the receiving ship, steaming side by side roughly 140–160 feet apart in an open, usually rough sea. I was in awe of the replenishment operation from the first time I saw it. I had seen the wrath of the Atlantic Ocean during hurricanes while in the merchant marine, and soon became convinced the Pacific Ocean was certainly no pond, especially after having been through typhoons packing winds of over one hundred knots. Emergency breakaways (in which the ships disengage) and executing turns in unison make the operation even more challenging and potentially dangerous. The replenishment operation as described herein may have changed in today's navy, but this is the way it was in the navy of my youth.

The exercise begins with the oiler getting steady on a predetermined replenishment course at a given speed, usually around twelve knots. The receiving ship then makes its approach on the oiler so as to position itself alongside. As the two ships close to, say, 150 feet, there is increased water turbulence and velocity between them that sometimes causes the vessels to yaw (swerve from side to side). This makes keeping course even more difficult. Once the carrier is on station alongside, a shot line is sent over from the oiler. The shot line is followed by hose slung in four saddles and a span wire (cable) to support the entire rig. Each saddle is connected to a saddle winch on the cargo deck of the oiler, which is tended by a sailor. That sailor has to carefully tend the line to ensure the saddle line is taut thereby keeping the hose suspended and out of the water. Multiple transfer rigs as described above are often used to transfer multiple types of fuel.

During one such replenishment, as a seaman started to operate one of the saddle winches, a snake sprang out from around the foundation and tried to bite him. Startled, he jumped back, and in doing so he let go of the line. That was his undoing. The line began to unravel off the winch head. This caused the saddle and hose to immediately drop towards the water with considerable speed and force. As the line unraveled, he grabbed it as it ran out. The line immediately looped and tightened around his arm and pulled him through the air roughly thirty feet, slamming him into a lifting block with such force that it crushed his shoulder and broke his neck. He died soon after they got him to sickbay. With no doctor on board he never had a chance; none of us, including the hospital corpsman chief petty officer (CPO), who was roughly equivalent to a senior registered nurse, could do anything to help him. The vessels executed an emergency breakaway.

The other aspect of this story that is so tragic, is that it happened in full view of his brother who was a crew member serving in the steward's department. As he was on a break, he wandered out on deck to watch the replenishment operation. There he was leaning over a rail looking out on the cargo deck with one foot on the lower rail, sipping a cup of coffee. Suddenly, he watched in horror as his brother was pulled to his death in an instant. There is a recurring myth that navy policy prohibits siblings from serving on the same ship. It is a myth I also subscribed to until I did this bit of research. Unfortunately for this family, the navy has no such regulation. However, according to the Naval Historical Center, in the event that siblings are enlisted in the navy, and all but one of them is killed, the surviving member will be transferred to non-combat duty. This incident proved to be the unhappiest moment of the deployment for all of us. It clearly demonstrated how utterly random and unfair life can be, a lesson I would witness time and time again in my life.

During another replenishment operation with, yes, another aircraft carrier, we were to face more bad luck. The carrier made a fine approach and got on station in good order. However, after thirty minutes or so, she began to yaw. In and out she weaved. It got steadily worse, and soon she was closing to within fifty feet of us. It was downright intimidating to see this 45,000-ton behemoth, high in the water, almost on top of us. Now we were so close that the sea between the two vessels became very turbulent. An emergency breakaway was ordered, but too late. We were free and clear of each other, but then came the terrifying sound of steel meshing with steel as the flight deck of the carrier cut into the steel sections of our aft house superstructure. I liken it to peeling back the top of a sardine can. At least that's the way it looked to me, as I stood in the aft well deck, in full view of what was happening.

During replenishment operations my collateral duty was that of cargo control officer stationed in the cargo control center near the aft well deck, with responsibility for all cargo movement. A well deck is a space on the open weather deck of a ship, lying at a lower deck level between adjacent raised decks. From where I stood, I could almost reach out and touch the carrier's hull plating. Steel, glass, and sparks flew everywhere. Luck was on our side: the sparks did not ignite the cargo, which included aviation gasoline, jet fuel, and fuel oil. All of the damage was above deck, and we were therefore not taking on any water. The ships remained locked in their unnatural intercourse for a minute or so, with steel screeching so loudly as to make our vessel sound like a wounded animal. Take it from me; the steel of a 45,000-ton vessel grinding against the steel of our 25,000-ton vessel was frightening. It's what happens when a heavyweight clashes with a middleweight: no contest. We took a beating while the big guy steamed away virtually unscathed. It seemed like an eternity, but finally the wounded vessels maneuvered clear of each other and went on their separate courses. Miraculously no one was injured—most of the crew was either out on deck or at their duty stations, not inside the aft superstructure. We soon received orders to proceed to a shipyard for repairs and much-needed R&R.

Not long after repairs were completed and we set to sea, we had another incident. This time we were refueling a heavy cruiser, the USS *Rochester* (CA-124). As I came out on deck that morning at daybreak I could see the sleek vessel cutting through the water making her approach to get on station. With her nine eight-inch guns striking such a menacing image, the vessel had such an awesome and intimidating presence that I said to myself, *God, I'm glad she's on our side*. The sea was quite rough that day. The hydrodynamic forces were now causing a great deal of sea turbulence between the two ships as they neared each other. Huge waves reached up to the sky and smashed violently onto our decks. The well decks were constantly awash and therefore dangerous to transit. Many of my gang had to be out on the forward and aft well decks during replenishment to work the cargo system and machinery. The aft well deck was particularly ornery because it was so densely populated with equipment, piping, valves, and stanchions that supported the cargo deck above—so much so that it was affectionately referred to as "the jungle." Petty Officer Third Class (PO3) Jim Golbe, was doing his best to work in this environment when a wave hit the aft well deck, swept him up and slammed him into the stanchions. He was so badly injured he could not help himself, so a few of us rushed out from the cargo control center to prevent him from being washed overboard.

When we got him up to sickbay, the hospital corpsman CPO examined him and concluded that his pelvis was probably broken. In addition, his leg was broken and so badly deformed it looked like a pretzel. He had extensive bruises and cuts. The CPO was able to treat some of the wounds and ease his pain with painkillers. However, the pelvis and leg needed medical attention soon, or there was a risk he might lose the leg. Under the circumstances the most expeditious way to handle it was to transfer him to the cruiser we were refueling, because they had a doctor on board. We never saw Jim again, but were relieved to later learn that he did not lose his leg, and but for a dip in his walk, made a full recovery.

The ship was not jinxed, we told ourselves. But during another replenishment a seaman was washed overboard, and this was *not a drill*. Here was a chance to put all of that good training to use, and where it could pay off. The rough seas plagued us with a lot of turbulence between the vessels. This time the victim was Seaman Bob Hensley, who put himself at considerable risk by pushing a shipmate clear of being washed overboard. At that instant, Bob got hit with a huge wave that lifted him off the deck and washed him clear over the deck rail. During these replenishment exercises it is normal operating practice to have a destroyer on station several hundred feet aft of the replenishing vessels to pick up anyone washed overboard, but that does not mean a "man overboard" incident was not inherently risky. The first thing to do is hope you aren't injured by the initial fall overboard. The next thing to avoid is being sucked into the ship's propellers, which Bob was able to do. He of course had a life jacket on, and therefore was in no real danger of drowning, or so we thought. Then a strange sequence of events occurred.

As he drifted out of the wake of both vessels, the destroyer cautiously closed in on him. It then turned broadside to him to facilitate the pickup. It was going well until he got alongside the destroyer. As the ship rolled to one side his life jacket got caught on an appendage of the hull, thereby lifting him up out of the water, and then dunking him into the water when it rolled back. It happened several times and each time he came closer to drowning. Finally, they were able to get him loose and safely onboard. He was returned to our vessel unharmed. It's the kind of story with a happy ending that I bet Bob is still telling his grandkids.

8

DEADLY FLASH POINT

Those who cannot remember the past are condemned to repeat it.

—George Santayana, Spanish philosopher, poet, and novelist (1863-1952)

Santayana's refrain is a familiar one and an important one as it relates to communism. Most of my navy days were spent at sea plying the mighty Pacific Ocean in and around Japan and South East Asia. It was the fall of 1958 when we found ourselves on the brink of a potentially deadly military confrontation with Communist China over a 240-mile long island, Taiwan, formerly known as Formosa. Following the Communist victory on the mainland in 1949, retreating Nationalist forces under Chiang Kai-shek established the Republic of China on Taiwan. The United States faced a flash point for what could have become World War III, and the ignition spot would have been in the narrow Straits of Taiwan separating Mainland China and the democratically governed island of Taiwan. In 1958, the conflict, referred to as the 1958 Taiwan Strait Crisis, began with a massive artillery barrage on the evening of August 23, and was directed at the islands of Quemoy and Matsu, ten miles off the mainland shore. The People's Liberation Army (PLA) patrol craft prevented relief supplies from reaching the islands. The U.S. Seventh Fleet, which was on station in and around Taiwan, was under strict orders not to fire unless fired upon. The artillery attack and the naval blockade gave a stark warning that a full-scale invasion of Taiwan was about to be launched.

President Eisenhower remained resolute. He committed U.S. naval and Marine Corps forces to the defense of Taiwan. On September 11, 1958, Eisenhower addressed the nation on television and radio to explain his actions, and told the American people that the attack was a "test of the free world's courage in resisting aggression." China, in its determination to capture Taiwan, began the artillery war in what most people thought was the prelude to an invasion. U.S. relations with Taiwan were governed by the Taiwan Relations Act, which stipulated that the United States is bound to assist Taiwan in defense against attack. Communist China's offensive ended in early November when ships from the U.S. Seventh Fleet escorted a relief convoy to Quemoy and Matsu without interference from the PLA patrol craft. Intermittent shelling of Quemoy continued, however, until January 7, 1959. We'll never know how close we came to starting a war with China, which would have probably sparked a world war. It could have taken nothing more than a miscommunication, a misunderstanding, or a misjudgment. Yet, like any war, this one was not without casualties. The forty-four day "artillery war" cost the lives of three thousand civilians, one thousand military personnel from the Republic of China on Taiwan, the destruction of four thousand homes, and the loss of countless military equipment. Some of it we witnessed firsthand. We were constantly on the fringe of the incessant shelling, but fortunately never got hit, thus avoiding a major conflict.

We received orders to stand by a Taiwanese naval landing ship tank (LST), because it had received a direct artillery hit and was in dire need of assistance. As we rendezvoused we saw the entire superstructure was gone. Everyone on board was killed except for the six people who were in the forward part of the vessel. It was eventually towed to the U.S. Naval Base in Subic Bay, Philippines, and fully restored. The United States remained resolute, and it is widely held that the presence of the Seventh Fleet in close support of Taiwan's naval forces may have averted World War III, thus preserving freedom in the region.

To this day Taiwan remains a time bomb, as China continues to claim it as its twenty-third province, albeit a delinquent one. The dangers that still exist in the Straits of Taiwan will take the same firm determination and devotion to the ideals of freedom to keep Taiwan free. As I look back on the experience, I think of our effort as trying to referee a firefight between David and Goliath while sitting on a powder keg. For my service while stationed on board a U.S. naval vessel in the immediate region throughout this period I was awarded, many years later, the Badge of Honor from the Minister of Defense, Taiwan. After my navy and naval reserve service, I also received the National Defense Medal, the Naval Reserve Medal, and five military service ribbons. Years later I would receive the Outstanding Volunteer Service Medal for my work at a VA hospital.

Those times were grim for Taiwan in many ways. It was mostly agricultural then, and poverty was rife. While on station in Taiwan we docked in Kaohsiung, a city in the south. While at anchor one sweltering afternoon, Bill Eckert and I were leaning over the ship's railing chatting and munching apples, which we threw in the water after they were eaten. The water was murky and foul-smelling; much of the city's sewage dumped into the harbor. Then we saw kids dive off their rafts for the eaten apple cores. At first we thought it was for sport, until we saw them eagerly devouring what they recovered. Bill and I said nothing, but the look on his face, and probably mine, said it all—for the first time in our lives we struggled to understand the realization of poverty. It sunk in when we saw local workmen scavenge every last bit of leftover food and garbage they could get their hands on to take home to their families. We saw much the same thing in Hong Kong during our calls there. Those images stay with you for life, and reminded me of something kids of the 1950s often heard from their parents at dinner tables across America.

The artillery shellings during the Taiwan Strait Crisis had given us a taste of military engagement. I came away from that experience asking myself if I had seen enough, or if I was thirsting for more. Did I possess the warrior spirit? The dangerous but unrelated shipboard accidents whetted that curiosity, too. Even in those non-combative situations we experienced death and destruction—the ship itself seemed to put us in harm's way almost as much as military aspects of our engagement, albeit on a smaller scale. These deliberations would greatly affect my later choice between going career-navy and reverting to civilian life.

†

Channel fever. Nearly everyone who puts to sea will at one time or another get a case of it; usually a day or two out of port after being at sea for an extended period of time. Sleeplessness, restlessness, and anxiety are all symptoms of the affliction. So it was on our ship as we were about to complete a six-month deployment in the Far East. Even the wisps of morning fog, so typical in Long Beach Harbor, couldn't calm the edge we were all feeling that morning as the vessel entered the harbor.

Homecomings were usually joyous occasions. Families would be waiting on the dock waving and cheering to their loved ones as the vessel maneuvered to get alongside. Streamers would be flying, and sometimes there would even be a band playing. Then came the excited dash down the gangway into the open arms of loved ones. What a marvelous feeling it was to be back with family, friends, and familiar surroundings. As my ranking officer used to say, it was honeymoon time all over again. This time the joy of our return would be heightened by my forthcoming promotion to lieutenant, junior grade, and an auspicious occasion.

Typically, while my ship was deployed operating with the Seventh Fleet in the Pacific, Ronnie would return home to Brooklyn and live with her parents. We wrote often and missed each other during these long absences. When the vessel returned to Long Beach for a six-month stateside deployment, she would come back to Long Beach where we would rent a furnished apartment. She worked at one of the local hospitals as a registered nurse, and I continued with my shipboard duties, training and supervising never-ending ship maintenance and repair. However, this time our social life picked up, mostly at the officer's club and with other navy families. The weather was usually great and there were lots of things to do and exciting places to see, especially in and around Los Angeles. We even got a chance to see my old Brooklyn (Los Angeles) Dodgers at the Los Angeles Memorial Coliseum, where they played from 1958 to 1961. Even some of the old names from the Brooklyn Dodgers glory days were there—Hodges, Reese, Furillo, and Snider. But make no mistake, the magic was gone.

We heard that one of the "things to do" was to see a bullfight in Tijuana, a Mexican town just across the U.S. border from San Diego. After all, this was a unique opportunity because Mexico is one of the few remaining countries where bullfighting is still legal. Motivated mostly by curiosity we ventured south to see the spectacle firsthand. Considered by many people to be a cruel "sport," we were disappointed to find that it was worse than cruel—it was barbaric, especially if botched by the matador.

The first two fights went pretty much as expected; there were two clean kills. The third, however, was enough to curdle one's blood. The object is for the matador to kill the bull with a swift, clean thrust of the sword by placing the sword in a coin-sized area between the bull's shoulders. If done properly (i.e., in one stroke) the animal dies in a matter of seconds. However, the butcher we saw took several strokes to finally put the bull out of its misery, but not before causing considerable blood to flow and bubble through the poor animal's mouth and nose. The bullring was such a gory mess that on one occasion the matador nearly lost his footing. It was a ghastly sight that brought Ronnie to the verge of tears. Since the bull put up such a courageous fight it was considered the winner, and as tradition dictates, its dead carcass dragged around the bullring, still bleeding, but to a standing ovation. The matador was so hapless that he was pelted with seat cushions as he left the ring. Our curiosity more than satisfied, we promptly exited the ring never to return.

Supporters of bullfighting regard it as an integral part of their national culture. Nevertheless, statistics show it is losing popularity even in cultures where it has been ingrained for centuries. See it once, whether done properly or not, and you'll probably join the majority of naysayers. It is easy to understand why bullfighting is criticized by many animal rights activists—I wish them every success.

The auspicious occasion was the change of command ceremony to welcome a new skipper. All hands were decked out in dress uniform—spit and polish was the order of the day not only for ship's personnel, but for the vessel. I had never seen the twenty-two-year-old lady looking so pristine. No fog this time, just a picture-perfect day with lots of sun. The harbor and piers were full of naval vessels making the kinds of noises one only hears around ships—chipping hammers, whistles, horns, and loudspeakers blaring out orders of the day. Small workboats were bustling throughout the harbor taxiing people, stores and supplies from ship to ship, and ship to shore. Stubborn tugboats pushed, pulled, and clung alongside their payloads as if to defy the laws of physics. It was the kind of dynamic atmosphere that would once again get my "navy" juices going. This was the navy I loved, and moments like this made me realize the difficult decision I would soon have to make whether to re-up or pursue a shore-side career. I never had difficulty making decisions, but I dreaded this one.

Our anxiety about the change of command heightened when we heard of the new skipper's celebrity. Captain John D. Bulkeley, U.S. Navy, was about to take command of the "Leaky T," as we affectionately referred to her. He was replacing a "Captain Queeg" type if there ever was one, who was an alcoholic to boot. This was the "deep draft" command Captain Bulkeley needed to climb from the rank of captain (four-striper) to admiral eventually. His reputation had preceded him. During the dark days of World War II in the Pacific he and his PT boats evacuated General MacArthur and his family from Corregidor in the Philippines to Midanao Island through waters infested with Japanese ships. After this harrowing trip the general was flown to Australia to assume command of the Allies in the Southwest Pacific. MacArthur, always with a flair for the dramatic, told Bulkeley, "You have taken me out of the jaws of death." For this and his service in the Philippines over a four-month period, during which he was responsible for sinking enemy warships, Captain Bulkeley was awarded the Medal of Honor, bestowed upon him by President Franklin D. Roosevelt.

It was not until the change of command ceremony that I had ever seen the Medal of Honor, and how impressive it was draped around his neck. His exploits in the Pacific were immortalized in the book and subsequent film, *They Were Expendable*, starring Robert Montgomery as Bulkeley. I found the book so engrossing that it is the only book I ever read cover to cover without putting it down. I recall him telling me that he had received $200,000 for his services as technical advisor in the making of the movie. Typical of his generosity he also mentioned that he donated all of the proceeds to the Navy Relief Fund, forerunner to the Navy–Marine Corps Relief Society. We all learned a great deal from him about leadership, responsibility, and devotion to duty. Unfortunately, his tenure on board was short-lived.

The six months passed too quickly. Before we knew it Ronnie was on a plane heading east, and I was at sea once again en route to the Far East, this time for my last Pacific deployment.

En route Captain Bulkeley became seriously ill. Our hospital corpsman CPO, who by this time must have been the most challenged hospital corpsman in this man's navy, could do little to help him. It appeared as if Saint Peter the patron saint of sailors had completely forsaken us. Captain Bulkeley needed medical attention, and quickly. The problem was that we were in the middle of the Pacific Ocean. Moreover, it would take us a week or so to steam to the nearest landfall. So we did the next best thing. We rendezvoused with a U.S. naval destroyer and transferred him to the destroyer at sea. The destroyer proceeded at flank (top) speed to Pearl Harbor, where in the naval hospital he underwent surgery and fully recovered. As he never returned to the *Tolovana,* I assumed, wrongly, that I would never see him again.

His war did not end in the Philippines. In 1944 at Normandy, Lieutenant Commander Bulkeley led torpedo boats and minesweepers that cleared the lanes to Utah Beach. His boats sank German E-boats and prevented others from attacking allied landing ships. Even the prickly Charles de Gaulle recognized his achievements by awarding him the French Croix de Guerre "for his conspicuous gallantry and extraordinary bravery in action as commander of motor torpedo boats operating off France." He continued his courageous exploits as skipper of his first large ship, the destroyer USS *Endicott,* which was deployed for the invasion of Southern France. Approximately two months after D-Day, with only one of Endicott's guns working, he attacked two German corvettes at point blank range and sank them both. During the Korean War, Commander Bulkeley commanded Destroyer Division 132, and found himself again under the command of the legendary General

MacArthur. After the war, he served as the chief of staff for Cruiser Division Five.

In 1963, Rear Admiral Bulkeley took that same toughness and determination to Cuba where he faced off with Fidel Castro while commanding the disputed Guantanamo Bay Naval Base. There he met Cuba's threat to sever water supplies in response to the Bay of Pigs invasion and other assaults by ordering the installation of desalinization equipment to make the base self-sufficient. To further rouse Castro's ire, he had a giant shield of the Marine Corps insignia illuminated with floodlights as a reminder of the American presence in Cuba. I thought to myself, *That's just like the old war horse.* The shield proved to be a constant source of aggravation to the Cuban Premier, who eventually had a $50,000 dead-or-alive bounty placed on Bulkeley's head. It remained there until the day the admiral died. He retired from active duty in 1967. However, his intense interest in and familiarity with engineering was instrumental in him being recalled to serve as the commander of the navy's Board of Inspection and Survey. In 1988, he retired after fifty-five years of service.

Vice Admiral Bulkeley died April 6, 1996, and was buried with full military honors and a chest full of medals that could sink one of his PT boats. In tribute to this dynamic and resourceful warrior, the navy paid him the ultimate honor by naming an *Arleigh Burke*-class guided missile destroyer after him: USS *Bulkeley* (DDG-84), commissioned December 8, 2001. That was sixty years to the day after the opening of hostilities in the Philippines. Such was the ending to a career that spanned six decades. Never the politician, and always a maverick, here was a man who lived in a time before the term "politically correct" was omnipresent. In final praise of him I would resurrect that old saying: They broke the mold after they made him. Knowing him as I did, I feel certain that the highest compliment anyone could pay him is to say, "He was all navy." And he was.

†

At the end of every six-month deployment we would return to our homeport Long Beach via Pearl Harbor. Upon entering the harbor there would always be the solemn passage by the USS *Arizona* Memorial. It is the final resting place of 1,102 of the ship's 1,177 crewmen who lost their lives on December 7, 1941. The 184-foot Memorial spans the mid-portion of the sunken battleship and contains the shrine room where the names of those entombed in the *Arizona* are engraved on a marble wall. Fuel oil still seeps from the vessel. It is traditional for every U.S. Navy, and Coast Guard vessel to participate in what is known as "manning the rails." Military personnel serving on these ships stand at attention at the ship's side rails in full dress uniform, and salute the USS *Arizona* Memorial in solemn fashion as their ship slowly glides into port. During our last port entry I recall standing next to newly commissioned Ensign Lambertson, whose father's name is inscribed on that marble wall. His tearful eyes were testament to just how heart-wrenching it was for him to witness his father's final resting place so far from home. He promised he would someday return with his mother.

An interesting aside, in 1999 the battleship USS *Missouri* was moved to Pearl Harbor from the West Coast and docked forward of and perpendicular to the USS *Arizona* Memorial. On September 2, 1945, upon the deck of the USS *Missouri* in Tokyo Bay, the Japanese surrendered to General Douglas MacArthur and Admiral Chester

Nimitz, ending World War II. Thus, a visitor to Hawaii can board both vessels and proclaim they set foot on the very spots where the United States' involvement in the world's bloodiest war started and ended.

†

As joyous as the homecomings were, we did experience setbacks. During one such setback I had the ill luck to be on duty as the command duty officer (CDO). He is in charge of the ship and is the responsible officer for any incidents that take place when a ship is docked in port. I took over the watch at 2000 hours. As I recall it was around 2200 hours when the phone on the quarterdeck rang. The voice at the other end sounding very distressed asked, "This is Father Lopez, may I please speak with the captain?" When I told him that the captain was ashore and that I was the CDO, he hit me with the devastating news. One of our chief petty officers had just committed suicide by putting the muzzle of a gun in his mouth, blowing the back of his head off. The reason was all too familiar in navy annals. Poor guy walked in on his wife in bed with another man. The incident in itself was not shocking; these things happen. We know that. The thing that is shocking is the insensitivity with which this one played out. Didn't they know the poor guy was coming home? Couldn't they have gotten it on somewhere other than his home? And what about their two kids who were in the house at the time? We never got answers to those questions, not that it was any of our business. It was, however, our business to make the necessary arrangements between his family and the appropriate naval authorities, which we did.

Among my more mundane duties was to arrange for the vessel to be completely fumigated. Not only was it necessary

ight: A prevalent U.S. Vorld War II poster varning that loose lips ank ships. (Poster by nton Otto Fischer, 1943).

elow: Surf Avenue in oney Island, Brooklyn rca 1912. (By Irving nderhill, Brooklyn useum/Brooklyn ibrary Collection).

Top: Grandfather Michael alongside one of his most prized ship models.

Right: Mom on board her namesake, *Dolores*, a 34-foot Elco cabin cruiser.

Bottom: Dad on board *Dolores* moored in Bensonhurst, Brooklyn, NY.

Aerial view of United States Merchant Marine Academy at Kings Point, N.Y.

Lions resting. Taken in the Okavango, Botswanna, 2007.

Lone lioness finishing off a zebra kill with her mouth around the animal's throat. Taken in Masai Mara, Kenya, Africa, 2007.

Lion and cub eating a cape buffalo in Northern Sabi Sand, South Africa. (Photo taken by Luca Galuzzi - www.galuzzi.it

Author on safari alongside single hump, dromedary camels.

Villagers waiting for the barge.

River-crossing barge.

SCENES
FROM
TUSCANY

Top left: Florence Duomo after sunset. **Top right:** A classic view of the rolling Tuscan landscape with farmhouse near Pienza. **Bottom left:** A view of Pienza. **Bottom right:** San Gimig

Top: SS *United States* in her glory days on the North Atlantic (1952-1969).
Bottom: SS *United States* today in Philadelphia, a mere shadow of her former glory.

USS *Tolovana* (AO-64) underway heading out to sea from San Diego, C circa post-1958. (Erich Utecht, USS *Tolovana* 1968-70).

USS *Tolovana* receiving cargo from sister fleet oiler, USS *Guadelupe* (AO-32),1954.

USS *Tolovana* refueling USS *Franklin D. Roosevel* (CVA-42) and USS *Black* (DD-666) in th Gulf of Tonkin, 1966. (By Michael O. Smith

Inset: Tension Span Wire Rig – refueling rig between oiler and receiving ship.

Vice Admiral John D. Bulkeley, U.S. Navy. (Photo by Robert Lucier, 1988).

Former New Jersey Governor, Christine Whitman, and the author in the Governor's office of the N.J. State House, Trenton, May 6, 1996. The occasion was the inauguration of the USS *New Jersey* auto license plate.

Author's "Best-of-Show" 1987 Mercedes-Benz 560SL Roadster. Destined for vintage status, this elegantly styled 2-seater was in production a record-breaking nineteen years.

The Starace family onboard QEII returning to the U.S. from England. (From left: Michael, Ronnie, Dorine, the author and Nicky III).

Above: Kodaiji Temple, Kyoto, Japan, was constructed in 1605 in memory of the great political leader, Toyotomi Hideyoshi by his widow.

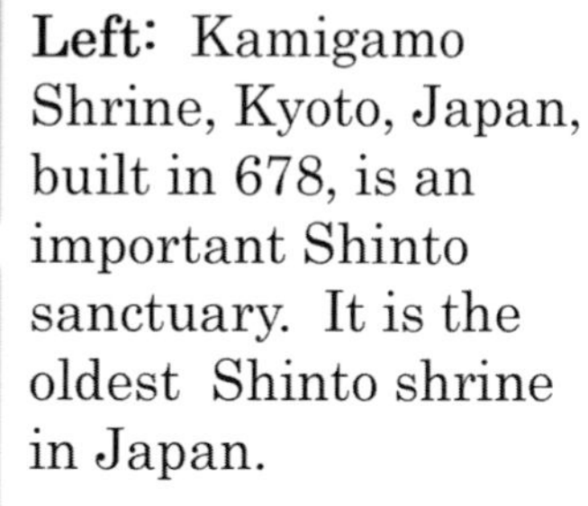

Left: Kamigamo Shrine, Kyoto, Japan, built in 678, is an important Shinto sanctuary. It is the oldest Shinto shrine in Japan.

Bottom: Kinkakuji Temple, Kyoto, Japan.

Right: Geisha at the moated Nijojo Castle Festival, Kyoto, Japan. (By Andrew MacColl, 2008).

Above: Woman dressed as a Geisha. (By Christopher Mark Poulton-theCMP.net).

Right: Women dressed as maiko (geisha apprentices) on the grounds of the Kiyomizu-dera temple, Kyoto, Japan, 2004. (Photo by Michael Reeve).

Above: Himeji Castle is considered to be Japan's most spectacular castle.

Left: Cherry blossoms in Japan.

ight: herry lossom eason with Iount Fuji n the ackground.

Left: Author and Ronnie with their housekeeper, Chioko-san, in her bridal attire.

Below: Genbaku Dome. The Hiroshima Peace Memorial in Hiroshima, Japan commonly known as the Atomic Bomb Dome, is the only bomb-damaged building still standing.

The author with his prize sailfish, Acapulco, Mexico, November, 1976. The catch weighed in at 158 pounds and measured 10 feet, 2 inches tip to tip.

Hauling the catch on board.

The sailfish breaking water the first time.

Above: The legendary Raffles Hotel, named after Sir Stamford Raffles, an early British colonist.

Right: Orchard Road lit up at Christmas.

Left: Sri Mariammar Temple, built in 1827 is the oldest hindu temple in Singapore. Its gopuram (entranc tower) shows that it is in Dravidian Style (south India). Sacred cows dot the temple boundary. (Photo by Michael Caviglia, Switzerland).

to ensure there were no more snakes on board, but the roach infestation was getting worse and had to be eliminated for the vessel to remain habitable. I was no stranger to roaches, but the problem was beyond imagination. If you walked into any pantry on the vessel at night and turned the light on, the place was alive with dozens of roaches. When you walked into a pantry, you felt them crunching underfoot no matter where you stepped. Bill and I were roommates in a cabin directly across from a pantry. We frequently saw and felt their creepy presence, especially at night while sleeping. And take it from me, these guys were heavy hitters. After the fumigation, the vessel was clean as a whistle—no more roach guts on your shoes, or nightly bed visitors crawling in your ears.

The navy presented another crossroads in my life. As I approached the end of my term, I agonized over whether to get out or to make a career of it. There were so many factors to consider. Would the career be challenging enough? Was I willing to accept all the risks associated with a military career, not to mention the extended periods away from home? This was especially important because we had every intention of having children.

Ronnie was very much in favor of remaining on the West Coast, for its fair weather and chic lifestyle. I leaned toward following the best maritime career opportunity, no matter where it took us. Remaining on the West Coast would probably have meant leaving the navy for a shore-side job in industry. However, whether it was the navy or a shore-side job, I knew that I had to be careful because there are times when I think my self-assertive style may come across as threatening. The challenge would therefore be to temper my tone without compromising the mission. The dilemma in making a career path choice caused some of the first strains in our marriage. Life was beginning to get complicated and made me yearn for the hard-working simpler life I knew and loved at Kings Point. Those feelings were to come over me time and time again.

I finally decided to leave to pursue a career in the maritime industry. However, I agonized about going back to pursue a naval career for almost two years after leaving. Had I chosen the navy, I would have again been looking at a different career path and lifestyle. In so doing, I would have re-entered the navy with the rank of lieutenant, having continued service in the U.S. Naval Reserve after leaving the regular navy. The noblest aspect of such a choice would have been serving the nation. Prodding me in that direction was an ex-navy career guy who was working with me in the same office, and he nearly pushed me over the edge. However, all these many years later I don't fret about it, but I do from time to time think about it in a melancholy "what if" sort of way. To this day, having served is one of the proudest things I have done in my life.

†

During one of my last home leaves while still in the navy, I returned to Brooklyn, and came upon a rare opportunity. The Brooklyn Dodgers' organization would make it possible for me, one of its most disheartened fans, to obtain a genuine piece of baseball history to remember it by.

Shortly after the Dodgers' exodus, the wrecking ball was brought in to bring down the storied ballpark. Wreckers swarmed into Ebbets Field and leveled the stands and everything else that stood in their way. Soil that had felt the spikes of The Boys of Summer was no more. When I read the demolition announcement in the newspapers

I could feel the tears welling up in my eyes. All manner of bits and pieces from the park would be sold to any of the adoring fans that showed up on the announced dates. The memorabilia included things like bases, seats, and sections of the foul poles and virtually anything else that could be moved. How fortunate for me to be on leave at this opportune time. So one bright morning I headed out to the old ballpark with a heavy heart for what was to be my last visit. By the time I got there the wrecking ball had done most of its dirty deed. The place was a shambles. However, from the items that were still left I picked out a box seat and purchased it for the princely sum of $2. I still remember the white number "24" painted on the seat. It gathered dust in my basement for nearly forty-five years before I began to realize that when the wrecking ball finally got to me in the not-to-distant future, my kids would look at this thing and would quickly dispose of it as junk. They could not be expected to know of its possible monetary value, not to mention its sentimental value, at least to me. With that in mind I contacted an auction house specializing in sports equipment and memorabilia. I was amazed at the $1,500 starting price they suggested. After a one-month auction I was even more amazed at the $3,300 sale price. Percentage-wise it turned out to be the most profitable investment I ever made. But I would give back every cent of it to see "Dem Bums" return.

Strange, but the demolition of Ebbets Field became a metaphor of the decade that followed. Here was a baseball shrine that had seen glory, passed its prime and been destroyed. Was a nation about to go through a similar fate? In reality, the next losses would hit far closer to home.

Three months after I was discharged from the navy, my father died from complications from an ulcer surgery.

It was almost as if he was waiting for me to return home safely before letting go of this world.

By the time I arrived at the hospital my mother was already there, and my father had passed. When I entered his room, he was already enclosed in a clear plastic tent. He looked so emaciated and ghostly, it was as if I was seeing him for the first time. I regretted not having seen him before he died because there were so many things I wanted to say to him and should have long before this. I wanted to tell him that in spite of the bumpy road our relationship traveled, I knew he always acted in my best interests, as he saw it. I wanted to tell him that when I look to the sky from the deck of my boat, I will always think of him, and thank him for instilling the boating passion I still feel in my bones. I wanted to thank him for playing catch with me on the Brooklyn Roads. I wanted to thank him for the Brooklyn Dodgers games we attended. I wanted to thank him for giving me his father, whom I so adored, and who so enriched my life. And I wanted to say to him something that, sadly, I had never said before: "Dad, I love you."

9

THE FREEPORT YEARS

When sorrows come, they come not as spies, but in battalions!

—William Shakespeare, Hamlet

The saga started with my first shore-side job after leaving the navy. The job was uneventful, and provided little headway on the path I wanted my career to take. I didn't want to be stuck in Nowhere, U.S.A., for the rest of my life, and was restless. Actually, we lived in Freeport, New York. In the early '60s, Ronnie and I were both working, and we bought a home one block from the water. Our Freeport years were probably as dizzying as the 1960s themselves—you might even say our lifestyle was a microcosm of the country.

The country was restless and changing dramatically. Bob Dylan sang *"The times they are a-changin',"* and they were. He pioneered music that had something to say; the bubble gum stuff was coming to an end, as was our innocence. Frankly, I have to admit that the 1950s, often referred to as the Age of Innocence, is a bit overstated. In fact, I would go so far as to say that there are those of us who actually believe our parents had sex. Dylan was saying things like, "Your children are not yours to command." That is pretty mundane by today's standards, but I can tell you this—during the sexual revolution of the '60s it was downright radical. And Ronnie and I were going to have to deal with these issues at a very personal level because from 1961 to 1964 we were blessed with three children, Dorine, Nicholas III, and Michael. The five of us were to stand witness to a host of irreversible changes to our nation. The civil rights movement was in full swing. For some, progress wasn't happening fast enough. Most of us, however, were pleased that progress was being made. Vietnam was festering, and would soon come to a head. When the My Lai Massacre was exposed, it prompted widespread outrage. Later there was the U.S. invasion of Cambodia. The unsuccessful Bay of Pigs Invasion demoralized the country, and was made worse by the Cuban Missile Crisis a year later. Juggernaut Japan was stampeding through world markets and revolutionizing the auto and consumer electronics industries. People all over the world were stunned by the assassinations of John F. Kennedy, Robert F. Kennedy, and Martin Luther King Jr.

Later in the decade the Woodstock Festival exemplified for many the idealistic hopes of the age. By the late '60s and early '70s we saw the U.S. trade figures go from plus to minus for the first time, and stay negative nearly every year since, reaching over $700 billion in 2007. As an expression of anti-Vietnam War sentiment, the decade was capped by the Kent State shootings in 1970. We appeared to the world as a nation at war with itself. Most of us felt despair and frustration at not being able to prevent America from falling apart at the seams, which is what it looked like as we lived through it. Yet, not all the news was depressing—America landing a man on the moon in 1969 showed there were still ingredients of greatness.

†

It was at my second job that my career began to surge. It also became my vantage point on the age. I interviewed twice for it, after which they kept me dangling on a string for nearly a month before giving me the nod. The job would become a vital link between Kings Point and my seagoing service, and the next job where I would carve out the career for which I was destined.

In 1963 I was hired by one of the world's largest independent ship owners, Daniel K. Ludwig, who at the time was the richest man in the United States and perhaps the world. At the height of his career he was the biggest individual ship operator, owning a fleet of sixty ocean-going tankers. An innovator in ship design, construction, chartering, and financing, his ships set the standard for size, quality of construction, and operating performance. His leadership in the progressive and continual expansion of tanker size pioneered the construction and development of supertankers and enabled substantial reductions in the cost of moving crude oil internationally. This yielded significant savings to end-users of oil worldwide. A humanitarian as well, in his later years he dedicated virtually all of his fortune to cancer research. In the four years I worked for him, he and his staff would give me the knowledge to launch my career into the supertanker era.

One of my first assignments was to head down to Chester, Pennsylvania, to visit a ship docked on the

Delaware River, and sort out some technical problems they were having. I drove by myself to Chester on a cold and rainy morning. As I entered the town I was following a car that had two people in it. Both guys were white. I followed the car for about one mile along a two-way street. As we approached an intersection with a traffic light, the light turned red. I started to slow down in what was probably a thirty-mile-per-hour speed zone. At that instant two young black girls, probably on the way to high school, started to cross the street. The car in front of me did not slow down. Notwithstanding the rain, visibility was good. As the girls got to the middle of the road they looked right and saw the car in front of me approaching them. They kept on going, assuming the car would stop for the red light.

It did not stop. It rolled right through the intersection and deliberately ran over both of them. The girl nearest the car got the brunt of the impact and was thrown about ten feet into the air, landing on the pavement near the curb. The other girl was hit and dropped to the ground. The car never braked.

I pulled over right away and got out of my car to lend whatever assistance I could. I lifted the girl that had been thrown and carried her to the steps of a nearby brownstone house. She was bleeding and seemed to be hurt pretty badly. The other girl was bruised and in shock, but managed to get up on her own and joined us. There wasn't much I could do except get help. As I turned away to do so, I saw a few people beginning to gather. Then I heard somebody say, "Hey, he did it!" and point at me. Now a few more people showed up and joined the "he did it" chant. The hostility towards me was building fast.

When a few of them starting shoving me around, I knew it was time to make tracks.

I made a dash for my car, managed to get in and speed away while they hurled stuff at the car. Believe me, I considered myself lucky to get away with a few scratches and a broken rear window.

Under the same circumstances, I'd do it again. I do not fully comprehend the vast complexities of human prejudice, but you cannot ignore people in distress.

†

Our major attraction to Freeport was proximity to the water, in a town that used to call itself the "Boating Capital of the East." Unfortunately, we never owned a boat while living there. Desire notwithstanding, we simply couldn't afford one. Besides, I was busy carving out a career and going to night school for a master's degree and prepping for the New York professional engineer's (PE) license examination. I eventually received the degree. I also passed parts I and II of the PE exam, but foolishly declined taking part III because my career was on a management track rather than engineering.

At home, Ronnie was the mainstay of our family. By this time she had given up her job as an industrial nurse to raise our three children—*and* me. We were feeling a distinct shift away from the conservative 1950s—the social and moral fabric of the country was rapidly changing, and in the process, presenting new challenges to parents everywhere. We had to cope with a more liberal approach in dealing with our children and all the related challenges that face parents and couples in any modern decade. For many of us, that did not come easy. Take my word for it; there was a lot more to the '60s than hippies. And in some respects, our experience was similar to what any couple just starting out would go through, then or now.

For one, it was our first time owning a home. Our first spring season in the house, this city slicker was about to take his first crack at mowing a lawn. Everything was going well until I bumped into my first dandelion. There it was standing so pretty, bright and yellow. I thought it was a real enhancement to the lawn, and therefore decided to mow around it. I also thought about how generous the previous owner was to have planted it. Then of course it died of its own accord as all weeds do, and I kept wondering what I had done to bring about its demise. Years later a neighbor said, "Nick you looked so intent on what you were doing that I didn't have the heart to break your heart. But my wife and I sure got a laugh out of it."

Another incident reflects some of the craziness of the times. My neighbor's wife had been after her husband Rich for months to fix a leak under the kitchen sink. He refused to admit he had no idea how to fix the leak, and got so fed up listening to her that he called in a plumber to do the job, but neglected to tell her about it. (He might have planned to take the credit himself.) In any case, the plumber showed up and my neighbor explained the leak, and went off to do something in the backyard. So, there was the plumber on his back with his head up under the sink with just his legs sticking out from the kitchen cabinet. Lo and behold who arrives home but my neighbor's wife. She enters the kitchen and assumes that the guy under the sink is her husband, who has finally gotten around to doing the job. Elated, she reaches down and in one quick motion grabs the plumber by his ding-a-ling through his pants, gives a pull and a shake and proclaims, "Better late than never honey." The poor guy under the sink went ballistic, bolted up and cracked his head on the underside of the sink.

Her husband hears the commotion and rushes in to find his wife apologizing profusely, and the plumber bleeding profusely. They had to call an ambulance, and he eventually needed seven stitches to close the wound. The clincher is that when the paramedic asked the husband how the accident happened, the paramedic laughed so hard that he slipped on the stairs and dropped the stretcher, and the plumber. The plumber never came back to that house and never even sent them a bill.

Another neighbor loved to tinker with his car. Trouble was he was a heavy smoker and an even heavier drinker. Working on the carburetor of his car he collected a quart of leftover gasoline. The ever-present can of beer was close at hand.

After the job was finished he poured the gasoline into the toilet next to the garage, but must have been distracted because he did not flush the toilet. As his wife tells the story, later that day while sitting on the toilet taking care of business he lit a cigarette, and threw the match into the toilet. The gas fumes exploded, singed his buttocks, and propelled him off the toilet like one of Hitler's V-2 rockets into the opposite wall. She knew something was wrong when she heard his urgent screams for help. She called an ambulance, and got him to a hospital. Then she locked up the beer.

†

Because we didn't own a boat in those years, I readily accepted an invitation from my other neighbor, Fred, to spend the day fishing with his father, Jim, on their thirty-eight-foot cabin cruiser. I wasn't looking for the thrills of deep-sea fishing, or, for that matter, any kind of fishing. I simply could not resist a day relaxing on the water. Weather-wise it turned out to be a perfect summer day, although the sea was a bit choppy.

Fred's father knew the ropes in terms of equipment, bait, where to go, and how to catch fish. However, he may have gotten a bit over-zealous. After an hour or two they were having pretty good luck—they landed a few bluefish and some flounder, the latter being one of my favorites. There were tuna out there as well, but so far, none on the hook. As the day wore on Jim's experience was beginning to show—he was getting most of the hits and hauling them in. Fred ran a poor second, and as anticipated, I wasn't in the running. At one point Jim thought he had something on his line, but then lost it. So he pulled it in and started to re-bait the hook. At that moment Fred and I heard a terrifying yell from the stern area where Jim was fishing. I was on the foredeck and Fred was down below getting something to eat. In the process of cutting bait, Jim had slashed his left hand and two of its fingers. Later he would tell us that at the moment he was cutting the bait, the boat took a sudden roll thereby causing the accident. The cuts were right to the bone. He was bleeding so profusely that we were not able to control it; there was a first aid kit on board, but its capabilities stopped short of surgical. I had never seen so much blood in all my life, and could not imagine anyone losing so much blood and yet surviving. There was so much blood on the deck I kept slipping and sliding in it. It seemed that our crude, poorly applied tourniquet was doing little to stem the bleeding. It reached a point where I was beginning to think there was more of his blood on me than in him. Clearly, we were losing the battle and it showed in the blazing eyes of Jim's ashen-gray face.

Fred got on the very high frequency (VHF) radiotelephone to get help. He was able to get through to the nearest U.S. Coast Guard station and advised them of our position and the gravity of our situation—and God bless the Coast Guard, the unsung miracle workers. You never hear much about them, and therefore most of us do not realize how dedicated these people are and what a vital role they play in saving lives, often at considerable risk to their own. Within twenty minutes they had a helicopter hovering above us. They lowered a basket to lift Jim off the boat to get him to the nearest hospital. The lift-off process took roughly fifteen minutes and went very smoothly thanks to the expertise of the helicopter crew. With Jim safely tucked on board the helicopter, we breathed a sigh of relief. From the spot of the accident it would have taken approximately two hours for us to get back to the marina even at top speed. As it turned out, that time would have been critical in saving Jim's life.

†

Do you remember where you were November 9, 1965? Probably not. But I know where I was. I was still working for Mr. Ludwig in New York City, still honing my craft, and soaking up as much as I could about designing, building, and operating giant ships. Being the innovator that he was, he had leased a shipyard in Japan from the Japanese government, from which he launched one of the most ambitious shipbuilding programs the world had seen up to that point. This reunited me with Japan, and was to crystallize a lifelong relationship.

I left the office for my usual commute home to Long Island. It was evening rush hour. I'd later find out that the power lines from Niagara Falls to the city were operating near their maximum capacity. At about 5:15 p.m. a main transmission line relay failed, triggering a massive cascading power failure that darkened the entire Northeast and parts of Canada. All of a sudden the lights went out, first in southern Canada, then in Boston, then in New York. Within minutes, before anybody knew what was happening, the greatest blackout in history engulfed a vital area of the Northeast. At least twenty-five million people over an area of eighty-thousand square miles were caught in the dark shroud. It touched people for periods ranging from a few minutes to days. In one of the greatest industrial complexes on earth, almost everything came to a standstill. And that included the Long Island Railroad commuter train.

I was trapped in the bowels of a subway tunnel under the East River. Someone had a pocket transistor radio, but reception was nil. This of course was before cell phones. It was also before terrorism, as we now know it. Nevertheless, to be stuck in a tunnel in the dark, without knowing what was going on, was agonizing. Flooding was the most prevalent thought on our minds. Had the tunnel caved in? Were we going to be drowned like rats? As it turned out there was no cave-in, there was no panic, no disorder, and no widespread fear except for the one or two diabetics who did not have their medication with them.

We sat in that tunnel in pitch darkness without ventilation for nearly five hours. A claustrophobic would have gone mad. The air became very stale. Finally, the flashlight of a conductor pierced the darkness as he came through our car, informing us that there had been a blackout. It was not good news, but at least it alleviated our fears of drowning and gave us a glimmer of hope. He also informed us that there was no relief in sight.

At approximately 3:00 a.m. of the next day we began to hear rumbling—a diesel locomotive that had been sent into the tunnel to tow trains back to the New York train station. Only problem was that since we were halfway through the tunnel there were many trains ahead of us to be towed back. I guess it was around 5:00 a.m. when we felt our train nudge and jerk backwards, which meant the locomotive was being hooked up to our train, and by 6:00 a.m. we were in tow back to the station. By the time we got there, the station was a caldron of intense emotions. People were seething with anxiety and frustration. Others slept on the floors, on steps, in phone booths, on restaurant countertops and every other nook and cranny imaginable. I couldn't sleep soundly, but somehow managed to find a corner where I could at least sit down on the cold marble floor and catch a few winks. There was not a bit of food or beverage to be had.

I will not try to describe the conditions in the restrooms, but I was reminded of it when I read accounts of the deplorable sanitary conditions that existed in the Louisiana Superdome after Hurricane Katrina. But through it all, there was little of the rude jostling that was a part of normal commuting. New York often gets a bad wrap for its burliness, but I know of no other city in the world where so many different kinds of people come together and live in relative peace. The station that night was a microcosm of that image.

It wasn't until 10:00 a.m. that trains started to move people out of the station to their destinations using diesel locomotives. We pulled into the Freeport Station that afternoon. When I walked in the front door all Ronnie said was, "Where the heck have you been?"

Those days were full of first experiences—and some of them reflect poorly on me. Case in point: I had to make a business trip to Portland, Maine, and was driving my car to LaGuardia Airport to catch the flight. I was running late, and doing around seventy-five miles per hour in what was a fifty-five-mile-per-hour zone. As bad luck would have it, I got pulled over by a motorcycle cop.

When I returned from the trip I reported to the courthouse, as there was no option to handle it by mail. Bad omen. When I went before the judge I explained my situation, not that I had a very good excuse for speeding. He abruptly sentenced me to a $50 fine or five days in jail and five days in jail. I was so delighted with the leniency of the "$50 or five days," that the "and five days" didn't sink in. As I moved on to the clerk's window she asked me if I wanted to pay the $50 or do the five days. I coughed up the $50, and after paying, started to walk away.

As I did I felt a hand on my shoulder. As I turned around it was a police officer who politely said, "This way sir." I thought he didn't realize that I had paid the $50, so I explained to him that I did in fact pay it. He then explained to me that the sentence handed down had provision for an additional five days and that there was no option: It had to be served. I frantically said there must be some misunderstanding and proceeded back to the clerk's window. She merely reconfirmed what the judge and the police officer had said. To make matters worse I had no recourse for legal representation. The only consolation was that the offense would go on my record as a speeding violation only. I was allowed to make one phone call, which was to Ronnie. She couldn't believe they were going to put me jail for speeding.

After I made the call, a police officer in the room tried to console me. He said, off the record, that the judge who sentenced me was especially harsh on speeders because his daughter was recently killed in a traffic accident that involved a speeding driver. He also said I wasn't the first to get hit this hard and wouldn't be the last.

They took me to a cell in the basement of the courthouse where I sat for a few hours. They brought another guy, and who was very disheveled, and asked me, "What are you in for?" Sounded like something right out of a Cagney gangster movie. I said speeding, to which he snickered and turned away. Guess I just wasn't in his league. Then it hit me. Of course they were only trying to put a scare into me. They were going to let me sweat it out for a few hours, teach me a lesson, and let me go.

Not so. An hour later they loaded the two of us into a police car and carted us off to the Raymond Street Jail in Brooklyn. They put me in a big room, sort of a detention center, with maybe twenty beds. That night I had my first meal *in stir*. After dinner we started talking with one another, comparing notes. It turned out that most of the group were in for the same violation—speeding. We all had had the worst possible luck in drawing that judge, whose decision in my view was more emotional than judicial. The time rolled pretty quickly; we had a friendly bunch of guys who talked a lot, played cards and so on. My saving grace was that I was booked on Wednesday, which meant I could go home that Friday, having served only three days. The house rules were that if your sentence expired on Sunday, as mine would have, you could leave on Friday, as the place was not fully staffed on Sunday. And so on Friday I was *sprung*.

Ironically, I did make my flight that day, but only because the flight was delayed.

A year or so later I pulled into a gas station near my home. I thought I recognized the guy who came out to pump gas. He looked like one of the guys I met in detention. I got out of the car and asked him, "Do you recognize me?" He scratched his head a bit, looked at me quizzically and said, "Yeah, I remember you. We *did time* together." Not exactly what I wanted to hear, but we shook hands, reminisced and had a few laughs. On that fateful day his parents were arriving at the airport, and he was going to pick them up. He too was running late and got nabbed for speeding.

†

During my years for the company, I traveled in airplanes more than I ever expected or wanted to. The near fatal experience on Pan Am Flight 830 that Ronnie and I would experience fifteen years later was not my first brush with air disaster, nor would it be the last.

My first close call turned out to be innocuous, but for a few brief moments I thought I was going to die. It was a business trip from New York to Sarnia, Canada, via Montreal at a time when I was still an inexperienced flyer.

Unbeknownst to me, there was a scheduled stop between Sarnia and Montreal on the return flight. This was a small aircraft that carried approximately thirty passengers, during a time when aero-technology and operating procedures were not nearly as advanced as they are today. As the plane started to descend for its landing, I began to think we were in some kind of trouble, but the pilot didn't want to announce it for fear of panicking the passengers. As the ground got closer and closer, I was holding on to my seat for dear life and beginning to sweat. I wanted to yell out, but I was too embarrassed; the elderly woman next to me was as cool as a cucumber, reading a newspaper. In fact, everybody on board was as calm as could be. I began to wonder, "What are these people made of? We're on the verge of a crash landing and there's not so much as a murmur out of anyone. What kind of a wimp am I? C'mon, somebody say or do something. Anything to make me feel like I'm not losing my mind."

By this time the woman next to me sensed my terror and calmly asked, "Are you OK, sir?"

"Yes," I said with a quiver in my voice. "How are you?"

"Would you like my paper to read?"

I thought, HOW CAN ANYBODY READ ANYTHING AT A TIME LIKE THIS? Down and down we go, but no runway, only farmland. There are horses grazing out there that I can almost touch. The pilot came on the intercom and calmly asked everyone to fasten their seatbelts. God, this guy is cool!

Through it all, my seatmate is still calmly reading her stuff. Another announcement: "PASSENGERS PROCEEDING ON TO MONTREAL ARE REQUESTED TO REMAIN ON BOARD ..."

Idiot me!

That night, after getting back into the city from the trip, I needed a break. I decided to have a quick dinner at a Chinese restaurant near the office. As the place was full, the host suggested I have a drink at the bar until a table became available. While sipping my drink, I looked around and noticed the actor Van Johnson having dinner with a well-dressed producer-type. I looked over several times and

I guess it came off as a flirtation, because when he got up to leave without his guest, he walked directly behind me and gave me a gentle squeeze on my right rib cage. I turned around and gave him a warm, "Hi Van, I've enjoyed your work." He walked out only to reappear ten minutes later. He sat down again, but at the far end of the bar. Every time I looked over at him he was staring at me. Realizing what was about to happen unless I defused it, I stopped looking over. Fifteen minutes or so later he got up and started to walk out. As he passed by I got another gentle squeeze, this time on the right hip. When he got to the door, he gave me a nod as if to join him. It was certainly the best offer I had all night, but I declined.

At that moment a table became available. I sat down and placed my order. Ten minutes later the waiter showed up with a glass of wine. He said, "This is with the compliments of the gentleman at that table." I looked over and it was the producer-type that had been dining with Van. Guess this was my lucky night. Rather than offend him I accepted the drink by raising the glass, and nodding a thankful toast in his direction. This time there was no staring on my part. I kept my eyes glued to the salmon on my plate. He finished his meal long before I did. As he got up to leave he walked by my table and said, "I'm going to have a nightcap at the bar. Why not join me?" I politely declined, finished my meal and went on my way. Thankfully, all I ended up with that night was the Daily News.

†

A few years after the Sarnia flight I had my second close call in flight, this one real, not imagined. Ronnie and I were on a flight from Bermuda to New York, returning from a bit of R&R, when we started to smell smoke in the cabin.

The pilot came on the intercom explaining that there was an electrical fire, and that steps were being taken to control it. Just when some of us began to have difficulty breathing, down came the dangling oxygen masks. Oh no, it was Hail Mary time all over again.

There were no injuries as yet, but a bit of panic was beginning to set in, especially for the passengers with children. I do not recall the name of the carrier, but kudos to the crew whose performance was exemplary in maintaining order. Now we began to lose altitude. At this point I remember asking myself how I could be experiencing another in-flight trauma so soon after my Sarnia "ordeal." We were at an altitude of 20,000 feet, with a fire on board, and the sea coming up swiftly to capture us.

The pilot came on the intercom again, this time imploring us to stay calm, while assuring us that the situation was under control. After leveling off at 10,000 feet the flight attendants began to demonstrate how to brace ourselves for the impact of a belly-landing at sea. Evacuation procedures were also explained. There was still smoke in the cabin. Some of the children began to cry. Flight attendants kept scurrying around the cabin trying to keep people calm. I started agonizing over what it would be like "clawing at the window" to get out after we hit the water.

But fortunately, our prayers were answered. We welcomed the pilot's announcement that the fire was under control, and almost extinguished. Now the smoke was not as dense. It eventually cleared, but the stench remained in the air, and later, in our clothes. But who cared? We would be arriving in New York in one hour, a bit late, but unscathed. We even managed to have a couple of much-needed drinks before we arrived, on the house.

As I continued to do a lot of business travel, I gained more comfort in the air, but still had close calls. I reached a mental state whereby I used to have dreams about watching planes that were on fire while in flight. I was always watching them from ground level. Invariably they would crash and explode in a ball of flames. I felt so helpless not to be able to come to anyone's assistance. I began to think this might be an omen of things to come.

†

During these years, I would be gone for days, sometimes weeks at a time, for business trips. My priorities shifted more and more to the job and away from the family. I should have put a check on it, but was overpowered by ever-increasing management responsibility and ambition. Striking a balance between work and my personal life became increasingly difficult. This put an enormous load on Ronnie, and of course an even greater strain on the marriage.

But it wasn't all shock and pain. There was gratification, and there was much for which to be thankful. When I left the company in 1966, my boss Wally Brian paid me one of the nicest compliments I think I have ever received. We had just come back to the office from a farewell luncheon and I had said all my goodbyes except for him. After we shook hands, he said, "We are sorry to lose you, because you could have developed into one of our key people." Then he held up his left hand, with his forefinger and thumb barely separated. He looked me squarely in the eye and said, "Nick, I want you to know something. There isn't this much bullshit about you." It harkened me back to the motto of my alma mater: *Acta Non Verba.* Yes, I was getting it right!

10

ON THE ROAD AGAIN

But to see her was to love her, love but her, and love forever.

—Robert Burns, Scottish poet and lyricist (1759–1796)

In 1966 I reached another milestone. I accepted a job working for a major oil company in their marine transportation department. It brought a significant salary increase, but more important, the job put me back on the right career path. I would be working in the maritime industry for a multinational company that was about to embark on a huge multi-billion dollar shipbuilding program worldwide. Now I would get to see the world again. It didn't take long. Two years later we accepted a two-to-three-year assignment working and living in London. Jackpot!

As we approached the departure gate of the TWA flight to London, a spunky four-year-old Michael looked up at his grandfather, who was there to see us off, and said defiantly,

"We're going to London and we're not coming back!" Nearly three years later when we repatriated, I had wished he was right. Life for us in the U.K. was probably as good, if not better, than any other time in our marriage. The three kids were comfortable in English schools. We had a lovely home on a hill in the quaint and rustic village of Kingston-on-Thames, just six miles southwest of London. My office was a mere three miles from our home, and my work was perfectly in tune with my goals.

Relocating to a foreign country is always toughest on the stay-at-home spouse. The kids quickly settle into the new environment; the working parent has his or her job with which to keep busy. In our case, it was Ronnie who had to make the biggest adjustments while still holding things together on the home front, but as time passed, we got into a social groove. With the clarity of distance, I realized that we had never felt stable in Freeport. Happily, we found ourselves jolted back to a more positive mindset, and things felt like they were improving.

Life in Kingston-on-Thames always satisfied my addiction to the lovely English countryside—it was an experience in genteel living. The community was very old and quaint. Do you want to know quaint? Some of the nearby homes had thatched roofs. There were rhododendrons around our ranch-style home that were as high as the roof, really. Everywhere there were lush, magnificent gardens and graceful climbing vines that surrounded the scattered ivy-covered stone-built cottages nestled into the hillside. All of this was set in rolling hills with silver trickling streams and winding roads without sidewalks. It's a view of England you certainly won't get in London. Then too, there was always the omnipresent pub overflowing with the customary good cheer. We even had a livery stable nearby where Dorine spent much of her time riding and attending to the horses. When she came home at night her "fragrance" left no doubt as to where she had been.

†

As the first Christmas in our new home approached, we began to prepare for Santa Claus, or Father Christmas as he is known in the United Kingdom, in much the same way as did in back home. We could think of no gift more appropriate for the kids than a puppy to complete our English lifestyle. Off we went in pursuit of our favorite, the toy Yorkshire terrier. They are feisty, adorable little creatures whose yap is a lot worse than their bite. It didn't take long to come up with an adorable little Yorkie at a local kennel. As a puppy, he was so small he fit in the palm of Nicky's hand. Everybody had different ideas of what to name him, but Nicky had the idea of naming him after the nearby town where he was purchased—and so Esher came into our lives.

Our neighbor John across the road had a vicious Alsatian that he normally kept chained in his garage, or would keep under close surveillance at his side. On evenings when there was thunder and lighting, the barking and howling of that dog could send shivers up your spine. Now, Esher was a lap dog, and we did not let him run loose outside the house. However, one day he darted out an open door into the front garden. John was out working in his front garden with his dog close at hand. (Close your eyes this is not pretty). When his dog saw Esher, he darted across the road before John had a chance to restrain him. From Esher's appearance, it looked like the Alsatian only needed two or three bites to bring the curtain down on our poor little guy. From inside the house we hadn't noticed any of this, but there was a knock on the door. We opened the door to find John standing there with Esher in his hands, and tears in his eyes. He was almost as devastated as we were. He apologized profusely, and we knew he was sincere.

The kids cried for days over the loss of our little friend, but we tried to make it all better by burying him in the back garden with a ceremony and all the trimmings. I didn't bury him deep enough, though, because while I was out back one day I noticed the grave had been dug up and poor Esher was gone. I didn't have the heart to tell the kids that an animal had probably made a meal of him. So we told them Esher simply went to heaven like all good dogs.

When the neighbors got wind of what happened they started to pressure John about the dangerous behavior of his dog and the possible risks to their children. After all, today a dog, tomorrow possibly a child. John acquiesced and voluntarily had his dog put down. He had owned the dog for many years and loved it dearly, but being a parent he knew their concerns were indeed valid.

Gluttons for punishment, we went out and bought another dog, another Yorkie, another Esher, from the same kennel. We were determined not to let anything put a damper on our new life. We even went so far as to dine on roast beef and Yorkshire pudding every Sunday, patronize the local pub, and devour as many museums as possible.

†

Sometimes I would take the bus home from my office, which was near Kingston-on-Thames. I loved the way some of the locals jumped off the bus before the bus came to a full stop. Ever notice that when you're in London? They'd do it even while carrying packages. In particular, I used to watch this elderly woman do it—she was so ginger and graceful about it. I said to myself, *If she can do it, so can I.*

One evening on the way home I mustered up enough courage to finally approach the deed. She was on the bus, too, and though we never spoke, I sensed that she knew she was my bus-warrior mentor. God forbid I should fail. I would look and feel like a complete fool. As we approached our stop, she jumped off in her usual gazelle-like manner, landing cleanly and without incident.

Now I was feeling like a young paratrooper, jumping for the first time. Humbled, but not deterred, I jumped off right behind her, timed it all wrong, and went tumbling along the ground with my attaché case bouncing on ahead of me. I landed spread-eagle. The fall caused my pants to tear, and my case to open and my papers to go flying all over the ground.

My mentor noticed the bumbling Yank, of course. In her very ladylike manner she approached me, graciously offered me her hand, and said, "Are you OK young man? Not so easy is it?"

Bruised and humbled I meekly trudged homeward. However, like any good trooper, I tried it again and eventually got it right. By the time I left the U.K., believe me I was flying off those buses like a native and showing it off every chance I could.

The trick is to hit the ground running.

†

The company I worked for had contracted with nine shipyards to build a fleet of supertankers in Europe and the U.K. I was part of the team sent to London to create a project management office, which would oversee the design and construction of the ships. It also had responsibility for contract administration, including budget control.

One of the first issues our office was to face would remind me that I was in a different culture, despite the easy transition I had made to my new lifestyle. One morning I received a call from the shipyard in Northern Ireland that was building two of the four U.K.-built ships. There was a work stoppage, which could seriously disrupt the building schedule. The hull paint delivered to the shipyard was orange, thus, all the Catholic workers refused to handle it and walked off the job. They would not and did not return to work until new paint of a more "neutral" color was delivered to the shipyard. Let me put it this way—it was akin to an American wearing a Ku Klux Klan hood and robe on Martin Luther King Jr's birthday.

The national flag of the Republic of Ireland is a vertical tricolor of green, white, and orange. The green represents Roman Catholicism while the orange represents Protestantism. The white in the center signifies a lasting peace between Green and Orange. Many Irish Catholics consider orange as the color of oppression just as the Protestants consider green the color of sectarianism. As a result, war has raged periodically between the two factions for the last two centuries. It is not surprising, therefore, that a few hundred tins of paint should set off such a tempest.

The problem was resolved without causing a delay, thanks to some red paint, though in the end, the ships were delivered late anyway for a whole host of other reasons. I've often wondered if the Protestant workers would have walked off the job had the paint color been green. History tells us they would have. It also tells us it is time for Orange and Green to mend centuries of hate by finally moving into the "white" zone. In the meantime, the bad feelings persist.

The job had its perks. On May 2, 1969, Ronnie and I attended the launch of the biggest vessel—and the first supertanker, at 253,000 tons—ever built in the U.K. up to that time. As a member of the owner's project management team, we were invited to the christening ceremony. The sponsor for this auspicious occasion was to be none other than Her Majesty Queen Elizabeth II.

Ronnie and I began to wonder how we would fit in. By this time in our marriage she had evolved into a free spirit, continuously gaining confidence as she took on more and more responsibility in and outside the home, with a devotion that drew the admiration of everyone we knew. Given my extensive business travel, she had become the effective head of our household, and clearly demonstrated the leadership qualities to pull it off. In the process, she blossomed beyond her parochial education, and became more inclined to rightfully challenge my dominant personality. The ceremony was about to hit an emotional cord that signified a family in its heyday.

Nevertheless, I have to admit we were a bit awe-struck to be a part of such an auspicious occasion. After all, being in the presence of royalty, especially the Queen of England, was a new experience for us wee folks from Brooklyn. Who ever dreamed? And yet it was about to happen—or so we thought. Fate had other plans for the queen, and for us.

Given the queen's demanding and tight schedule, the launch date had been set well in advance. As the date fast approached, the shipyard predicted that it might not make the target date. Production was stepped up. That effort notwithstanding it soon became apparent the shipyard was not going to be ready to launch on time, no matter what.

Upon contacting the Royal House, shipyard management was advised that her schedule was firm and could not be changed to suit a new launch date. Nevertheless, a new launch date was set and the queen had to cancel her appearance. In her stead, the Royal House hastily proposed Her Royal Highness Princess Anne as a substitute for her mother. This seemed quite a good accommodation, as it would still give the event prestige. That was important, as Britain sought to further promote its image as a leading seafaring and shipbuilding nation.

Finally the big day arrived and with all preparations completed, it appeared the big ship was ready for launch. Stands were set up all around the ship for spectators. Media coverage was extensive. Despite the gray weather (what else?) the ship and launch site were festooned with brightly colored streamers, and decorations of every sort and color. After all, when it comes to pomp and ceremony, nobody does it better than the Brits.

Nor do the tailors of Savile Row in London when it comes to tailoring the finest English fabrics. Never a clothes horse, I was not one to get concerned about my clothing going out of style. But I simply could not resist the apotheosis of elegance, taste, and style that was and is the hallmark of Savile Row-made clothing. By the time of the christening I was all decked out in my finest tailor-mades. A double-breasted, full-length, camelhair coat that the tailor told me would never go out of style. A three-piece suit with a gold pocket watch in the vest pocket, and a gold chain festooned across the waistcoat front, with a fob dangling from it. The jacket had a cash pocket just above the lower right hand pocket. Later, I would develop a fetish for wearing ascot ties, which I still do occasionally. Ronnie too was festooned in London's finest English fabrics and styles, and looked stunning in a black velvet, full-length flared coat, and a striking wide-brim black hat on top of her beautiful long red hair. There is nothing in women's apparel more appealing to me than a hat, and I have never seen one that I did not adore from the simplest to the most elegant. In our own humble way, we tried to measure up to the occasion—and did.

The christening was considered such an important event that local schoolchildren were given the day off to witness an inspirational piece of British maritime history. Thousands of spectators lined both banks of the river. This launch was to be one of the last slipway launch sites in the world for a ship of this size. In other words, the vessel, as huge as it was, would actually slide down the ways into the water, as opposed to the more modern technique of floating a vessel in a large graving dock. Since the river into which the vessel was to be launched was relatively narrow, the shipbuilders had tons upon tons of heavy chain hanging over the sides and bow of the vessel, extending to the ground. This was supposed to act as a drag to impede the launch speed and thus prevent the vessel from hitting the opposite bank. As zero hour approached, all preparations were finalized and the christening party including Princess Anne and other VIPs assembled on the christening platform adjacent to the mighty ship, which was almost 1,000 feet long.

At 10:30 a.m., Princess Anne stepped up to the launch stand and said, "I name this ship *Esso Northumbria* and may God bless her and all who sail in her." She then pulled the lever that released the bottle of champagne into the vessel's hull. As expected, the bottle struck the hull producing a resounding BANG to go with the spurting champagne and flying streamers. There was huge applause and the band played the national anthem "God Save the Queen."

Then the unexpected. We waited for the vessel to move ... and waited ... and waited. We could hear people scurrying around the underbelly of the vessel. Hydraulic jacks pushed feverishly to get her started down the ways, but without success. We were told to stand by while the shipyard workers tried to sort out the problem. More scurrying, more jacks—but the big ship wouldn't budge.

After an hour or so, a light rain began to fall. Snacks, coffee, and tea were brought. During the intermission, most of us had a chance to meet the princess. She was charming, gracious, and seemed genuinely interested in the ship. She inquired about how a ship navigates, how much fuel it consumes, and whether it could sink if it hit an iceberg. (I wonder what prompted *that* question.) Shortly thereafter, word came down that they were going to have one last try. We watched as the launch crew again worked to get the big ship moving, but still to no avail. Finally the shipyard management, terribly embarrassed by now, decided to call a halt to the proceedings and asked everyone to return to the site in the afternoon.

Later that day, around 3:00 p.m., we mustered on the christening platform as before. The princess was asked to go through the same procedure, and once again, the bottle burst on cue. Everybody held their breath. Nothing. No music or applause this time. We heard a few frustrated moans and groans here and there. More scurrying down below. More anxiety, but this time we began to hear faint creaking as the steel plating of the hull bottom meshed with the greased slipway. As the creaking got louder we saw the first slight movement—the mammoth black hull inched away and moved down the slipway. It began to gain momentum. Now there was a huge uproar as the crowd cheered the big ship on the day of its birth.

As the vessel moved away from us, the chains being dragged along with the vessel shrieked and rattled loudly and kicked up a huge cloud of rust-dust. Finally she hit the water like a pregnant whale and went into the waiting arms of two tugs. Happily the tugs and chains were able to prevent her from hitting the opposite bank. All is well that ends well.

†

In 1970, I was reassigned back to the United States, and of course decided to take Esher II with us. As the time approached for us to repatriate, we began to ponder immigrating to the U.K. By now, Michael was more English than he was American, accent and all. It would have been easy for us to remain. I made inquiries with a prominent British steamship company and a leading shipyard in Scotland. There were distinct possibilities.

It didn't happen for several reasons; above all, our family ties to the United States. But I can tell you this—the day we vacated that house on the hill was one of the saddest of my life. As the limousine drove away from the house I kept looking back up the road until the house disappeared from view. When it did, I turned around, careful not to let the kids see my watery eyes. I asked myself, *Are we making a mistake?* It took me years to get over that move.

The legendary superliner, *Queen Elizabeth 2*, was the Cunard Line's flagship from 1969 until 2004. We were originally booked on her maiden voyage, but were delayed and had to reschedule the journey. When we repatriated back to the United States in 1970, our family of five occupied two adjacent cabins. Walking her decks was enough to make us long for a return of the heyday of trans-Atlantic liners. She was by far the most dazzling vessel of her day—the sight and feel of her surging through heavy seas and gliding over calm seas was unforgettable. Her sleek, stylish design was beautifully balanced with her black-colored hull, white superstructure, and black and red stack. To those who could see her from afar at night, with her strings of sparkling portholes, she must have looked like a gem; a miniature constellation fallen from the sky. Onboard, she had an endless array of food and ubiquitous creature comforts. The cuisine matched the surroundings, featuring English favorites such as shepherd's pie, Beef Wellington, steak and kidney pie, and the quintessential British favorite, roast beef and Yorkshire pudding. Equipped with all of the latest amenities, she even had a kennel onboard for us to board Esher II. The kids could visit him every day and even walk him around deck.

†

Not long ago, I faced the sad realization that in my lifetime, I had come full circle on this great lady, the *QE2*. I was there at her beginning, and was about to witness the legendary queen's demise. After forty years of catering to the most discriminating passengers, her days on the high seas came to an abrupt end in late 2008, when she was retired from active service and scheduled to become a floating luxury hotel at Port Jumeirah, Dubai. Fortunately, she will not experience the worst possible death for a ship—the breakers—but like the rest of us, she'll have to suffer the indignity of being a shadow of her former self.

On the evening of January 13, 2008, near the Statue of Liberty, the *QE2* and *QM2* met with a third grand dame, the new Cunard superliner, *Queen Victoria.* I viewed all three ships in their only port appearance together in New York Harbor. This was no coincidence. Cunard orchestrated it carefully, realizing that with the *QE2* soon to be decommissioned, such an opportunity would probably not come again. Thousands of people crowded the waterfronts on all sides of the harbor. Fireboats spouted massive streams of water into the air. Small boats and shore-side cars tooted their horns. Each of the three ships put on fireworks displays and sounded their whistles. Their smoke stacks glowing in the moonlight, towered majestically above everything else. The miniature constellation of portholes was tripled that night, and glittered over the water. There were flybys of all sorts. Even the weather cooperated, and the evening came together in a spectacular panorama, a homage to the three grand-dames of the high seas, a vision of British maritime prowess never to be forgotten, or probably ever seen again.

11

HOW MY WIFE BECAME MY STEPSISTER

What made America great was her ability to transform her own dream into hope for all mankind.

—French President Nicolas Sarkozy
before Congress, November 7, 2007

After a while, the reverse culture shock of returning to America took hold. The inbound adjustment phase was almost as difficult as the one going outbound. And the same could be said for my family. Sure, we were on home turf again, but everything seemed so different. Or were we different? Living and traveling overseas had given me a broader, more mature outlook on life and the people around me. I looked upon travel as a doorway to foreign politics and cultures. I therefore looked upon myself as a quasi-ambassador, and as such it was important for me to always be on my best behavior when traveling abroad. I had also become more aware of my weaknesses and sensitivities, and this awareness would only continue to evolve as I continued to broaden my horizons.

As if re-entry wasn't difficult enough, we encountered a disturbing incident right off the bat, a rude awakening into our so-called new home. After disembarking from the *QE2* we checked into a hotel in Manhattan. My mother came over one Sunday to join us for lunch in the coffee shop; there were six of us including Ronnie and our three kids at the table. My mother, whose chair was at the head of the table, got up to go to the ladies room, and as she stepped away from the table left her mink jacket on the back of her chair. (Yes, remember the days when women actually wore furs?) The villain in this episode must have been eyeing our table for some time, because right after Mom moved away from the table, he swooped in, lifted the fur from the chair and did a quickstep towards the door.

Even though we were busy talking and eating, I saw it all happen from the corner of my eye. I'm certainly no hero, but I recklessly and instinctively went to intercept him and caught him just as he was passing the counter. I was able to pin him against the counter where we struggled and then wrestled each other to the floor. I was able to hold him long enough until security arrived on the scene. The thing that amazed me was that in less than two minutes the place was crawling with house detectives and police—security was tight. In retrospect it was kind of a dumb thing for me to do, but I distinctly remember wanting to avoid the anguish my mother would have felt if her precious mink jacket were to be stolen.

We retrieved the jacket; the guy was apprehended and taken away. All of this happened within the time span that my mother was gone. When she returned, the jacket was there as if it hadn't been touched. Being as high-strung as she was, we decided not to tell her what had happened. The whole affair soon blew away in the wind—pressing charges against the guy, as described by the police, sounded so complicated that we simply left the scene and never mentioned it again.

†

We eventually settled into a newly purchased six-bedroom English Tudor in Westchester County, with our English dog, our English wardrobes, and our English-accent kids. Repatriating back to America was like seeing it as does a foreigner who visits here for the first time—you reach out to try and understand why things are different, much the way we did upon relocating to the U.K. We actually had to make social adjustments coming back to our own country, and that felt strange.

A month after we moved in, there was a knock at the door. It was a policeman from the local police station. Naturally, we invited him in and asked if there was a problem. He said no, and that he merely wanted to welcome us to the neighborhood. He went on to explain that for a fee he and other members of the police department are routinely available to act as sort of a sergeant-at-arms for teenager parties. He pointed out that "the kids" can get out of hand, especially when the parents are out of the house. He then said—and I remember this verbatim as if it were yesterday—"When they see the gun, it keeps them in line."

I could feel my heart drop. It absolutely blew my mind.

Brimming with our new-found British civility, we hoped for a kinder America. We naively hoped for a society where there was no place for rudeness and harshness in dealing with one another. The steady diet of violence in the media made us long for a gentler America. Most of all, we hoped for a society where there would be no room for the domestic "hired gun." Instead, we saw an impatient and hurried America. We made comparisons and wondered if English civility could enable these conditions to exist. We asked ourselves if we were seeing a crisis in civility here at home, or merely experiencing a mindset that would readjust and eventually pass.

Quite apart from wanting to chase the officer out the door, I was ready to get on a plane to anywhere outside the United States. *What, I wondered, had happened to this country in the short time we were away?* Had my grandfather's America slipped away?

In reality, it probably hadn't changed that much. Perhaps we had simply moved to a neighborhood where people could afford these kinds of "services," or where policemen were better salesmen than most. We politely asked the "gun for hire" to leave, and told him we would not be availing ourselves of their services.

The re-entry process was nearly complete. The English civility we had come to appreciate was an ocean away, and I wondered again, had we made a mistake in coming home?

A few weeks later, the process would be completed. I got home one night to find everybody crying. "What's wrong?" I asked. "Is everybody OK?"

"Yes," came the reply, "but Esher II ran out and got run over on North Street."

Well, what's a guy to do? Another burial in the back garden, another ceremony, and more weeping—but this time I dug the grave deeper and it was never disturbed. The last tie to our life in England had been cut.

†

We had not been living in our new home long when Ronnie became my stepsister.

That was the day my widowed father-in-law, Michael, married my widowed mother to become my stepfather. My father died when he was only sixty-three years old. My mother was fifty-six years old at the time. A few years later my father-in-law, Michael, who was about the same age as my mother, lost his wife. My mother and father-in-law kept in touch with each other through my wife and me, as you'd expect. In fact, he used to offer her a ride whenever he drove out to visit us. Enter cupid. Before we knew it, they were not just seeing each other, but actually dating.

Michael came to me first and asked me what I thought of the idea. I told him sharing their lives would be very special, and at the same time, keep it all in the family. I thought it was a good match. They enjoyed dining out as much as spending a quiet evening at home, and being with family, especially the grandkids, was the most important part of their lives. They enjoyed afternoon drives in the country and staying overnight at bed-and-breakfasts along the way. Most importantly, they seemed to share a genuine affection for one another.

Their relationship reminded me of a favorite lyric of mine from the song "People"—"People who need people are the luckiest people in the world." One of the saddest things in life is to not share it with someone; nature did not intend for the human spirit to be solitary. As they were both very lonely living alone, we were delighted to see them joined in holy matrimony. A pity, those of us who do not "need people."

I had been without a father since 1959 and welcomed the chance to experience another paternal relationship, albeit a quite different one. Dad was the serious, hard-driving taskmaster who always expected more of himself and the people around him. Michael was a jovial, mild-mannered, even-tempered man, who seemed content with his surroundings. Both of them were caring, and shared a common bond; they were both plumbers. I guess Mom had an affinity. My gut feel told me the contrast between the two men favored my mother having a happier relationship with Michael than with my father.

And so it came to pass that he proposed, and Mama, bless her soul, accepted.

They announced a date for the wedding, and as extra icing on the cake, we offered our big new home for the wedding ceremony and reception. It was spacious and had all the trappings for such an affair—and besides, it would give an extra measure of warmth and hominess. The wedding was small; family and friends totaled around thirty-five people. I think elegant was the best way for me to describe the bride. Mom was wearing a light blue, satin, full-length dress with a matching veil and elbow gloves. The silver earrings and double row of pearls blended beautifully with her black hair, which by then was flecked with gray. What an odd feeling it was for me to be giving my mother away. Funny too, because I always viewed my father's side of the family as being wacky and lovable, and my mother's side as being conventional and reserved. It goes to show you that reality can mock your assumptions.

As the host, in the back of my mind, a worry was stewing. We had hired a caterer to do all of the food preparation, setup at the house, and serving. They were supposed to arrive at noon to begin setting up for the guests who would be arriving around 1:00 p.m. As the guests had begun to arrive, frantic phone calls to the caterer went unanswered. By two o'clock, Mom was married, and there was still no sign of the caterer. In the meantime, hungry guests were taking the edge off their appetites with an overindulgence in alcoholic beverages.

At two thirty, there was a ring at the door and the catering manager was standing there drunker than a cross-eyed skunk. She hung on to the handrail, barely coherent, and mumbled for me to come to her van. Standing next to it was one of her employees, who was as drunk as she. I shuddered at the thought that one of these idiots even drove the van over to our home. From what I could understand from her slurred speech, her employees had let her down, and that she was not able to prepare the menu we had agreed upon. Instead she had quickly prepared food that she hoped would please us.

With that she opened the van rear doors to show me the sickest batch of hot dogs and hamburgers I have ever seen, not to mention the stale rolls and bread that went with them. I'm not a violent person, but I must admit that there are times when controlling my temper is a real challenge. This was one of them. It was all I could do to contain myself from putting my hands around her throat and choking her until her eyes popped out. That's exactly what I was feeling. Fortunately, a cooler head prevailed and I simply gave her a stern heave-ho with some choice zingers.

And now I had to go back in the house to explain to thirty-five hungry, half-sloshed guests what had happened. Being family and friends, they were of course understanding and sympathetic. Nevertheless, we had to face the reality that there simply was not enough food in the house to feed all of these people. Faced with the distasteful prospect of ordering in "Chinese" or ten pizzas, someone came up with the idea to call around to a few of the local restaurants to see if they could accommodate us. That was a long shot—after all, how could we expect a restaurant to put together a meal for thirty-five people on such short notice? Anyway, it was worth a try since we didn't have a lot of options. And halleluiah! We actually found a restaurant in Harrison—one of our favorites, in fact—that would accommodate us if we gave them one hour to prepare.

By the time we got there it must have been around four o'clock. They had set up two large tables in a section of the main dining room, which worked out perfectly for us. We didn't even have to settle for a set menu; we actually could and did order a-la-carte. We wined and dined and had a four-course meal that turned out to be superb. They even managed to put together a small wedding cake for us.

After the best man Uncle Mike made a toast, several of us made individual toasts. When it was my turn we held our glasses high, and part of what I said was, "I didn't feel like I was losing a mother, but more like I was gaining a father." And I meant it. I had a great deal of love and respect for my new father; now I was calling him Dad in earnest.

I later extended our heartfelt appreciation to the restaurant owner/manager, and told him what had happened—he and his staff had saved the day for us. Hopefully we made it worthwhile for him and his kind staff.

†

Curious as it may seem, in later years, I compared Mom's relationship with my father to Ronnie's and mine. I recognized many of the same negative forces at work in their marriage as in ours. They didn't divorce; we eventually did. When we did I'm sure Michael was looking down on us, and I'm quite sure we broke his heart.

The storybook romance had a sad ending. A year and a half after the marriage, after we had moved abroad again, Michael died. Ronnie returned home for the funeral, but I was especially saddened by his death because I was not able to return home to say goodbye. He used to like to say that once you got past sixty years old you were on a fast track. Sorry to say he finally caught that train. Dad, I'm sure you are enriching lives up there as much as you did down here.

I still cherish his memory, and when my family and I think of him now, we reflect on his life and one of the humorous stories we often told about him. He used to relish buying, erecting, and dressing the Christmas tree. One year he came home from the office party feeling quite celebratory, and then proceeded to untie the Christmas tree that had been purchased days before. He started to erect the tree, and while doing so, he continued the merriment with a few more drinks—and when we arrived at his house that evening, we found him lying on the floor, face up, out cold, spread-eagle like Da Vinci's *The Vitruvian Man*, with the tree sprawled on top of him. It's a good thing Santa didn't see him.

When he died, he left a void in my life. He had always taken an interest in my work, hobbies, and almost anything else going on in my life, and was an inspiring figure in my adult life. His presence was sorely missed for other reasons, too. Our kids had lost their English accents, but you never lose the need for the special kind of love that only grandparents can provide.

†

We lived in Westchester for a few more years. Life was mostly unremarkable and pleasant, with one exception.

One of the worst things about a break-in is the creepy feeling you get after it's over. The thought of someone having been in your home, going through your things, messing with your stuff, using your bathroom and even eating your food, leaves you insecure. It is even more frightening to think of what might have happened if you had walked in on the burglar, or had even been present at the time of the robbery. It's almost as bad as the loss you feel for the valuables taken, whether their value is monetary or purely sentimental. So it was with the two break-ins I experienced, the first as a youngster living at home with my parents, the second in our Harrison home. The second one unnerved us the most, as we had our children's safety on our minds.

It occurred around 2:00 p.m. on a weekday, precisely the time nobody was ever home. You didn't have to be Dick Tracy to conclude, as did the police, that they must have cased the house for weeks. The break-in was an easy matter of cutting out a small pane of glass in a kitchen's leaded glass window, and then reaching in and opening the handle from the inside. The rear of the house was so treed-in that the risk of detection was minimal. It must have been a cakewalk. They also knew exactly what they were doing—they didn't take any of our junk, costume jewelry and the like. They only took the good stuff, including items of great sentimental value and family heirlooms. That's what hurt.

When the police came in they did as much as they could, but were candid with us: they doubted anyone would be apprehended for the robbery. No one ever was. We never heard another word about the incident, but it put our neighbors on alert. A few of them had security alarm systems installed in their homes.

The incident made me reflect on just how far we had come from our poor and humble days in Brooklyn. Sure, we had more material prosperity. We lived in prestigious Westchester County. We had two cars. And yes, my bedroom was a lot more than a corner of the living room. Come to think of it, the living room in that house was as big as the total area of the Brooklyn apartment. But had we really come that far? The friends we knew back then were as close and genuine as the people we have met since. The values being instilled in our children at their school and at home were no less high-minded than they are today. And there can be no mistake about the degree of violence then and now. Even the thug who stole my watch and ate our food way back when was an amateur compared to the slick, bold operators who stole furs in broad daylight and executed well planned break-ins. Back in Brooklyn, we were hit only once in twenty years. Now we had been hit twice within twenty months. There were no easy conclusions about how far we had really come.

†

Soon, we were on the move again. Only a year or two had passed since we settled into our Harrison home when I accepted a new assignment to work in Kobe, Japan. We saw it as a great opportunity to live and work in a new and exotic culture.

As we prepared to relocate to Kobe for the three-to-four-year assignment, Uncle Pete and his wife Aunt Rita were kind enough to give us a sayonara party at their home in Brooklyn a few weeks before we departed. After the festivities had gotten underway and the attention was elsewhere, he grabbed me by the arm and pulled me aside.

"Nicky, are you crazy?" he said. "How can you possibly take your wife and three children to go and live in a place like Japan? Do you know anything about those people?"

As he spoke I remembered the conversation we had years earlier around that same kitchen table, when he talked about the war horrors he had experienced. It helped me understand his attitude. I tried to explain that the Japan we were going to was different from the Japan that had launched the enemy forces he fought so fiercely, so many years ago.

"These days, Japan is a close friend and ally," I said.

No matter. To him, the *Banzai!* battle cry of the Japanese warrior was still fresh in his mind, and would remain so for the rest of his life. Even so, I tried to reassure him that the overseas venture on which we were about to embark would be a safe and rewarding one.

And it was. We lived in Japan three and a half years and found it to be an enriching experience, personally and professionally. The only shadow that hung over my next several years abroad was that Uncle Pete would die before we moved home again. I was therefore denied the privilege of saying goodbye to another dear man whom I loved.

12

MEMOIRS OF A JAPANOPHILE

Were You There *when they crucified my Lord?*

—My favorite hymn, Negro spiritual, author unknown

My family and I lived in Kobe, Japan from 1971 to 1974. I was part of a project management team supervising another multi-billion dollar shipbuilding program. Japan would remain with me for the rest of my life, and this period would resume a fifty-year love affair with Japanese culture.

For Ronnie and our three children, Japan was a first-time experience. Ronnie and I attended a two-week, company-sponsored orientation course at the American University in Washington, D.C., that helped grease the skids into foreign society.

I was no stranger to Japan, having traveled there during my navy days and later on business. The kid's new school had an American curriculum and a good reputation, as we had ascertained before accepting the post. Our housing concerns were quickly put to rest, too, with a lovely Western-style four-bedroom home located halfway up a mountainside. It was an absolutely beautiful setting, and our front door overlooked the entire harbor. Everything was convenient—the school was a mere fifteen-minute walk up the mountain, and my commute couldn't have been much more than that by train or car. Kobe was known for its abundance of Western housing and school systems. It offered a unique balance of city and suburban life, and it teemed with English-speaking foreigners. Country clubs offered a full range of activities similar to what would be available at home.

Before we knew it, Ronnie and the kids had sailed through culture shock with barely a whimper. After six months our social life was more active than it had ever been anywhere else. That was important—I was traveling nearly every week, and Ronnie needed an amicable social climate. Most of our friends were European and American. Nearly all my business associates were Japanese. Life was good. Sure, there was always some quirky stuff going on; the ever-present critters in our house, for instance, but after no time at all we were taking every day of our new life in stride.

†

Living and traveling in Japan is a stimulating experience, offering scenic beauty and the opportunity to observe one of the world's most unique cultures. However, I'd be remiss if I didn't hasten to add that, quite frankly, Japan poses a sometimes downright frustrating experience to the foreigner, especially if he is an American. I know of no other country in the world where fixtures of American life have been so readily adopted—industrialization, fashion, and baseball, to mention a few obvious ones. Quick to elevate and laud their heroes, they are even quicker to denounce their failures. Generally speaking, because they are comfortable in their own ways and possess a strong devotion to Japan, I sense they appear shy or even insecure around foreigners and in foreign countries. Yet, to their great credit, their natural instinct is to resist any influence that would seriously disrupt their core beliefs and culture. I have always been impressed with that aspect of Japanese society.

Equally to their credit is the fact that this is a country that climbed from almost complete isolation and feudalism to the second highest GNP in the world. With no mineral resources of her own, Japan also climbed out of the rubble of World War II and rebuilt the country in approximately twenty years, despite "expert" predictions that the process would require fifty years. A comparison can be drawn between Japan and postwar Germany. Both countries attribute their modern industrial competitiveness to their new and therefore highly productive factories. America, despite having escaped the ravages of war on its home turf, was at a disadvantage—we had to compete in the market while manufacturing goods in old, less productive factories. (In recent years that gap has narrowed.)

As part of my adjustment, I was attracted to anything that catered to Westerners. It was here, in early-'70s Japan, that a seed was planted for what would become my part-time modeling and acting hobby. This showed me that one of the ironies of life is to expect the unexpected.

I answered an ad in a local newspaper. An agency was looking for Westerners to do modeling work: NO EXPERIENCE REQUIRED, it said. A co-worker dared me to answer it.

As a lark, I called the agency and explained that I had no modeling experience, but had a full-time job in an unrelated field. I further explained that since I had a job, I would only be available evenings and weekends, and even that time would be limited by my business travel. Nevertheless, they encouraged me to come in—if they could use me, they would work around my schedule. After a short interview, they informed me that I was photogenic enough to fit into some of their upcoming projects. I began to think perhaps this mug of mine might come in handy after all. I can't say I worked often, but enough to gain experience and make a few yen on the side. I modeled eyeglasses, jewelry, and clothing, all of which appeared in national ads.

Later on, my family got involved. My two sons Nicky and Michael did a bit of modeling for clothing and toys. The agency even used my home and our entire family to model a line of Japanese home products, for which the company wanted a Western setting. That led to the five us being hired to model in Western-style homes for a local a developer. I found the work glamorous as well as profitable, and I decided I wanted to continue after we returned to the United States. However, a very active primary career and other family responsibilities made it impossible, so I would put it on hold for many years.

†

Although a car wasn't essential in Japan, we bought one for the extra measure of convenience it provided. It gave Ronnie an easy way to get back and forth to the two clubs we joined, and to visit some of our many friends. Playing bridge, dining out, movies at the clubs, sightseeing, looking after the kids, and a whole host of other activities kept her busy—so much so that it sometimes got too hectic for both of us. However, I was doing so much traveling that she needed to stay active and stave off boredom. And there were the times, too, when I was not traveling, but just as absent.

Several weeks after we placed the order for her car, we received a call from the dealer telling us that it had arrived from the factory and that they were now going to prep it for delivery. Days went by; we heard nothing more. I had a coworker who spoke Japanese call the dealer to find out the status. We were told it would be a few more days before we could expect to take delivery. After a lot of frustration and confusion, we found out there was nothing wrong with the car or the dealer. To my surprise and satisfaction, the normal practice in Japan at that time was for dealers to hold on to cars for approximately one week to thoroughly test and check them out so that when a car is delivered, the dealer is confident there will be no defects. After we took delivery, indeed, the car did not have a single defect or recall item for the entire three and a half years that we owned it; only routine maintenance. And what a beauty it was—a new Nissan Cedric two-door hardtop in gold with a white vinyl top.

Many years later, we would recognize the same quality in the Japanese-built cars we purchased in the United States. We would also be grateful to Japanese auto manufacturers for bringing much-needed quality control to the American auto industry. Upon taking delivery of a U.S.-manufactured auto, it was quite common to have many defects; loose moldings, rattles, dents, leaking windshields, handles that came off, scuffed paint—you name it. It took Japanese manufacturers to bring us cars that would run the first time out, thanks in large part to their quality control standards. Marketing is another cornerstone of the Japanese industrial success story—they excel at it. They enter a marketplace with the purposeful intention of designing and building products that fit that particular market. The strategy, while initially expensive in design development cost, is geared to establishing a permanent market presence, while recognizing that profits will not be immediate. That compares to the short-sighted strategy of some American companies that try to force-fit existing products into markets for which they were not designed. While that may reap short-term profits, it is a sure-fire formula for eventually losing market share. I saw firsthand evidence of this when I was assigned to Singapore as Director of Business Development, Far East, an assignment I will discuss later.

As I write this, the United States is weathering the most serious financial downturn since the Great Depression. The automobile manufacturing industry, one of the business sectors responsible for the downturn, has been losing market share for the last forty years. The playing field, however, is not level. Japanese auto plants in the United States have achieved profitability by setting up their factories in Southern and border states, where they can avoid the United Auto Workers union. In their efforts to compete, Detroit's Big Three continue to seek government financial assistance—GM and Chrysler have already received part of a multi-billion dollar federal bailout package. As a taxpayer, I have a problem with that. Yet, I am realistic enough to know that since one in nine workers in this country holds an auto-industry-related job, it is in the general interest for that assistance to be forthcoming.

One can hope that such assistance will impose sweeping reductions in UAW compensation and benefits packages. For example, concessions need to be made to narrow a $25–$30-an-hour gap between labor costs at UAW-represented plants and nonunion U.S. factories run by Japanese automakers. What they need to avoid are the kind of bad management decisions and union demands that resulted in nonsensical situations—for instance, workers made $27 an hour to play cards because their contracts had a "no-work" clause, which guaranteed they would be paid even when there was no work to do. I think that is representative of the kind of union strategy that has focused on a dreaded four-letter word. That word is MORE. It is perhaps presumptuous, even contentious of me to say so, but I cannot help but to wonder if labor unions will continue to survive in the changing economic environment.

In all fairness I should also mention that the U.S. auto industry has made considerable progress in the last twenty years. They are doing a better job at delivering quality cars that are more fuel-efficient. Living abroad has given me a broader perspective from which to make objective observations.

There is, however, a long way to go not only in the auto industry, but with other critical issues. Perhaps more than ever before, government needs to come up with solutions to problems that have been long-standing. For example, when will we have a coherent energy policy? When will we finally do something about a trade deficit that keeps growing, not to mention the staggering level of national debt? Should we be taking global warming seriously? How about ever-spiraling health care costs? When will we begin to see fiscal responsibility when it comes to government spending? And there is a fairly new challenge—illegal immigration? We debate this one to death, and twelve million immigrants later, we still do not have a coherent policy. To make matters worse, Washington continues to demonstrate an inability to get things done in an efficient and timely manner, and that it is inapt to the task of reducing government. At the same time, we continue to lose the competitive edge in worldwide markets, and the politicians keep doing what they do best—talking about it. But like every coin, there is another side; and it has to do with the American worker. In my view, there are simply too many of us who do as little as possible for a day's wage. That too has to change if we are going to remain competitive in worldwide markets.

Getting back to my car purchase in Japan, the other astounding aspect of the purchase was the dealer's complete trust in us. The dealer accepted a personal check in payment for the car, not in advance, but on the day of delivery. The all-important component in the transaction was my word given over a handshake. Another important factor was my business card. The exchange of initialed business cards was tantamount to an informal contract, and I came to learn that your signed business card is your bond. Working for a major oil company with a recognizable name certainly helped—and I'm not naive enough to think they didn't check us out in their own way. Nevertheless,

I was amazed that I could drive our car off the lot after paying for it like a bag of groceries.

Vehicle inspections were rigorous, expensive, and required every two years after the initial three-year inspection. The dealer who sold us the car came to the house and not only picked up our car, but left a loaner. They kept the car for three days and handled all the paperwork that needed to be done with the Department of Motor Vehicles. When they delivered it to our home, the car was immaculate and in tip-top shape inside and out—washed and waxed, and with all the mechanical and electronic jobs completed to our satisfaction. The cost of oil, filters, belts, and so forth was out of sight, but with such service, who could complain? The $500 we paid for the entire job seemed well worth it. (Today, the cost is between $750 and $1,500.) That car ran like new right up to the day we sold it.

Driving on the left side of the road was not a problem because we had gotten used to doing it years earlier in England. It did, however, require complete concentration. If you drive and talk or get distracted in some other way, there is a tendency to drift back to your *right side* ways, and possibly cause an accident. If you make a mistake, there is some solace in knowing that Japanese drivers generally tend to be well mannered. For example, when a taxi pulls up behind you at night, the driver will typically dim the headlights to avoid the glare in your eyes.

My International Driver's License expired after a year in Japan. I had to obtain a Japanese driver's license. With a measure of pleasure, I slipped it into my wallet alongside my licenses from New York, New Jersey, California (and later the U.K.)—and with a measure of pride, noted they were all some of the toughest places in the world to drive.

†

My mother came to visit. We already had a habit of taking every opportunity to see as much of the country and its culture as possible, so with my mother in town, we suggested staying at a traditional Japanese-style inn known as a ryokan. She enthusiastically agreed, for she would not have otherwise experienced such a thing, even in her wildest dreams. Despite her humble surroundings in Brooklyn, Mom was a very good, tireless traveler who was anxious to see and do it all. I had never seen her so excited about travel—her verve was not diminished in the least, even when she realized she'd forgotten to bring that ratty fur jacket with her.

We chose a ryokan near Kyoto, a city considered to be the cultural capital of Japan. One difference from a Western-style hotel that we noticed was the expectation that shoes be removed before entering; everyone walks around in slippers. This is true in the Japanese home as well. A ryokan also provides you with a yucata, which is a kimono-like robe. Yukata can be your nightwear, but can also be worn lounging outside your room and even in the town streets. The design of each room is strictly Japanese-style too. The floor is covered with tatami mats made of straw. The room is partitioned by sliding fusama screens that are made of thick decorative paper. You sleep on a futon mattress, which is laid upon the tatami floor. The maid spreads out the futon after dinner and puts them away in the morning. Your room will either have a private bath or there will be a public bath in the ryokan. If public, you will be expected to soap up and rinse outside of the large tub because the hot water is for soaking and used by other guests, too.

We booked two rooms for a weekend. On the day we arrived, we settled in pretty quickly and arranged to have a lovely Japanese dinner at the inn. Everything seemed calm. But as my wife and I were getting dressed in preparation for dinner, suddenly there was a very loud, unfamiliar rumble followed by movements of the floor and walls around us. The ground was shaking. We knew we were in trouble when the hanging lamps began to sway and the furniture started bouncing up and down. Walls cracked. Dust erupted. We fell down, but were still in one piece. We were frightened, but didn't panic knowing that what we did in the next few seconds and minutes could be the difference between life and death or serious injury. Could it be? Yes, we were experiencing an earthquake. I thought I had seen it all, but this was a first. Then I thought, *What about Mom?* Small in stature and strong in spirit, and very excitable in emergencies, she could not have been doing well.

I dashed to her room and found her lying on the tatami mats, trembling, holding her rosary beads. She was frozen in place not sure whether to leave the room or stay. Afraid the ceiling might fall in on her, she wanted to hide, but there was nothing she could hide under. Instead, she just prayed, choking her rosary beads, with a look of fright on her face that I will never forget. All she could say was, "My God, what happened?"

Poor woman—she came all the way to Japan only to get caught in, of all things, an earthquake. I do not remember the Richter scale reading, but it lasted fifteen seconds and was the real thing. Fortunately, none of us were hurt except for a few minor scratches and bruises. Very quickly the staff anxiously came to offer assistance and assure us that everything was under control. Shortly thereafter, Mom brushed herself off, fixed her hair, touched up her makeup and was ready for dinner. That was just like her.

I'm happy to say the rest of our stay was uneventful and quite relaxing, especially after a few drinks of sake. Our meals were served in a traditional tatami room with one table. As I recall there were twelve small courses, each served artistically. We dined on all our favorite Japanese dishes such as sukiyaki, batter-fried tempura, shabu-shabu, sashimi, and sushi with rice and tea. We ate the typical breakfast served in a ryokan consisting of rice, miso (bean paste) soup, tofu, greens, fruit, and a variety of fish. Even though Mom was normally an adventurous eater, I think she was put off by the little fish heads floating around in the soup.

On the day of our departure we were given the usual courteous send-off by the staff. After they brought the car out front, three of the staff lined up outside the ryokan facing us as we stood by the car. Each of them bowed ceremoniously several times, and so did we. As we drove away, I looked back and they were still bowing. This is a deeply rooted and beautiful custom, and like nearly everything in Japan, it is a ceremony. Mom commented that she had never seen anything like that before, and was impressed. She also said that during her stay she had never been treated so courteously in her life, or experienced such exemplary service.

†

No matter where you are in Japan, take it from me, food is an obsession. For most Westerners, the taste needs to be cultivated, but once you have it, you'll want more of it. There are sushi bars, tempura shops, delectable coffee shops, steak houses, *teppanyaki*-style restaurants, pastry shops, *shabu-shabu* restaurants, shops that specialize in deep-fried delicacies, ramen and *udon* noodle stands where you can slurp to your heart's content, and a host of others I can't begin to remember. Why, even the vending machines offer twelve kinds of tea, hot and cold.

Let me tell you about what I consider to be the ultimate Japanese culinary experience. During our sojourn in Kobe we ate whole, fresh carp. The challenge for the chef is to carve the body on the bone into edible portions, while leaving just enough life so that when it is served to you, there is still a slight quiver of life in it. The trick is to then pick off pieces of the *live* fish with your chopsticks and *enjoy*. At some point the poor creature finally capitulates. Here, I think Mom was put off, as the fish was too fresh even for her, and believe me she was usually a stickler for fresh food. You then save the best for last, which in this case are the eyes. Considered a delicacy, fish eyes can be the source of a dining ruckus at a Japanese table as there are too few to go around. We did not have such a problem. In my vast dining experience in the Orient, I have on occasion tried them, and would liken them to chewing grainy, tasteless, pit-less olives. Pigeon eyes, which I have also tried, are not much better.

†

Not long after Mom left Japan we found ourselves looking forward to the delights of the cherry blossom season. Can there be any aspect of Japanese culture more endearing than *sakura zensen,* the cherry blossom season? The flowers are a delightful respite from the rigors of everyday life. Celebrated for centuries, cherry blossoms have come to symbolize for the Japanese the transience of life because of their short blooming times. The season lasts a mere two weeks, depending on the weather conditions and where in Japan you might be at the time.

We and many of our expatriate friends got as caught up in the festivities as the locals. Our favorite outing was to visit a local park and sit with friends under the blooming cherry trees, picnicking with sake and Japanese delicacies, while listening to Japanese music. Equally enjoyable was watching the locals going through the same ritual, enjoying it as much as we did. Sheer delight! Although I have never seen it, I understand that Washington, D.C., undergoes the same kind of festive transformation every spring.

On special occasions like this, or whenever we hosted family or friends, we would drive forty-five minutes to Himeji Castle, Japan's most spectacular castle. Perched high on a hill, it is distinguishable by its tall stone foundation, multi-layer roofs, and whitewashed walls. Unlike many other Japanese castles, Himeji Castle was never destroyed in wars, earthquakes, or fires, and therefore survives in its original state—dating back to 1609, when it was completed. Located approximately seventy-five miles west of Kyoto, it is also accessible by the bullet train.

To visit during peak blooming season is a two-for-one delight because the grounds surrounding the castle are festooned with hundreds of cherry trees. To stand at the bottom of the hill looking up at the castle is like seeing a grand ship afloat on a sea of flowers. The whole scene reminded me of Puccini's *Madame Butterfly*, which contains what I consider to be the most beautiful music ever composed—*Un Bel Di*, or *One Fine Day*. (His aria, *Nessun Dorma* from *Turnadot* runs a close second.) *One Fine Day* brings me to tears every time I hear it. Our routine was to visit the castle in the morning, have lunch at one of the Japanese restaurants in town, and return to the castle to finish the tour.

These kinds of excursions gave us a chance to practice our Japanese. After taking classes two to three times a week, I muddled through, enough to order food in a restaurant and get travel directions. The kids were studying it in school, and were pretty good at it by the time we left Japan, especially Dorine.

†

In addition to staying at a ryokan, we would occasionally take day-trips to Kyoto to soak up as much of the culture as possible. With a population of 1.5 million people, it is Japan's most popular tourist destination and a major part of the Osaka–Kobe–Kyoto metropolitan area.

Before visiting Kyoto we had never paid much attention to the temples and castles scattered around the city. There are many, but two stand out in my mind as well worth visiting. The Kodaiji Temple, built in 1606, is one of the most imposing sites, as is the moated Nijojo Castle. Then, too, there is the wide array of antique shops. And if you are lucky, you'll also be able to do some geisha-watching.

You can't miss the geishas' white makeup, sandals, red lipstick, traditional hair bun and brightly colored kimonos. These Japanese entertainers are extensively trained and skilled in the arts of traditional music, dance, and conversation. Some foreigners associate geishas with sexual gratification. Not so! These elegant ladies graciously entertain guests with song, dance, food and beverage service, and conversation. Be careful though, because if you are so inclined the fees for such entertainment will run into the hundreds, even thousands of dollars, depending on the size of your party.

Staying at a ryokan can also be expensive. But a visit to Kyoto is not complete without staying at one. It is the perfect mixer to make the "Kyoto Cocktail" complete.

†

I am a licensed U.S. Coast Guard Captain and have crewed sailboats many times, but I was never qualified to operate a sailboat on my own. However, there was a time in Japan when my machismo got the better of me. We were vacationing at Lake Nojiri. The lake, with water that seemed clean enough to drink, was set high up in the mountains and surrounded by greenery and trees so tall they seemed to reach beyond the sky. To say the place was pristine would be putting it mildly. Near our cabin was a small sailboat rental house with a fleet of eighteen-foot sailboats. There wasn't much to the place other than the boats, a rustic old dock house, a few broken-down slips and the elderly gent who ran the place. All you had to do was pay the rental fee and bring the boat back whenever you were done with it.

Nicky was twelve years old. He was anxious to venture out, and was beginning to show an interest in ships. In fact, in a couple of years, and without any encouragement from me, he would start building model ships. He was intelligent and obedient, and tended to be shy and somewhat of a loner. Although we didn't recognize it at the time, the "loner" aspect of his personality may have been the first symptom of the dreaded illness that would take his life fourteen years later. Sadly, in the next two to three years there would be no doubt in our minds as to what we were up against, and the suffering he was about to go through.

That day at the lake, I sat outside the cabin for two hours talking and trying to decide whether we should rent one of the sailboats. The weather wouldn't get in our way; it was sunny with a nice breeze blowing. Finally, this old salt worked up enough courage and decided to do it, and take the both of us out for a run on the lake.

I admit I was not brimming with confidence. For the first thirty minutes, things were going great. I even tacked successfully, twice. The third time, Nicky and I were facing each other, sitting on opposite gunwales. A wind gust hit us as I came about. I knew I was pushing too hard when the lee gunwale dipped underwater. Over we went. The look on my Nicky's face told the whole story as he slipped beneath the water: shock. With life jackets on, we popped up and hung on to the boat. In the calm water and not being far from shore, I was able to wave for the owner. He rescued us and dragged us back to port, wet and embarrassed.

In retrospect this incident could have had disastrous results. Fortunately, with our life jackets on we quickly bounced up, clear of the boat. It is not difficult to imagine the results had one or both of us gotten tangled in the lines.

I have not manned a sailboat since then.

†

While living in Japan we took vacations to exotic places that were not normally convenient. One such trip took us to Egypt via India and Pakistan, and the flight once again brought us too close to danger. The last in this bad patch of flying incidents occurred on a flight from Karachi (Jinnah) International Airport, Pakistan to Cairo.

We were in the air a mere thirty minutes when the pilot came on the intercom announcing that we were having "technical difficulties." We've all heard that at one time or another. Everything seemed quite normal—no vibrations, smoke, or unusual noise. We did notice, however, that the plane had slowed down and that we were circling. Certainly not a good sign. I began to wonder if this Jonah's dreadful luck was ever going to change.

I have known hundreds of people who have flown for years without experiencing a single incident. Here I was, in a span of ten to twelve years, about to embark on my fourth. However, there was an uncomfortable difference this time. I do not want to cast aspersions on the crew, but I have to say their performance did not inspire confidence. They were not especially helpful. They appeared quite jittery. They did not seem knowledgeable about the plane, its equipment, and its safety procedures. Nor were they well informed about what was going on. Moreover, the captain was reticent. We circled around for approximately thirty, maybe forty-five minutes after the first announcement without hearing a word about our situation. Not knowing what you're up against is frightening. Finally, the captain made a vague announcement about engine trouble, but couldn't be more specific about it, or what was being done to get us out of the mess. Circling around in the dark as if rudderless made it even more ominous.

The plane's speed was so low it seemed to be gliding. Its cabin was eerily quiet. Right then and there I swore never to ever, ever fly again. This was it. How many more times could I possibly tempt fate? My frustration was that I was not in control of my fate; I was in the air, out of my domain. If I were on the sea, where I belong, I would at least stand a chance of surviving. I could make decisions to control the final outcome. However, I had little choice in this matter so I prayed to God to just get me through this flight, and I would never again set foot on another bloody plane. "Oh dear Lord, it's Nick. Are you listening to me?"

Then that dreaded intercom broke my spell—our fearless pilot again. But this time he had some specifics for us. One of the four jet engines had abnormally high lube oil temperature. More waiting, more circling. At least the beverages kept coming. By this time I had lost track of time, but at some point he came on again to tell us we were going to return to the airport in Karachi at reduced speed. More importantly, he assured us we were in no immediate danger and that we would be on the ground safely in about one hour.

And so it came to be. They put us up for the night at considerable inconvenience, and off we went the next day without incident. I broke my promise to the good Lord and continued flying for many years thereafter. He must have forgiven me because I never had a single air incident after that. After all, how else could I keep my job? I was working for a multinational company in the international maritime business. That spells TRAVEL.

†

Before we left Japan to return to the United States, I was determined that my family visit Hiroshima. I wanted to leave them with a vivid impression of the horrors of war, and could think of no better way to do it than to visit the site of the first atomic bomb attack. As young as the kids were at the time of the visit, the powerful images they witnessed made an impression that has lasted to this day. I had visited Hiroshima and Nagasaki (the second atomic bombing site) some years earlier during business trips to nearby cities. This, then, was my second visit to Hiroshima and it created an even more vivid, enduring impression.

The bombings of Hiroshima and Nagasaki were nuclear attacks at the end of World War II that took place August 6, 1945, and August 9, 1945, respectively. To date they are the only instances of the use of nuclear weapons in warfare, and hopefully will be the last. I think anyone who visits either one of these cities, especially Hiroshima, will share that view. Our family was most impressed with the displays in the Main Building of the Hiroshima Peace Memorial Museum that include atomic bomb artifacts and materials, some of which are bone chilling. Things like charred shoes, barely recognizable toys, and melted eyeglasses give vivid and lasting impressions of the carnage. The East Building uses huge wall-mounted photography to show the city's annihilation, and there, the carnage is even more evident than in the Main Building. The other highlight is the Atomic Bomb Dome, a European-style building near the museum. The nuclear explosion was almost directly above it, making it the closest structure to withstand the explosion. It has been preserved in the state the bombing left it, and is the single-most recognizable symbol of the Hiroshima bombing. It stands as a constant reminder of nuclear devastation and the hope it will never happen again.

Controversy over the bomb still remains intense, and probably always will. The most common and compelling defense for the bombing campaign is that it hastened victory and probably saved the lives of an estimated one million

American servicemen and countless Japanese, compared to the toll of invading and conquering Japan using traditional warfare.

Living in Europe and Japan, and seeing Hiroshima again, brought out in me a sensitivity that I'm not sure I knew existed. Like most people I had opinions regarding politics, religion, and apple pie. But now I was seeing and doing things that ignited an inner awareness. I might even call it guilt. I was acquiring knowledge about the world that was changing my perspective and opinions. And for the first time in my life I would look at America with an objective, even critical eye. I challenged myself to find ways, no matter how humble, to bring about positive change. These feelings would intensify in the years to come as I traveled the world. I would see poverty and destruction that I could not have otherwise imagined. Sharing it with others—through conversation, through writing—assuages the pent-up feelings I harbor about such matters. It ripped the mask off the guilt I was feeling about things like Hiroshima and poverty. Even though I was not directly responsible, the echoes of a lingering passive attitude continue to haunt me.

The end of 1974 saw the end of our sojourn in Kobe. And while the drive down the mountain wasn't as heart-wrenching as the drive down that hill from the home in Kingston-on-Thames, it was still a somber experience.

13

DON'T BOTHER TO UNPACK

Grandchildren are God's way of compensating us for growing old.

—Mary H. Waldrip, English writer

Repatriating to the United States from Japan wasn't the same reverse-culture shock that we had experienced upon returning from England. This time it required a process of adjusting to the many vicissitudes we saw in American society. We had been away for nearly four years. The national zeitgeist had moved away from the turbulent '60s into a more tranquil decade that would see the end of the Vietnam War and the beginning of the oil shortages, first in 1973 and to a lesser extent in 1977. We were living in Japan during the first energy crisis, and fortunately missed the long lines for gas. The crisis served as a wake-up call to many Americans, who for the first time realized the central role energy plays in our lives. For the first time, at least in my recollection, tinhorn governments were pushing us around. I thought, *Hey, they can't do that to us.* But they did because they held the trump card: Oil.

These days, the stranglehold seems to be coming from not another tinhorn government, but none other than our old cold war adversary, Russia. The political and economic goals they were not able to achieve in the cold war, they are pursuing in the oilfields. With the recent government takeover of the national oil industry, Russia's oil output continues to grow dramatically. With it, we are seeing Russia emerge as a new kind of threat, as an energy giant and world power.

Back in the '70s, conservation became the order of the day. Before then, who had ever even heard of conservation in an energy sense? To make matters worse we were reeling from the effects of the Watergate scandal. The Nixon administration was disgraced and resigned from office. And how strange that I should remember that the word Negro had all but disappeared from the American-English vocabulary. However, the civil rights movement continued into the '70s, and is still a work in progress. We also seeded the environmental movement. Nuclear power got a start, sputtered, and has been stymied because of safety issues. (In recent years there has been a resurgence.) Guys and gals were wearing bell-bottoms. Junk food had arrived en masse, and it showed—walking through the airline terminal the day we arrived from Japan I recall having the same reaction as many foreigners; gosh, these people are *heavy*. Rotund bellies cascaded over the waists of jeans. Men shuffled along in sweat pants that looked as though they—the pants *and* the men—had never been washed. Baggy clothing appeared to be at least two sizes bigger than a normal fit. It almost seemed as though the richer we became, the more slovenly we behaved.

Before we could move into our home in Harrison, we had to move into rented quarters until the family renting our home vacated it. We decided on a four-bedroom condominium in Rye, New York. The building's tenants included TV personality Gary Moore. A long-time Rye resident, he had moved there after his wife died. As we both were avid yachtsmen, we hit it off pretty well.

Our next-door neighbors were a couple in their mid-thirties who had been married for several years, and to say it was a wobbly marriage would be putting it mildly. These two quarreled incessantly, and since the walls were thin, we were privy to details. One night at around 2:00 a.m. we awoke to the yelling of a fever-pitched battle. As it got louder we caught the drift of what was being said. She kept talking divorce; he kept threatening suicide. On and on it went into the wee hours. We pounded on the wall, to no avail. Then we heard a low rumble—the glass door leading to the small veranda. Ronnie and I thought his threat to commit suicide might be serious. The veranda overlooked the parking lot. That's when it hit me like a bolt of lightning: My own new Cadillac Coupe de Ville was parked just below his window. He had agreed to let me use his parking spot for the Caddie as I was using my spot for a second car. I stormed out of the apartment in my pajamas, car keys in hand to move my gem out of harm's way.

After a while tempers finally cooled and we got some sleep. A few days later we joked about it. He said something like, "Hell Nick, why did you move it? It would have broken my fall."

The fight was close to home in more than one way. My own family was embroiled in similar strife. Ronnie and I were quarreling more often, after which we would not be on speaking terms for days, sometimes weeks at a time. I was not being as supportive and attentive as I should have been, and given all the business travel I was doing, I asked myself if I was spending enough time at home. Should I have been more present with the kids? I began to doubt my ability to make a marriage work. Was I too demanding, too critical, and too self-centered? In a whirlwind lifestyle, did we ever stop long enough to say, "I love you"? It reminded me of something my sister Anne used to say—that it takes a great deal of effort to make a marriage work, and you have to keep at it continuously. Clearly, I was not getting the job done, and my single-minded focus on my career was proving to be especially tough on the relationship.

†

We welcomed in the 1975 new year by moving back into the Harrison house. We got on with our lives, and began to shift gears as best we could. But before we knew it, we would be looking at another major move, and another "drive down the hill," although not as traumatic. As if on cue, we received advice in the fall of 1975 that the company would be moving to New Jersey. Although we had the option to remain in the Harrison house, I didn't want to put myself through a three-and-a-half-hour car commute every day. The family agreed, and so we started to shift gears once again for a move that was expected to take place in the latter part of 1976.

As we began to slowly make preparations to pull up roots once again, we worried about transferring the kids to a new school system in another state. This was especially difficult as they were at middle and high school levels. They tried not to show it, but we knew they were disappointed. We were also disappointed to see that although Nicky had not as yet been diagnosed with schizophrenia, the symptoms, in retrospect, were evident. Hostility developed between him and his brother Michael. Before, they had been such great pals—they shared everything and enjoyed playing together. But Nicky was beginning to shut people out, and Ronnie and I didn't know how to cope with the situation. We needed to get professional help, soon.

Of lesser concern was having to give up our 1927 English Tudor home. It was magnificent, set in the rolling hills of Westchester County, in a neighborhood of stately Tudor homes surrounded by towering trees. It had many of the wonderful architectural features found only in Tudor style homes such as oak paneling, leaded glass windows, a twenty-four-foot sunken living room, and a huge stone fireplace. We loved the house, creakiness and all, and hoped we could duplicate it in our new state.

However, our New Jersey odyssey began with the purchase of a colonial split-level home in Short Hills, in the fall of 1976. We tried to buy another Tudor, but couldn't quite connect with the right property. So we remained in the home we initially purchased, where I still reside with my daughter and her son, Nicky.

†

Other changes in 1970s America emerged gradually. Along with the shift toward fast food, came a wider public awareness of physical fitness.

One of the perks at the company's new location was a first-rate fitness center. I initially hesitated to join, but with the support and encouragement of my good friend and co-worker Allan Jenks, I soon signed up. He then got me on board with classes in step aerobics. I have belonged to fitness centers for the past twenty-one years doing step aerobics, floor aerobics, weight training, treadmill running, stretching, toning and a host of other activities, two to three times a week.

Allan also got me back into golf. We were playing a round of golf, when for the first time in my life I shot an eagle—I sunk the ball in two on a par four hole. The tenth hole was approximately 420 yards long, and I got off a strong tee shot that landed in a good position for my next shot to the green. Using a 3-iron for my second shot, I watched the ball fly directly towards the green. However, since the green was above my eye level I did not see the ball go in the hole. As our foursome, which included his charming wife Joyce, got to the green we looked for my ball in the traps, in the rough, and all around the green, but it was nowhere in sight. After a few minutes I heard Allan yell out, "Nick, your ball is in the hole." That was an incredible thrill. Even my all-time favorite sports figure, golfer Tom Watson would have been proud of me. Later, it was "drinks on me" at the clubhouse.

There has always been a steady stream of lifetime activity—being on the go from morning to night, no matter what I was doing, no matter how important or frivolous. If my day is filled with getting things done, I'm having a great day. I have never, ever been satisfied with being idle. Clearly, I'm happiest when I'm working. I recall having to spend four days in a hospital to cure my third bout with diverticulitis. Other than writing this book or reading, there was nothing constructive for me to do except take intravenous antibiotics. After day two, I was intent on jumping out the window. Shortly thereafter, as a result of the diverticulitis, I spent another five days in the hospital to have ten inches of my large intestine removed (sigmoid resection). After two days I had the same flying leap inclination.

Although it is unfortunate that I have never learned how to relax, an active lifestyle, exercise, and a proper diet have been my formula for physical fitness. I have always prided myself on being physically fit, having worked at it very hard all my life with one form of activity or another. Sports have always been an integral part of my life, be it football, golf, baseball, tennis, handball, or softball. Even though I was not overly skillful, I was always a conscientious player making the most of what I had, no matter the sport. That was certainly true of softball that I played all of my life. I played weekly on the company softball team, which participated in a corporate league.

Twenty or so years later when I semi-retired, I would stay in touch with the game by playing softball twice a week in a senior softball league, whose players would demonstrate the meaning of senior physical fitness and sportsmanship. One year the league nominated a team to play in the Summer National Senior Olympic Games in Pittsburgh. I was lucky enough to be assigned to the team, but unfortunately my participation was curtailed due to a hand injury requiring nine stitches, on the first play of the first game.

The company I worked for was also diligent about providing annual medical examinations for all its employees. And so it was at the new work location. Grateful for the opportunity, I never missed taking these examinations. There was one instance, however, where I had my doubts. Without exception I had been accustomed to male doctors for any and all medical treatment. That wasn't deliberate;

it's just the way it was. On this one occasion I had to report to the medical office for an examination with Dr. Grasso. Of course I could not tell gender from the name alone, but soon discovered the doctor was a *she*.

She walked in and began to conduct the examination in much the same manner as any doctor would. I don't know if it showed, but I began to squirm a bit. To make matters even more awkward, she was young and attractive. She asked the usual questions and then asked me to get into the usual garb—the gown that ties in the back. She discreetly left the room with the promise to return in ten minutes or so. Now I was really squirming and starting to sweat. I was not quite sure if I should call it quits or go on. Then I thought maybe I should tell her I was not feeling well and ask to be excused. However, I decided against that, because it would only give her more reason to examine me. There was no way out: I had to go through with it, coward that I am.

When she came back, I was sitting on the exam table grinning sheepishly, trying to be cool, but not fooling anyone. I remember that I kept pulling the gown down so it would cover my knees. Imagine that. She must have thought, *What a wimp*. Anyway, in typical fashion she started from the top and worked her way down, feeling, poking, probing as she went. *Too late to back out now*, I thought. Things were going pretty well though until she asked me to stand up and UNTIE THE GOWN. Oh God—I knew what was coming. It was the hernia test. She stood next to me, reached down, nestled her forefinger next to my privates, and asked me to cough, facing away. Then again, and again. Then the other side. She said, "Please cough. Again. Again. Thank you." (Although the results were negative, I would not be as fortunate in the future, having had three hernias surgically repaired.)

When she put lubricant on a finger of the rubber glove I thought my world was about to come to an end. She politely asked me to bend over the exam table with my rear exposed. Before assuming the position, I meekly asked if this part of the examination was really necessary, as it was done during last year's examination. She humored me, of course, and then carried on. It was over in a flash, and I have to tell you it was as gentle as I had ever experienced. Perhaps because women have smaller fingers. I wouldn't go so far as to say I enjoyed it, but you know what I mean—or at least the guys do.

When it was all over I got dressed and she went over the results with me, professional as could be.

As I got up to leave, we shook hands and I said to her, "Doc, now I know how you ladies have felt all these many years."

Her head rocked back as she laughed and said, "Nick, you're in great shape. See you next year." The following year, I did see *her* again, but the *her* was another female doctor. When we introduced ourselves she actually gave me an out by saying that if I preferred a male doctor, she would arrange it. Had I been made that offer for the previous examination, I probably would have taken it. This time, it didn't bother me a bit.

†

During six relatively calm years in the United States, I had taken on a wide variety of assignments in marine transportation gaining invaluable experience. Although there wasn't the dynamic growth that we had seen in previous years, there were still challenging opportunities in the company's shipbuilding programs and fleet operations. At one point I was the Division Manager in charge of the company's worldwide ship construction program. Then there was a two-year stint as Fleet Operations Manager with responsibility for forty ships, which was half of the international tanker fleet. I also spent time in the ship chartering side of the business.

In 1980 it was time to hit the road again. I was going to be assigned to Taiwan for approximately two years as a vice president in charge of ship construction.

This time, Ronnie would not join me. The news was not good—Nicky had been diagnosed with schizophrenia, was being counseled and taking medication. The prognosis was not good either—it was a stretch to think he could ever live a normal life again, but we were determined to do everything in our power to make his life as close to normal as possible. His condition had deteriorated to point where he needed close supervision. So the plan was that I would commute home as often as possible, and Ronnie would remain behind and take periodic trips to Kaohsiung when she could.

14

THE ONE THAT DIDN'T GET AWAY

Life's greatest gift is to give.

—Nicholas F. Starace II

During a relatively quiet six-year respite in New Jersey, one of the first things we did was to take a vacation trip to Acapulco, Mexico.

Paradoxically, this story has a very sad ending, even though I caught the big one. It was November 11, 1976, and Ronnie and I, along with our best friends Dick and Jeanell departed on a one-week vacation. After checking in at our hotel on the beachfront avenue, the reasons for Acapulco's popularity soon emerged: Bars blared out pop tunes, souvenir stores sold loads of silver jewelry, hucksters sold cart-and-horse rides, and the omnipresent beach peddlers hawked their tinsel trinkets hollering, "Hi *amigo*, 100 percent discount today!" We also got the distinct feeling that while in our hotel, we were staying in a luxury bubble, removed from the town's seedier side and isolated from the local culture that distinguishes Acapulco from resort towns in the United States. The bulk of our money was spent on lavish meals, organized day-trips, massages, and even golf, all confined to the hotel's manicured grounds.

For this reason, I was eager to go deep-sea fishing. In Acapulco, one must follow the lure of deep water, in pursuit of the tenacious sailfish. After making a few inquiries at the hotel, we located several boats for charter and at reasonable rates. For Dick and me, this would be our first attempt at deep-sea fishing, and I was eager. The thought of landing a huge fish conjured up a whole host of exciting images like the first sight of it breaking high out of the water, streaking to the sky. My father was an avid fisherman, but I did not share his passion. I'd simply tag along, fishing off a pier or his boat for the local catch. This was like playing in the big leagues.

We cast off that morning about 7:00 a.m., thus liberating our wives for a daylong shopping spree. In our party were the captain and the four of us who chartered his boat. There were three fishing chairs in his forty-five-foot fishing boat, which meant that the four of us would rotate about every half-hour through the three chairs while the fourth guy took a break. No sooner had we cleared Acapulco Bay and started to troll and chum than we got a hit. It was a small dolphin—not a sailfish, but enough to provide us with the freshest fish I had ever eaten, with the exception of live carp in Japan. The captain filleted and cooked it for lunch. I recall thinking enthusiastically that this must be a darn good omen.

On the contrary. We cruised and trolled and chummed and fished and ate and drank for nearly five hours, without even a nibble. At two o'clock the captain told us that this was the time he would normally head back, but since we hadn't caught anything other than lunch, he would stay out for another half-hour. Just about then, I was coming off a break. The four of us had gotten pretty chummy with all of the booze, and were more consumed with chatting, joking, and horsing around than the fishing we had come out to do. After all, there were no fish. Or so we thought: I was in the chair for about ten minutes and it turned out to be the right chair at the right time. Even though half-crocked, I sobered up when that fish hit my line. I thought it was going to pull me right out of the chair and off the boat. I could not have imagined what I was in for and for how long. It wasn't until the huge fish broke water the first time that I realized how beautiful it was. Sure enough it was a sailfish flying high into the air, just like in the travelogues. This was the real thing, and I was exhilarated. I struggled with that beast for approximately thirty minutes, needing a lot of help from the captain as well as muscle from the guys to help pull her in. Back and forth, back and forth, we pulled and tugged, struggling for just inches of line at a time. Finally we got her alongside the boat. I was more exhausted than my catch. The ache in my arms over the next few days would remind me of the fight.

As I looked at the near-still figure floating next to the boat, I marveled at its coloring. It occurred to me that I had never seen such a beautiful blend of colors in my life, as if a rainbow were swimming on the end of my line. They were so vivid, made even more striking by the fact that they adorned a living creature. That admiration turned to shock when all of those colors disappeared as soon as the big fish was gaffed and hauled on board. The entire body turned a bleak gray, even though there was still life left in it. How sad, I thought, to destroy such a beautiful creature. It was even sadder to learn sailfish are not edible. That meant we had killed this poor creature solely for "sport." Already I was beginning to feel great remorse, not realizing the worst was yet to come.

Having finally landed a big one, the captain decided it was time to head back. The day had not been a total loss after all. As we got underway, one of the guys called out—he spotted another sailfish swimming astern of us, as if it were heading right into the boat. We could not believe it, but it seemed to be following us back to port. A frenzy quickly developed as the other two guys stumbled over one another trying to get into chairs to resume fishing. The captain brought the fishing poles out again, and to satisfy his customers, starting trolling and chumming. I'd had enough and sat motionless. Dick was indifferent at this point; he had seen and drank enough, too. The others thought, *Could we be this lucky?* and continued fishing for about fifteen minutes. Nothing, and I mean nothing, would deter that fish from swimming a constant distance astern of us and on the same course. It followed patiently without pursuit of the bait. After another twenty minutes or so, the captain stopped all fishing and resumed normal speed back home. When we asked why, he said it was hopeless—because in his view, the sailfish following us was probably the mate of the one we had caught. My heart sank. Now I was truly devastated.

That poor fish followed us in to the entrance of Acapulco Bay, at which point it broke off and headed out to sea, alone and without its mate.

When I look back on that trip and think about that fish being separated from its mate, I wish I would have seen it as a warning of things to come. I, too, was to be separated from my mate, but for very different reasons. Fish don't argue much, but Ronnie and I did. We liked many of the same things, such as the theater, dining out, and the ballet. Moreover, she had exquisite taste when it came to decorating and purchasing things for the home. Most of the time we were on the same page insofar as what to buy, and for how much. The rub came when I sometimes fretted that things were too expensive. It caused dissent that was a part of the bigger issue of my absence.

After we tied up, the dock was alive with photographers and taxidermists. They could tell we had a catch on board from the pennant the captain was flying from the yardarm. That's the customary practice; one pennant for each fish caught. Before we arrived, we had all speculated as to the weight of our fish, and I say "ours" in the broadest sense, as surely this catch was a joint effort. Now we would know for sure since part of the ritual is to put the fish ashore and hang it by its tail from one of the many dockside scales. The final number was 158 pounds. Unbelievable by any standard, but even more so when you consider the record for Acapulco at the time was 192 pounds. Our fish was a mighty ten feet two inches from tip to tip. As distressed as I was, I had the gall to stand beside the dead beast and have a photo taken.

Next came the mad scramble of taxidermists who were anxious to stuff my prize and ship it home, for a handsome fee of course. Although my heart wasn't in it, I was getting a lot of encouragement to give it consideration. I was torn, because if I displayed it at home it would be a constant reminder of what turned out to be a painful experience.

However, before I could even consider it, I would have to get my wife's blessing. I therefore called the hotel and explained the situation to her. She left no doubt in my mind. I suggested we mount my prize in the living room, to which she said, "Over my dead body." Always a glutton for punishment, I then suggested the bedroom, to which she intimated that if she had to sleep in a room with that fish, I too would end up sleeping with the fishes. We went from room to room, and when I finally got an OK for the garage, I gave up, which is probably what I wanted all along. So all I got for the day's adventure was heartache and an 8 x 10 color glossy.

I'm certain that fish eventually got stuffed and ended up in a seafood restaurant or the lobby of a seaside hotel. I vowed then and there to never fish again, and I haven't. I'm repulsed by the pain I think it inflicts on the fish. The only exception, if you can call it that, is the occasional crabbing I do with my grandsons Benjamin, Brian, and Nicky. However, they understand that we only keep them if we plan to eat them. Otherwise, back they go. Ironic too, as I own a forty-four-foot yacht, but fishing is still taboo. Nevertheless, the sight of that fish following us in to Acapulco still haunts me.

†

During my tenure aboard the SS *African Moon*, which was long before the trip to Acapulco, I had another fishing experience that was quite memorable, but for a different reason. The sailfish as you know did not get away—fortunately, this one did.

We were docked in Port Elizabeth, South Africa, when I found myself with spare time. Having nothing better to do, I decided to borrow fishing gear from a crew member and do a bit of fishing off the end of the pier where we were docked. After an hour or so without even a nibble, I was about to give up when I got a hit. However, it wasn't your typical back and forth kind of struggle. It was more like a dead weight hanging from the end of the line. Whatever it was, there was no fight in it. It was as if my catch had given up straight away. I guess I spent fifteen minutes hauling it in before it hit the surface. As it broke water I was shocked by what I saw. Could it be ...? A passerby had noticed my efforts in hauling this creature in and was watching when it broke water. Not quite a man-eater, it looked like an octopus or a squid. We couldn't get a clear view to determine the number of tentacles it had. I'm guessing it was at least six feet across, tip to tip.

Now the struggle really began as it wrapped its tentacles tightly around the pier pilings. The pier was approximately ten feet above the water level so it appeared that it was going to be a long drawn-out struggle. As I kept tugging at it, it took an even tighter hold on the piling. I began to say to myself, *What the hell am I going to do with this alien even if I do land it?* I certainly wasn't going to eat it, nor was I going to have it mounted, God forbid. Those thoughts discouraged me to a point where I decided to give it up. Just as I was about to cut the line and let everything go, the line broke loose from the creature. As best as I could determine, the flesh between two of the tentacles gave way, and it was gone in an instant. Unlike the poor sailfish I caught in Acapulco, this one happily got away and that made for a happier ending indeed. No remorse this time—yet I couldn't help but think that I wouldn't have even gone fishing in Port Elizabeth if I'd already experienced the Acapulco fiasco.

The octopus certainly doesn't have the majestic beauty of the sailfish, but why waste another creature?

Recalling that anecdote aroused my curiosity and therefore prompted me to do a bit of research to determine the difference between the octopus and the squid. Both are members of the cephalopod species. Octopuses have eight tentacles. We all know that, but did you know that squids have ten tentacles? OK, but what else is there to differentiate one from the other? Well, I learned that squids have very long and fleshy tentacles; their bodies are elongated. The tentacles of the octopus are short and meaty with large suckers. The hoods (heads) are also different in that the octopus is sort of bulb-shaped and short, whereas the squid is longer, straight, and somewhat streamlined. And, oh yes, both are considered delicacies in the wonderful world of Japanese cuisine, which is something I found out from my days living in Japan. Having done the research, I would say what I caught was an octopus, but I'll never know for sure. Just think, with that bit of knowledge your sleepless nights are over.

15

I SHALL RETURN

One should not pursue goals that are easily achieved. One must develop an instinct for what one can barely achieve through one's greatest efforts.

—Dr. Albert Einstein

Like my well-known general-compatriot of Philippines fame, I too returned, not as a conquering hero or in a navy uniform, but in a business suit. And once again I would find myself at risk. Ironically, I would be living in the same city I knew as a young naval officer—Kaohsiung. There were business trips to Taipei and sightseeing to some of the scenic outlying areas, but my focus was Kaohsiung, an obscure, small city that most people have never even heard of.

I had been assigned to Taiwan for approximately two years as vice president in charge of ship construction. The oil company I worked for had contracted with China Shipbuilding Corporation (CSBC), to build four medium-size tankers. Our office was set up in Kaohsiung, where the shipyard was located, to administrate the contract and supervise the design and construction.

It was 1980, and in the twenty-two years that had elapsed since my last visit, I was amazed to see how much the population and city had grown. Thankfully, much of the poverty was gone, but there were the other dreaded "P" words: pollution and pests. The city had industrialized, and in the process, was choking itself to death. Huge black dust plumes hung over the city every evening. This outpouring of dust layered with smog, industrial and vehicular fumes, and micro-particles seemed to infiltrate all aspects of everyday life. It was so bad it seemed that more than half the population wore crude gauze masks to help keep their lungs clean. One of the main culprits was the omnipresent motorbike. Not only were they belching their poisonous fumes, but also creating an astounding noise level.

They were everywhere, all the time. On a corner near my apartment, I often saw an entire family of a mom, dad, and three kids merrily chugging along every day to school and work on one motorbike. There were not many cars other than taxis—just motorbikes, buses, and trucks. Add to it the stench that permeated parts of the city every day, and you had an unpleasant atmosphere to wake up to in the morning. The stench emanated from the human waste that dumped into the rivers that flowed in and around the city, especially the main one called, of all things, Love River. There were emission standards and sanitary codes. However, as a local official once explained to me, if the authorities ever tried to implement those regulations, the city would soon come to a grinding halt. Better to keep business booming so that Taiwan, which had become one of Asia's Four Little Dragons (the other three were Hong Kong, Singapore, and South Korea), could maintain its high growth rate and rapid industrialization.

Pirating of copyrighted material was rampant. And most of it wasn't even underground. It was sold in the open, and was as cheap as it was shoddy. Even food products were pirated. For example, there were boxes of "Mitz" crackers on store shelves. They were packaged in wax sleeves in Ritz's signature red box, but lacked the signature crunch and buttery flavor. Then there were the "Hersey" candy bars. They, too, were packaged exactly like a Hershey bar using the same brown paper wrapper and the same blocky, silver font. One bite and you knew they were not the real thing. Sure, there were copyright laws, but the piracy was so widespread that the authorities had difficulty trying to enforce them, or so they claimed.

As I got better acquainted with the city, I decided its pollution problem must have been a factor in its rat infestation. Movie theaters seemed to be a favorite hangout. For a long time I couldn't figure out why, until one evening in a theater I could hear the sound of paper crunching next to my feet. It became obvious they were after candy droppings and therefore had to rummage through candy wrappings left on the floor by patrons. As I sat in an aisle seat, I could see shadows of dark figures scurrying across the aisle. These were big guys too, so the scurrying was not all that swift. On another occasion, I saw a rat's silhouette at the bottom of the screen lumbering from one side of the screen to the other. Poor guy somehow got onstage looking for a place to hide, and instead was lost. He put on quite a good show as evidenced by the loud *oohs* and *aahs* from the entertained audience. You'd even see the rodents darting across meat counters in the supermarkets. I'll never forget the look on my boss' face during one of his visits to Taiwan, as we sat down to breakfast at his hotel. As we forked into our meals, one of Kaohsiung's finest nonchalantly scurried past our feet. My boss bolted up from the table, and then asked me, "Nick, is this normal around here?" After that, the poor guy just wasn't up to finishing his breakfast.

There were roaches, spiders, and centipedes the size of which I could not have imagined, even though I had spent time in the Far East. I remember being a dinner guest at a very fine restaurant in town, when the host, a native, had to shake off a roach that was navigating its way up his tie. Later during the same meal I had to flick a roach off the dessert menu. An associate of mine got a fever and nasty infection from the bite of a four-inch long centipede in his living room. It's amazing though as to what you can get used to.

†

One of the guys, Bob Boorujy, and I used to quip, "What did we ever do to our mothers to deserve this assignment?" Bob struggled with the project for three frustrating years and was a prime factor in its success. Being culture-sensitive, I normally did not discuss the city's more repulsive subjects with the locals, although we expatriates often fretted over some of the things we saw.

For instance, Bob told me of a rat restaurant near his hotel. In a culture renowned for eating anything that moves, in an infested city, rats are fair game. I don't know if the restaurant was ever short of customers, but I can tell you this —it was never short of stock.

By Western standards, Taiwan does not rank high in its treatment of animals. One day I passed the window of a butcher shop, and found myself gazing at a carcass I couldn't identify. After staring at it for several long moments, it suddenly dawned on me: it was the skinned half-section of a dog. Man's best friend is considered a delicacy in Taiwan and other Asian nations. Some of the locals even claim it offers health benefits. Probing around the shop a bit more, I noticed a few caged dogs out back being fattened up, presumably waiting their turn before the last supper. I hasten to add that for anyone who has a taste for dog flesh, but can't afford dining out, there is a vast array of stray dogs in Kaohsiung to suit the palate.

One of the most hideous and inhuman things I have ever seen occurred at a mom-and-pop snake shop. I do not like snakes, but this was too much even for me. Upon entering the shop, you browse through the many caged, live snakes and pick out the one you like the best. It was then "dressed," cooked, and eaten right there at the shop. It was the dressing part that was the most sickening. After you picked out your snake, the owner would take it to the storefront and hang it by its tail. This was done outside, where a large table was set up so that passers-by could watch the gory proceedings, sort of like a public hanging. The *show* was a way of enticing would-be customers into the shop for a meal. One evening, as I passed by one such shop, a four-foot specimen was being prepared for the patron's dinner. After it was hanged by its tail and still quite alive, the owner slit the snake straight up and down the belly-line with an incision approximately three feet long. He then proceeded to skin it. I don't know if snakes feel pain or not, but at that moment, I felt a pang of sympathy. After the skin was off, deeper incisions were made at locations near the snake's organs. Out came the heart, liver, and other organs, and placed in a glass. Although there was still some wiggle left in the creature, I think, or at least hoped, it was dead by this time. Meanwhile, all of the dripping blood was collected in a tin cup attached to and hanging from the snake's head. Picture that for a moment. None of this bloody mess was wasted. Each course was more delectable than the previous, or so it seemed from the expression on the customer's face. First came the blood. It was poured into a glass, thinned slightly with another liquid I could not identify, and drunk down to the last "savory" drop. The skin was then cut up and mixed with greens to come up with what appeared to be a scrumptious snakeskin salad. Ah, then the organs were served in what appeared to be some type of stew with a side of rice. Lastly, the body was sliced, fried, and served with vegetables to close out this snake feast. This was the only part of the menu I could relate to, as I can recall having eaten snake meat somewhere along my many travels throughout Southeast Asia. Despite my squeamishness around snakes, I admit I had found it tasty. It's a good thing I knew nothing of its preparation, or it would have put me right off. At this point I darted away, nauseated by what I'd just seen.

Pet cats serve quite another purpose. On several occasions I would see a dead one hanging by the neck from a tree branch. Being a cat person, I shuddered. It puzzled me for several months before I worked up the nerve to ask the question without seeming offended. The most favorable explanation was that in some of the country's more remote regions, cats are not buried after they die. Instead they are wrapped, tied around the neck, and hung from a tree to ward off evil spirits. Only when it has completely decomposed is it taken down and discarded. To do so before then is considered bad luck.

Superstition ran deep in the culture. One morning we drove up to the shipyard where our ships were being built, to find a twelve-foot-high brick wall that had been erected directly across the main entrance of the shipyard during the night. A new entrance had been erected approximately three hundred feet to the right of the brick wall. The driver, who was befuddled by this, drove up to the wall, made a right hand turn and proceeded to enter the shipyard through the new entrance, then made a left turn to get back on the main entrance road. I inquired about the new and seemingly haphazard arrangement. I was informed this was done to ward off and prevent evil spirits from entering the shipyard. Shipyard management perceived these evil spirits as having contributed to the shipbuilder's recent financial woes and as having caused a disastrous fire on board one of our ships.

The fire occurred several weeks before. It started in the engine room, when a workman's welding torch ignited diesel oil that was raining down on them from an open fuel supply line. It should have been capped, but when work started that day, the supply line valve was opened to test diesel equipment, thus sending flammable liquid into the engine room. Within minutes the engine room became an inferno, killing sixteen workers. Had it occurred twenty minutes later, several of my staff and myself would have been on board and probably perished, too. Huge clouds of black smoke billowed from the vessel, and the fire raged until the diesel oil burned itself out, several hours later. It was not until late evening that things cooled enough to get on board. Evidence of the fire's intensity was everywhere: sixteen-inch girders twisted like spaghetti, mountains of electrical cable burned to rubble, ladders and gratings reduced to hardened pools of metal. Some of those who perished burned to death; others were scalded from burning oil, while the *lucky* ones died of smoke inhalation. Worst of all were the ghastly remains of three men on a landing at the top of a stairwell reduced to charred husks, stuck in a mannequin position completely black—a sight that would open the eyes of a blind man. In trying to escape the deadly flames, they climbed the stairs only to be trapped by a door that would not open.

After the fire, a mass funeral service was held for the family and friends of the deceased. The anguish and despair affected me deeply, as did the tragic carelessness that led to the fire. In the face of that knowledge, a twelve-foot wall across the shipyard entrance was absurd. I found it hard to believe this kind of thinking could prevail in a sophisticated corporation managing one of the most advanced, world-class facilities of its kind. I would see this mentality again a few years later in Singapore, when a major and reputable hotel chain was having financial difficulty with its upscale hotel. Sure enough, I walked by one day to find the main entrance changed; doors previously parallel to the sidewalk had been torn down and replaced with doors angled at forty-five degrees.

I called it superstition. Not so: It was foolish of me to think it was some kind ancient voodoo. I learned much later that shipyard management was merely following the ancient Chinese science of Feng Shui, which has been around for more than 3,500 years. The words literally mean *wind* and *water*. Most major cities in China follow the rules of Feng Shui for their design and layout. It is also commonly applied to businesses and homes. As I understand it, the ultimate goal is that all components blend in harmony to create balance in one's business or life. In *Essential Feng Shui*, Lillian Too says, "Feng Shui is a discipline with guidelines that are compatible with many techniques of architectural planning. Space, weather, astronomy, and geomagnetism are basic components of Feng Shui. Proponents claim that it has an effect on health, wealth, and personal relationships." To the non-believers, might I say that CSBC and the hotel are still doing a booming business. Moreover, its use is not limited to Chinese cultures. I discovered that Donald Trump and Prince Charles have used Feng Shui. Even businesses like News Corporation consulted Feng Shui experts regarding the headquarters of DirecTV, after acquiring it in 2003.

†

Enter Grace Kelly. It was April 1982 and CSBC was completing major renovations to two of America's heretofore merchant marine stalwarts—the SS *Independence* and the SS *Constitution*. These two grand dames of the once-proud American passenger liner fleet were well beyond their glory days. However, major ship-owner C.Y. Tung, based in Hong Kong, purchased both vessels with the intention of fully renovating them to modern-day standards and returning them to service plying the Hawaiian Islands. CSBC got the contract, which was concomitant with the construction of our four ships.

The new owners, having a sense of history, thought it would be a great idea to invite Princess Grace of Monaco to re-christen the SS *Constitution*, knowing her previous association with the vessel. Over two decades before, she booked passage to make a trip from socialite and movie star to outright royalty. She and her entourage of eighty, including family members, friends, members of the wedding party, nearly two dozen of the press, and her black poodle, Oliver, boarded the SS *Constitution* at New York's Pier 84 on the morning of April 4, 1956. The bride-to-be sailed with sixty, yes, sixty pieces of luggage and a trousseau befitting a princess. On April 12, the liner was met in Monte Carlo's harbor by Prince Rainier's yacht. Movie theaters and TV networks ran the images for weeks while covering her wedding.

Given her sentimental attachment, she gratefully accepted the invitation to re-christen the vessel. She was to fly to Hong Kong, meet with the owner, and proceed to Kaohsiung with the owner's entourage for the christening ceremony and all the pomp that goes with it—usually a three-to four-day affair with dinners and sightseeing trips. Lo and behold, no sooner did she arrive in Hong Kong than the ship owner C.Y. Tung died of a heart attack. The dilemma then was whether to cancel the christening or proceed as originally planned. It was decided not to proceed with a full-blown formal christening, but to do an abbreviated, one-day ceremony. She would arrive in the morning, go directly to the shipyard, christen the vessel, attend an exclusive 12-person luncheon, and return to Monaco via Hong Kong later that afternoon. During all this commotion, I had been back home in New Jersey on a business trip, as I was essentially commuting back and forth during my two-year assignment. Before leaving Kaohsiung, I had been invited to attend the christening and the formal dinner party afterward. While in New Jersey, CSBC contacted me to let me know the turn of events and of the new arrangements. I was still invited to the christening ceremony. However, I was to now play a pivotal role in the day's proceedings. I was invited to the luncheon as well, which would be attended by Princess Grace, ten of the CSBC and owner's executives, and myself. In so many words, my role would be to host and escort the princess.

I was to act as a buffer between her and the rest of the group. Dining and socializing with a group of businessmen who spoke little or no English was destined to be awkward, so my job was to give her a touch of home and offer small talk about the latest events in the United States, including happenings in her hometown of Philadelphia. I accepted my new role with delight, and finalized my travel plans to return to Kaohsiung.

Several days before departing, however, my boss came down with one of the worst cases of shingles his doctor had ever seen. He was scheduled to give several important presentations in Japan. It was expedient for me to take his place, but the heartbreaker was that his schedule conflicted with the christening date. I had to make those presentations, and I had no choice but to miss my day in the sun with the princess. I arrived in Kaohsiung two days after the ceremony, terribly disappointed.

On September 14, 1982, at age fifty-two, Princess Grace of Monaco died in a car accident just five months after her appearance in Kaohsiung. She reportedly had a stroke while driving, causing the car to plunge down a forty-five-foot embankment. She is buried at the Cathedral of St. Nicholas in Monte Carlo, Monaco.

After the christening, it remained for CSBC to complete all work and settle the bill with the ship's owner. In the course of the renovation, significant changes had been made in the scope of the work, thereby requiring an upward adjustment in the contract price. Negotiations carried on for days and weeks without reaching a settlement. CSBC then became concerned that the owner might try to sail the vessel to Honolulu, her destination homeport, without making the final payment. To avert this, CSBC positioned a large tower crane in front of the bridge house with one hundred tons of steel hanging from it, thus blocking the vessel from leaving its berth. After six weeks, the bill was finally settled and the vessel departed for its final destination in the sun. And so it came to pass that a princess had gracefully presided over a queen's return to her rightful home on the high seas.

†

In this period of my life, during my time abroad, I had many uneasy experiences. Taiwan was no exception.

I routinely flew to Kaohsiung from the United States via Hong Kong or Taipei. On other occasions I would fly back and forth between Kaohsiung and Taipei. After a while, I got into the habit of using the same late afternoon flight from Taipei to Kaohsiung. It was convenient and the timing was right. On one such occasion, upon arriving in Taipei from the United States, I found out that my usual flight to Kaohsiung had gone down three days earlier. No one survived the crash, which occurred shortly after takeoff. The authorities investigating the incident determined that before going into commercial service, the plane had been used for hauling cargo, that cargo being fresh fish. Turns out that over a period of time, the fish—or more specifically the sea water they were immersed in during shipment—corroded the plane's internal structure to a point where the plane imploded ten minutes after takeoff, killing all 132 people on board. I took the same flight anyway. I was, after all, practical, and recognized that the odds were against such a crash happening again. Sort of the same feeling I had on the next flight after our ill-fated Pan American Flight 830 to Honolulu, earlier that year.

During my two-year tenure traveling back and forth between the United States and Taiwan, I met an American who was assigned to Kaohsiung to supervise the construction of oil rigs. He had bought a forty-two-foot sailboat and asked me if I would crew it with him to Hong Kong, a two-to-three day sail. I jumped at the opportunity of such an adventure and timed it such that I could take enough vacation to fit in with his timetable. However, even the best-laid plans can run amuck. I had to back out due to a last-minute work commitment. As expected, he readily found someone to take my place. The upshot of this story is that they got lost en route to Hong Kong and landed in what was then called Red China. Both were arrested and the boat confiscated. I don't know how I would have explained that one to the folks back home. And I don't know when they got out of jail, assuming they did, or if he ever got his boat back. I had left Kaohsiung by that time.

†

One of the more gratifying moments in Kaohsiung was to work with Angela, one of the most hard-working and efficient secretaries I have ever encountered. When we set up our office at the shipyard, we looked to CSBC to provide us with local secretarial and support staff. We were most fortunate to have Angela assigned to our office. She was the glue that held our office of happy goons together; and she was the one who got me through the acceptance speech I made as the owner's representative for one of the ship christenings. I decided to give it in Mandarin Chinese, even though I did not speak a word of it. I prepared the speech, and she translated it and took me through a rehearsal, day after day. After I gave it for real, I asked for her to grade it a on a scale of 1 to 10—she gave me an 8.

Near the end of my tenure, I decided to recognize her commitment as best I knew how. I designated her to preside over the keel-laying ceremony of one of our vessels. According to shipyard executives, she was the first woman to do so in Taiwan. She struck the ceremonial champagne bottle to commemorate the birth of a new ship. Although not quite as prestigious as the christening upon a vessel's completion, it was just as thrilling to Angela and the rest of us. I hope that she still relishes that moment and everything it symbolized. The local press played it up in newspaper articles as a further promotion of women's rights. Having started a memorable tradition, we perpetuated it by inviting Bob Boorujy's wife Jean to preside at the keel-laying ceremony of a subsequent vessel.

I soon had reason to recall the stubborn tanker we launched in 1969 in England, the one that required two bottles of champagne from the princess and hours of extra labor. That English-flag vessel did not have a glorious history. Plagued with mechanical and operational problems, poor fuel economy, and finally the Oil Embargo of 1973, she was doomed for an early and ignominious grave. She was delivered to the breakers in Kaohsiung in May 1982. My office overlooked the harbor entrance to the shipyard and to the breakers. I saw her arrive one morning and later proceed to the breaker's yard, where she was scrapped. What an uneasy feeling that was. I assure you there was no band playing, nor was there any of the fanfare that surrounded her launch. There wasn't even a welcoming committee—fittingly, only I.

Over a period of a few weeks the tired old lady slowly vanished piece by piece, as her hull and superstructure were cut away. Her gigantic stack fell like a toppled redwood. Finally, she was only a carcass, scant evidence of her existence. How sad. I had been there for her birth and now I witnessed her demise while still working for the same company. I had come full circle, which was not a comfortable feeling to say the least. Was I getting old? Or had I just been around too long? Maybe *I* was ready for the scrap heap. In any case, during the ensuing months in Kaohsiung, I was to witness the scrapping of several other vessels which I had earlier helped build. It left me with an empty feeling, and at the same time made me think about what was going on at home.

The heartsick image of that once great ship fit the mood back in our house in New Jersey. When my role in the CSBC ship construction project wrapped in 1982, circumstances had kept Ronnie and I mostly apart for two years. Dorine was in college. Michael was in high school. By this time, Nicky's schizophrenia was getting worse. His mood swings became extreme. Paranoia, a core symptom of the disease, had set in, causing him to wall himself off from everything and everybody, including the immediate family. There seemed to be very little we could do to ease his pain and anxiety. He even quit the high school basketball team. Dorine seemed the only one who could get close to him and even that contact was limited. The medication he was taking caused side-effects, which included severe depression. To see your child gradually fall into an abyss without being able to offer much help is a wrenching experience.

To make matters worse, while I was away, Ronnie was treated for a brain aneurysm during which time I should have been at home. Instead, I was covering the job as best I could, working ten hours a day nearly every day of the week, while commuting home essentially every other month—a thirty-six-hour grind. She was able to join me for a couple of weeks after recovering through medication, during which time we took a holiday trip to China. It was an exciting experience, but our return flight home via Hawaii was the one with a terrorist's bomb. The result of all of this was a huge amount of stress for us and for our marriage.

Later, I began to feel guilty about Nicky's condition, thinking it was brought on by the many moves we had made. I thought the moves caused him to become emotionally disoriented. Not so. The makings of it had been there from birth. Psychiatric evaluations determined the disease would have surfaced under any circumstances. Much to the contrary, living overseas was a broadening experience for our children that enhanced their development. Many years later, Dorine would send me a touching father's day e-mail greeting with the picture of a little girl sitting on her father's shoulders. The message read, "On your shoulders I saw the world."

16

BLIMEY! WE'RE HOME AGAIN!

It had long since come to my attention that people of accomplishment rarely sit back and let things happen to them. They went out and happened to things.

—Leonardo da Vinci (1452–1519)

It would not be long before opportunity sounded the whistle again. I was on a fast track, but the train was moving too quickly for its passenger to see much of the scenery. I was offered an assignment working in the same office outside of London that I had left in 1970, but this time as the office manager. Given the wonderful first sojourn, and the great opportunity itself, the decision was a no-brainer. So off we went in 1983 to take on the new assignment with great enthusiasm, while we rented out our home in New Jersey.

Being the accident-prone family that we are, we of course had to have at least one before leaving for London. Michael, the "we're going to London and not coming back" kid, delivered one of his specialties. For an eighteen-year-old, it was (and still is) fashionable to cruise around town in your hot rod, which in his case was a yellow Mustang Mach 1. Unfortunately, he crossed swords with a much bigger vehicle; he and a Salvation Army box truck collided at an intersection just a mile or two from our home. Judging from the extent of the damage, I suspect both vehicles were speeding. No contest. The car was decapitated; the roof was completely torn away by the truck's undercarriage. We all know the benefits of wearing seatbelts, but on this day, luckily, he was being negligent. It saved his life, because without his seatbelt to restrain him, he was able to crouch down into the passenger seat, thereby avoiding the *guillotine*. Instead, he got off easy with some bruises and a few stitches in an ear. The car was totaled.

Off to college went the kids that fall, and off to London went Ronnie and I. We decided to live in central London instead of in the suburbs.

With my international driver's license about to expire I thought it would be advisable to finally get my U.K. license. I did all the paperwork and set up a date for the test. Just before I started the engine the day of the test, the inspector looked over at me and said, "You'll have to forgive me if my breath is a bit off, but I just had a couple of beers with lunch." I replied, "No problem, so did I." I passed, thanks to the guy's sense of humor.

Each of the two times we lived in London we always made it a point to travel to Scotland *on holiday* (Brits go on holiday, not vacation). Its history, and culture, makes Edinburgh our favorite target, especially when the Open Championship, aka the British Open, is at the Royal and Ancient Golf Club of St. Andrews. The club, a Mecca, hosts 2,400 members from all over the world. Although I am not an avid golfer, I have played at St. Andrews because of the mystic, almost sacred, surroundings—the grounds date back to the Roman occupation, when Romans brought the earliest form of golf to the British Isles in the form of their own stick-and-ball game.

In 1984 when the Open was at St. Andrews, we *motored* north to enjoy the legendary warmth and hospitality of the Scots (Brits motor, as well as drive). The unassuming Scottish attitude is refreshingly humble and charming. Our bed and breakfast further enhanced the experience, affording a cultural intimacy that we would not have gotten at a hotel for twice the price. One of the many things that the Scots are known for is their quintessential dish, haggis. Made from the stomach lining of cow or sheep, it is both loved and reviled by natives and foreigners alike. It is an acquired taste that, sorry to say, I have not as yet acquired.

After attending all four rounds of the Open, Ronnie, Michael and I, played golf on the old course and then headed south to Edinburgh, to my favorite hotel there, the Caledonian. (I believe it is now the Caledonian Hilton.) The hotel is in the heart of the city, in the shadow of Edinburgh Castle where the famous Edinburgh Military Tattoo is held every August. Rarely do you find a city, so steeped in tradition that combines such lovely people and stunning architecture. It was there that we had a harrowing experience—like something out of a Hitchcock movie.

One afternoon, after a day of sightseeing at the castle, we were resting our tired feet and looking out the hotel window to a building across the road. All of a sudden a child appeared at an open window. He then climbed out of the window onto a ledge that wrapped around the building perimeter. The ledge couldn't have been more than two feet wide. The kid was around ten years old. I could only assume he was by himself in the apartment or hotel room or whatever it was. He started to walk back and forth along the ledge, showing no sense of fear. He kept looking down, which in itself was maddening. He would then sit down for a while, dangling his feet over the ledge, get up and start walking again, teetering as he went. It was almost as if he was daring himself to fall. My heart was in my mouth as I thought of what might happen in an instant. He sat down on the ledge again. Suddenly, the sight of him on the ledge sent a shiver up my spine; it made me think of our children who were back home. Where were they? Were their lives dangling on the edge somewhere? Hopefully someone could do more to help them than I could for this poor boy.

I didn't dare call out for fear it might startle him and cause him to fall to his death. So I did the next best thing. I called the front desk, apprised them of the situation, and suggested they get help immediately.

Within five minutes emergency vehicles were on the scene. The boy remained on the ledge. The fire trucks began to hoist ladders to reach up to his floor. Then I could see a man leaning out the window pleading with the boy to come in from the ledge. They talked; the boy moved in his direction, then stopped. More talking. More cajoling. Then the man reached out and I could hear him say, "Take my hand, lad, please." Finally, he was able to grab the boy's hand. There was no struggle, no fuss. From the boy's point of view he had simply been on an adventure.

An hour or so later the police showed up at our door. They knew the hotel had called in the emergency, and the front desk identified me as having originated the alert. They had to talk with us for the purpose of their report, and to thank us. The day ended well, but for hours, I couldn't get the adrenaline out of my system. I kept seeing our kids up there. Was someone looking after them? More importantly, the nagging question I kept asking myself was what the outcome would have been had we not called for assistance when we did. It gave me shivers.

†

While living in London we were all well aware of the terrorist movements of the Provisional Irish Republican Army (IRA) in the U.K., much like the threat posed by Islamic extremists today worldwide. There is a reason of course: Much like Palestinian extremists, Irish terrorists formed militarized political parties in their respective post-colonial-era part of the globe. The phenomenon is somewhat the opposite of what I saw in the "navy of my youth," in that these groups committed violent acts in the service of their own sovereignty, rather than in defense of another's. Guilty of perpetrating bomb attacks, raids, and street battles in mainland Britain, the aim of the Provisional IRA was to establish a sovereign, socialist, all-island Irish state. A few years before we arrived, in 1979, they assassinated Louis Mountbattan, 1st Earl Mountbattan of Burma; and during our time in England, made an unsuccessful assassination attempt on Margaret Thatcher's life in Brighton, England. Since those turbulent times, the Continuity IRA and the Real IRA, which emerged from splits in the Provisional IRA, have been outlawed and classified as terrorist groups in the U.K. and in many other countries. Nevertheless, during our years in England, there was uneasiness about living in London, a city at the heart of IRA objectives. The most frightening aspect of the IRA presence was the despicable, often indiscriminate killing of innocent people.

It still affects me; my London years were one of the best times of my life, and I consider the city a second home.

Little did we know how close to home violence would strike, and how we would be personally affected by it.

The Harrods bombing was a car-bomb attack carried out by the IRA on December 17, 1983. The police received a warning that bombs had been placed in a car outside of the department store. The tip even specified the registration number of the car the device was in. Police officers approached the car and were caught in the blast as the bomb exploded. The device was planted in a blue, four-door, 1972 Austin sedan with a black vinyl roof. The bomb contained between twenty-five and thirty pounds of explosives. The explosion was so intense that the car roof was blown onto the spire of a nearby five-story building. If you ever get to London, take a look at the memorial that marks the spot where the three police officers were killed. It is located on the Hans Crescent (Street) side of Harrods. Remarkably, there was a second bomb warning made by the IRA to authorities at the time of the first explosion. It was stated that a bomb was placed in the C&A department store on the east side of Oxford Street in London. Police tried to clear the area crowded with shoppers and cordoned it off, but that claim was later found to be false.

Living in an apartment not too far from Harrods, we could hear the blast, but did not know what had happened until we saw it on television. We rushed to the scene and in spite of police barriers, could get close enough to see the gruesome sight of the car roof hanging from the building. There was chaos everywhere; fire trucks, ambulances, and the police tried to deal with crowd control. Six people were killed—three police officers and three passers-by. One of the latter was an American by the name of Kenneth Salveson. Although I did not know him personally, he was the son of a close business associate and friend, Gerry Salveson. We worked for the same company out of the same office in the United States. His son had just taken a job with an American firm in their London office. That fateful day he was walking into the side door of Harrods to buy a Christmas gift for his wife. He was planning to then go to Heathrow Airport to meet his wife, who was arriving later that day to join him. He never made it. She arrived, and when Ken didn't show up she proceeded to a London hotel where she heard the terrible news. As manager of the company office six miles outside of London, I received a call that evening from my boss in the United States, asking to me to offer whatever assistance I could. Gerry and his wife came to London immediately after their son's death to make arrangements to bring his body home.

†

With these scares high in my mind, the kids' visits never came often enough. By now all three of them were at private colleges, and looked forward to visiting with us once or twice a year. To add to our worries, Nicky was having a bumpy time of it, trying to deal with college and his illness at the same time. That took a great deal of courage given his condition. With his schizophrenic mind tormenting him, coping with studies and trying to fit into college social life must have been excruciating. It was even more courageous to voluntarily separate himself from medical and home care. But he did so knowing that college was a step he should take in spite of his illness, a step toward to a brighter future. I'm afraid I have a share in the blame for this, as

I always drove him hard and talked about the importance of being an achiever. So, because he was so eager to be as independent as possible, we tended to give him as much latitude as possible. That kind of spirited independence would, however, later contribute to his last breakdown.

Our next chance to visit was during the summer of 1984. I was getting antsy to have a boat under my feet. We wanted to see more of the River Thames than what flows through London, so to satisfy both urges we rented a thirty-four-foot powerboat from a nearby marina. We planned to spend a week on the boat, making our way westward on the Thames stopping overnight along the way. Our final destination was Oxford University, which is the oldest English speaking university in the world. We visited Diane, my daughter's best friend, who was attending the university on a one-summer program integrated with her U.S. college curriculum. Seeing Diane and Dorine together in a foreign country was an eye-opener. It helped me realize that the "kids" had grown up—Dorine was indeed seeing the world "on my shoulders." It also made me realize how broadening an experience it was for all our children to have lived in foreign countries and experienced different cultures. It showed their maturity, and made better citizens of them.

As you navigate the Thames there are numerous locks through which you must pass. You enter the lock, and then it is flooded to bring the boat up to the level of the river on the outlet side of the dock. One dock we entered took four boats in two rows. We were positioned in the back row with a boat forward of us. Ours was an old boat and therefore did not have an interlock between the starter motor and gearshift. In other words, you could start the boat with the engine in gear. I was well aware of this, having been cautioned by the rental shop when we took the boat. However, I failed to pass this important piece of information on to Dorine when I invited her to start the boat and navigate it out of the lock. After the dock was flooded and the gate opened, she happily went to start the engine, which I had inadvertently left in gear. The engine sputtered and started after which the boat lunged ahead, ramming the transom of the boat ahead of us. Fortunately no one was injured, and there was very little damage. Thanks to the owner's civility, we were able to eventually proceed on our way without confrontation, and with only minimal delay. I had explained to him that we were new on the river and that I was an American. He replied, "That's fine, we'll help you anyway."

That was not to be the end of our excitement. About halfway through our cruise up river, the engine failed. We drifted for a while, dodging traffic from both directions, before ending up on the riverbank. We called the rental shop to report our predicament, and by the next day, a technician was onboard to get us going again.

We lost a day and some sleep, but shortly after we got underway, we had another incident. My jokester son, Michael, decided to jump overboard, unannounced, as a lark. The river was narrow and heavily trafficked. It was, therefore, no easy task to coax a single-engine boat to make a U-turn, retrieve him, and then do another U-turn to get us back on our original course. Many years later when we had our own a boat, Dorine would pull a similar stunt, jumping overboard while we were anchored in the Hudson River. Even though she is a good swimmer, the swift three-knot current quickly took her downriver. In just several minutes all we could see was a small head bobbing up and down in the distance. We quickly weighed anchor and rescued her.

The only thing that saved the day, and probably her life, was her life jacket. These two incidents made me better understand why lions kill their young.

By the end of the trip, a sludgy realization had found its way through the back door of my mind: We were not functioning very well as a family. We had the collision in the locks, an engine breakdown, Michael doing his own thing, Dorine a bit bored with it all, while Ronnie and I argued over who should make breakfast. Nicky, the loner, stayed in the background, not saying much, just taking it all in, while trying to deal with the demons that were now stalking his mind.

†

All good things do come to an end, and so it was with our second London assignment. As the company continued to reduce its tanker fleet, relying more and more on chartered tonnage, the need for in-house marine engineering and project management services declined so far that the office became redundant. Our affiliated companies throughout Europe no longer required the services of our office.

As office manager, I had the unhappy task of overseeing the closure. We had to retire a cadre of local staff, some of whom had been with the company for many years. How sad, that like many of the ships I witnessed from construction to premature demolition, so went our office. I was part of the start-up team in 1968, and would now be the culprit to put the lock on the door in 1985.

From a personal standpoint, leaving London was easier this time. There wasn't the same degree of emotional distress—sure, there was disappointment, but somehow we seemed more detached this time around. Our lifestyle during the first sojourn was much more family-oriented; we lived in the suburbs and the kids were always at home with us, attending local schools. The children were as absorbed by the culture as we were, and we all lived like the locals. Also, during this second sojourn our "house on the hill" was a beautiful four-bedroom flat in the heart of London. The kids spent most of their time away from us, at college in the States. Ronnie and I lived alone in the city most of the time and behaved more like tourists than residents, catching up on theater, museums, ballet and the like. And when I traveled, she was alone—making it more of an irritant than it had been in Kingston-on-Thames.

17

THE SINGAPORE FLING

We must have a citizenship less concerned about what the government can do for it and more anxious about what it can do for the country.

—President Warren G. Harding at
the 1916 Republican convention

Shortly after we moved back into our home in New Jersey, I was offered what I thought was a unique opportunity. The oil company I worked for had acquired a multi-brand manufacturing company that produced large industrial electrical equipment. They asked me to set up a corporate marketing and sales office in Southeast Asia, a base from which to market their products. Given my extensive international experience, much of it in the Far East, and my many contacts in the region, I was asked to lead the operation and hire the staff needed to do it.

I chose Singapore as my base and opened an office there, later opening another office in Hong Kong from which to penetrate China. As Director of Business Development, Far East, I assumed responsibility for establishing a sales and marketing presence in Japan, China, and Southeast Asia. Marketing was new to me, but there is a commonly held viewpoint that marketing is half common sense and half instinct. I guess I had demonstrated a bit of both. So, always one for a challenge, I accepted my fifth overseas assignment in 1985. I could expect to return to my parent company upon completion of the assignment, which I did two years later.

As in the case of the Kaohsiung assignment, Ronnie was unable to join me in Singapore except for occasional visits—Nicky's illness made it impossible for him to focus on college studies, so he quit in his second year. Notwithstanding additional medical treatment and medication, his condition continued to deteriorate. By now he had isolated himself from nearly everybody. I think he knew he was losing the battle, but steadfastly tried to carry on hoping that somehow his condition would turn around. The pity was there seemed to be nothing anyone could do to ease his symptoms, but Ronnie believed he needed his mother to be in the United States, not Singapore.

I knew Singapore to be an ultra-modern, pristine island country. That's the impression you get as you are driven from Singapore Changi Airport to the city. Yet many tourists once drawn to the charm and excitement of fabled locales like Chinatown and Little India are disappointed to see how modernized some of it has become, and in some cases, that parts of the old city have even partially disappeared. Gone too are most of the famous rickshaws. Old landmarks and districts are disappearing in favor of endless shopping malls and towers of glass and steel. That's *progress*, I guess. But there's still the Raffles Hotel, where you can relive some of the colonial past by sipping a Singapore Sling near Somerset Maugham's portrait. He once called the Raffles Hotel the "legendary symbol for all the fables of the Exotic East." In many ways I think it still is.

Progress has its troubles. Development in and around Singapore kept eating away at natural habitat, thereby driving the island's wildlife to seek refuge in populated areas. Even so, I hardly expected the city to have a problem with wildlife. Was I right? How about pythons? How about a python nineteen feet long? Yep, near the building where I lived. And it was a tyke compared to the longest on record, which is thirty-five feet long. In this instance, the poor creature had somehow lost its way and slithered into one of the large open storm drains that are commonplace throughout the city.

I was part of the crowd that began to gather atop the storm drain to eye the huge creature. Except for the bull elephants I saw while on safari, it was the largest creature I had ever seen. After a while, two animal control units arrived to cart it away. They weren't big enough, so a larger unit had to be called in. Viewing it up close I estimated it must have been approximately fifteen inches in diameter. I was surprised at how docile it appeared; almost lifeless. Perhaps it was dying. As the vans drove off with their catch, everyone dispersed and got on with their business as if nothing had happened—just another day in the life of a vibrant, tropical city. I retired to my penthouse apartment, where I could look out on the entire metropolis and beyond. The view and the incident provided an interesting perspective of what can happen when contemporary clashes with primitive.

I would have another chance to experience that boundary line. Not only do *Mad Dogs and Englishmen* (written by Noel Coward) go out in the midday sun, but perverted golfers do, as well. One day, two business associates and I couldn't resist the temptation to play golf in the torrid afternoon heat. In such a climate, even Mr. Coward might have reneged on the idea. Nevertheless, the three of us were intent on playing eighteen holes of golf.

I was playing my usual game, spraying golf balls in all directions. On one hole, my tee shot went out of bounds, so off I went to track it down. I thought I knew the exact shrub it went into. When I got to it, I started to probe near a hole at the base of the shrub with my golf club. Before I could say "killer ants," I was covered from head to toe. And these guys were big—approximately a half-inch long. I couldn't believe how fast and aggressive they were; I had made the mistake of poking into their home turf, which caused them to swarm up my legs, attacking en masse. To make matters worse—a lot worse—they started stinging the hell out of me. I hit the ground, writhing frantically, trying to brush them off. By this time the two guys I was with, both Singaporeans, saw what was going on and came running to assist. There was a pond nearby, so they ushered me to it, where I jumped in and proceeded to take off all of my clothes except for my underwear. I was through with golf for the day.

I got medical treatment for the stings and quickly recovered. My attackers had not been killer ants, as it turned out, but red ants, sometimes referred to as fire ants. Killer ants, known as bulldog or bull ants, are indigenous to Southeast Asia and Australia, and can be lethal only if the stings are left untreated. I was never in any danger.

†

During one of Ronnie's trips to Singapore we decided to take a holiday trip to Bali. After all, we believed in taking full advantage of overseas assignments by seeing as much of the local culture as possible. Who knows when, if ever, you'll have the chance to do it again. So off we went to Bali, flying there via Jakarta. At the international airport in Jakarta, Ronnie ran into a minor snag. She got arrested.

To appreciate this tale one needs to understand that corruption was and probably still is endemic at all levels of government in Indonesia. The bureaucracy runs on greased palms. The commercial situation is not much different; unless you were willing to pay off the right people it was virtually impossible to do business. It got so bad that in 1986, the government tried to weed out corruption by firing almost six hundred immigration and customs officials in an effort to overhaul and reform its massive bureaucracy. The measure was effective for a while, but in a year or two the old methods and mentality crept back in. The rest, as the cliché goes, is history. It reminded me of my cynical view that if you took all of the money and wealth in the world and divided equally amongst everyone on the planet, in one hundred years or so it will have redistributed itself more or less as it was originally. Both situations say something about the human condition—beyond a set of inalienable rights, we're not created equal.

At the time we made this trip I was living and working in Singapore, trying to establish a sales presence in Indonesia. However, the place was so corrupt we found it impossible to do business within the framework of the company's ethics policy. As a result we terminated our efforts. It was unfortunate, because the country offered large potential profits.

I was not naïve about the difficulties of doing business in Indonesia, but I was unprepared for experiencing the corruption at a personal level. As we passed through immigration, an official quickly guided my wife to one side and into an office. I was told she was "being detained," and, "Her passport is not in order." I knew there was nothing wrong with her passport. But the more questions I asked, the more we went around in circles with no clear answers. I wanted to call the American Embassy in Jakarta, or my office in Singapore, but we were not allowed to make any telephone calls.

In the meantime, she was being *detained* for no good reason. That's a euphemism if I ever heard one. Moreover, they would not deal with her directly. In this country where women's rights are, shall we say, limited, the wheeling and dealing was up to me. As I went up the bureaucratic ladder it became abundantly clear that I would have to grease a palm or two. After a couple of hours, during which I was not allowed to see or talk to her, my hints in that direction were favorably received. Now it was simply a matter of how much it would take to spring her. I was the first one to throw out an arbitrary number, which I think was $50. ("Gosh," she said later, "am I not worth more than that?") It was all a game to steal as much money as they could, and the most frustrating part was that in such a situation, you have no legal recourse. You play ball or else.

Despite my fear for Ronnie, I found Henny Youngman's famous one-liner crossing my mind: "Take my wife ... Please." I would later joke with her that this could have been a golden opportunity. Just think, if I hadn't paid these guys off, I would have been free and clear. How often does an opportunity like this present itself? As I recall, it took $100 and a four-hour delay to get her released with her passport. In the taxi ride to the hotel, she jokingly said, "At one point I was beginning to think you were going to leave me there."

"Oh no," I said, "how could you even think such a thing?"

It was one of the last genuine laughs I remember sharing with her.

In January 1987, having accomplished all my business objectives, I booked our return to the house in Short Hills. Ronnie, Dorine, Michael, and my mother joined me in Singapore the last two weeks, after which we all returned home stopping in Hawaii for a bit of R&R. It was there that it became evident that Ronnie and I were not going to make it. I would lie awake at night wondering what could be done to save us. We simply couldn't learn how to live together in harmony, marriage counseling notwithstanding. The years together had not drawn us closer, but had instead driven us apart. We seemed to have less and less in common; were more inclined to go our own ways following our own interests. There was nobody waiting in my wings and none in hers—we just couldn't find a way to care for each other anymore. There was less and less cordial communication. Too often we'd get stuck blaming each other for matters important and trivial alike. She complained about the lack of attention, and me about the lack of affection, not to be confused with sex. The yelling and name-calling became louder and more frequent. We talked divorce on several occasions, but somehow always managed to patch things up without really solving anything. At first, divorce was unthinkable for Ronnie given her religious convictions. I knew, however, as I think she did, it was only a matter of time. To continue in the marriage would have meant destroying each other—there was too much pain.

18

THOUGH HE DIE EARLY, HE SHALL BE AT REST

You became a believer because you saw me. Blest are they who have not seen and have believed.

—Jesus to Thomas, John 20:29

In 1988, several years after the Salvesons lost their son Ken at the Harrods bombing, we were to fully understand the pain and grief they went through. We lost our oldest son, Nicky.

He had suffered from schizophrenia since he was fourteen years old. One characteristic of the disease is that all schizophrenics have suicidal tendencies. They tend to lose touch with the real world. And always, the paranoia—the deep-rooted belief that people are plotting against them. According to one psychiatric study, nearly 25 percent did in fact commit suicide in 1988. Leading up to his suicide he struggled to live some semblance of a normal life, but couldn't. By this time he had cut himself off from everyone—no exceptions. He experimented with drugs. He had serious self-esteem issues. He was rebellious in a way that was beyond what many teenagers experience and outgrow. His medications caused such severe side effects that he devised ways to avoid taking them without us knowing it. So severe were they that he would wander off and stay away for days at a time. It caused us to get very concerned about his physical well-being. In one instance he checked into a sleazy hotel in Newark, New Jersey, where two guys stole his motor bike at knifepoint. The next day a tenant went berserk and indiscriminately knifed a guy to death in the room above Nicky's. The guy then set the hotel on fire, killing several of the tenants who were asleep. Nicky was one of the lucky ones and made it out safely; we got the whole story from the police, who called us to take him home. When we got there he looked like something out of Michael Jackson's music video, "Thriller." Thereafter, his behavior had to be closely monitored, but his desire to be independent led him to go off again, this time to live on his own for a while, thereby cutting himself off from the treatment and family support he so desperately needed. On one occasion when we went to visit him, we had to virtually force ourselves on him before he would spend some time with us. While there I saw something that made me break down. He bought an old wreck of a red Mercedes-Benz sedan. The symbolic message was clear—Dad had a red Mercedes, so he had to have one, too. That is what made his death even more painful for me; he was a ship off the old block, sharing with me even my passion for all things nautical. He was more like me than any of my children, warts and all.

Alone, on a bitterly cold December night just before Christmas in his cramped two-room apartment, with no heat, no companionship, and only a few sticks of furniture, his world came to an end. At the blossoming age of twenty-six, no longer able to cope with his tormented life, Nicky broke our hearts—he committed suicide by putting a handgun to his head. The police report concluded that he did not die immediately from the gunshot wound. Instead, he bled to death over what must have been a torturous and agonizingly long period of time. Adding to the trauma was the fact that we received the news via a callous phone call. Ronnie and I embraced as never before, holding on for dear life, sobbing in complete shock. His life, not ours, flashed before our eyes. Twenty-six years of loving, of caring, of nursing, of worrying, gone in a heartbreaking instant. Gone too were all the dreams we had for him and his future. Where had it all gone, and *why*?

When it came time to identify his body at the coroner's office, we could not bear the thought of looking at his wounded and ghostly body. Instead, we opted to rely on dental records for positive identification. Nor could we bear the thought of looking at or receiving the gun he used to take his life. Instead, we instructed the police to destroy it.

And so my boy's tormented life was over. How fitting that his headstone should read, THOUGH HE DIE EARLY, HE SHALL BE AT REST. The thought of not ever seeing him again would eat away at me every day of my life. Now, age offers some comfort in the knowledge that each day brings me a day closer to seeing him again. Losing Nicky gave me an inner awareness of things I hadn't thought much about before. First among these was the need to be grateful for every day of life. It is something many of us take for granted, but I soon realized it is something to appreciate and cherish because it is so very fragile. Then too I became more cognizant of the need to be a more giving person. The need stemmed from a thought that plagues me to this day. Would his outcome have been different if I had given him more love and more of my time? Should I have been more tolerant and showed more patience? Would it have been any different if I had shared with him more of the things going on in my life? Did I take him to enough "Brooklyn Dodgers games," as my father did with me? Should we have done more things together, like playing catch? I put myself on a guilt trip, and vainly wished for another chance.

After we lost Nicky I was convinced his loss was the one thing that would finally cement our troubled marriage. Surely such a loss would be enough to crystallize any marriage. Not so. Just one and half years after Nicky died, Ronnie and I filed for divorce, counseling notwithstanding. In 1991 we were divorced, thus dissolving a thirty-four-year marriage. I looked for answers and found some by attending meetings of a child-loss support group called The Compassionate Friends. I discovered that an incredible 90 percent of all couples that lose a child end up divorced or separated. The many reasons are well beyond the scope of this discussion. However, a primary reason stems from the blame each parent puts on the other for the loss of the child. We didn't experience that one, though, because Nicky's schizophrenia was beyond our making and control. I attended eight to ten meetings of the support group before quitting. Problem was that I came away from most meetings more depressed than I was going in. Sitting with a group of strangers for a couple of hours, sharing the most intimate details of cause and effect, was no comfort.

†

In the meantime, Dorine was experiencing her own share of misery. In 1990 she was involved in a near-fatal car accident while pursuing a PhD in biophysics at Syracuse University. She was also working at becoming a proficient skier. As a passenger in the rear seat of a friend's car on the way to a local ski slope, they were broadsided from the left, where she was sitting. The car had been idling at a stoplight, and began to pull forward after the light turned green. The guy who hit them had jumped the red light, and plowed into them, spinning their car around twice.

As described by a passenger in a car behind them, the force of the impact was so severe that Dorine came flying out the rear driver's side window "like a rag doll." Her body was thrown clear of the car and came to a crushing stop against the curb. However, God was on our side that day, because in one of the cars behind them was a cardiologist who witnessed the accident. Dorine had stopped breathing, and he immediately administered mouth-to-mouth resuscitation, saving her life.

In Syracuse University Hospital, Dorine underwent several surgeries to remove her spleen and repair broken facial bones. The broken ribs had to pretty much heal on their own. To further complicate matters, she suffered a concussion. Although her healing was slow, and she lost her spleen, she made a full and courageous recovery.

†

The decade after 1988 would become the most agonizing of my life. I had always considered myself the classical Capricorn: that sure-footed mountain goat who stubbornly keeps climbing the mountain to overcome whatever obstacles may appear, and no matter what catastrophes may occur. But more illnesses and tragedy would leave the family questioning what else fate had in store for us.

The quadruple whammy came in 1997 when I was diagnosed with prostate cancer. It was up to me to select what kind of treatment I wanted. I could have the prostate gland surgically removed (prostatectomy), or have radiation therapy, or radioactive seed implants. Another option, hormonal therapy, was not recommended because the cancer had not spread beyond the prostate. Following my urologist's recommendation, I read *The ABCs of Prostate Cancer*, by Doctors J.E. Oesterling and M.A. Moyad. It became my bible. I read as much as I could on the subject, getting second and third opinions, and talking with other men similarly afflicted. I consulted with my niece (my brother's daughter) Patricia M. Camuto, MD, an Attending Physician, board certified in Anatomic and Clinical Pathology. Her assistance in confirming the urologist's diagnosis and proposed treatment plan was invaluable, as it gave me that extra measure of confidence I needed to make a tough decision. God bless her for it. Finally, I opted for the prostatectomy. For someone my age that seemed to afford the best prospect for longevity.

All of this came on the verge of my retirement. I was diagnosed with cancer the month before my retirement, and had the surgery two months after retirement. I thought to myself, *What a hell of a way to start my golden years*. It was as if I was being told to "Go Directly to Jail—Do Not Pass Go," or even worse, check out. But after successful surgery I had the newly earned distinction of "cancer survivor."

I was now living alone and went through a difficult period of convalescence after the surgery. With so much time on my hands, I found myself reflecting on the past.

As a young man, my capacity for handling disappointment and catastrophe was limited. I can remember how disappointed I felt when I dropped what would have been the winning touchdown pass during a high school championship football game. I was depressed for months thereafter. Then there was the failure to get into Kings Point on my initial attempt. That drove me to utter despair. These events were hugely important to me at the time. And I also believed that through disappointment and catastrophe, hope and even wisdom can emerge. In time, the thing that evolved in my character was a steely determination to work even harder to achieve my goals. No, I didn't become a better football player; I was as lousy a football player at Kings Point as I was in high school. But that determination, that stick-to-itiveness, made it possible for me to gain admittance to Kings Point on the second try. With that success came an added bonus. My confidence got a much-needed boost.

As I matured, life experiences strengthened my capacity to cope with real catastrophes. There is no better example of that than the rigorous mental and physical training at Kings Point. Next came the navy, and being faced with life-or-death situations. Even traveling and living overseas had an impact on my capacity to deal with crises. There was the terror of Pan Am Flight 830, and shipboard fire in Kaohsiung that claimed sixteen lives. I'm not what you would call a fun guy, but I do have a sense of humor that helped me through the tight spots.

I knew everybody's life is full of hard knocks. You look at life, and know it's not a cakewalk. But you must be able to bounce back and get on with your life because there is still much to live for. But as I lay healing, questions nagged me: Why do cruel and inexplicable things happen? Why is a young life taken? My gut told me that the pains and ills suffered in this life are predicated on our actions in the previous life, just as our destiny in the next life will be predicated on how we conduct ourselves in this life. How else can injustice be explained, other than to say it is beyond our comprehension?

Throughout my convalescence, I was reassured by the knowledge that statistically, the survival rate for prostate cancer was high. The challenge, however, was to get through the convalescence, and this is where Dorine saved the day. By this time Dr. Dorine M. Starace had earned her PhD and took a job at UCLA as a research scientist specializing in neuroscience. Much of her work focused on the use of biophysics in determining how the human nervous system functions. She wrote papers with titles such as "Voltage-Dependent Proton Transport by the Voltage Sensor of the Shaker K+ Channel," and, "Activation of Transducin by a Xenopus Short Wavelength Visual Pigment." Notwithstanding my technical background, I'm embarrassed to say that I could understand only about every third word, and even then, only the grammatical articles.

In spite of her busy schedule, she managed to slip away for two weeks to nurse me back to health. That so typifies Dorine's finest quality—generosity that springs from a heart of gold. She would later play a similar role for me after three more surgical procedures. For that kind of devotion I am eternally grateful. Her tender love and care made full recovery not only possible, but bearable. I began going to the fitness center again two or three times a week and maintaining a healthy diet, and as much as I was able, feeling that things were getting

Above: The Normandy American Cemetery in Colleville-sur-Mer, France. It covers 172 acres and contains 9387 American military dead.
Right: The sea of crosses at the Normandy American Cemetery.

Mannequin of paratrooper John Steele who was caught on the Sainte-Mère-Église church spire on D-Day.

The main street, Rue de Emile Desourteaux, in Oradour-sur-Glane, France, 1932.

The same street as above, Rue de Emile Desourteaux , as it looks today. Note the stairs on the right, circled in red, are the same stairs in the foreground, right, of the old 1932 photo abov

Burned and abandoned car in the remains of the original village of Oradour-sur-Glane, France. (Photo by TwoWings).

The site of the 1944 church massacre in Oradour-sur-Glane, France.

Two views of the *Sea Witch* model built by the author's son, Nicholas III, at 15 years old.

Model of HMS *Prince of Wales*,
a 98-gun British ship of the line.

Manned ship models at Port Revel Shiphandling, France.

Fully animated, generic creation of steamboat sternwheeler *Dorine*, circa 1865. Designed and built by the author.

Backstage opening night, before performance of *An Ideal Husband*, Paper Mill Playhouse.

Author in print ad for a well-known pharmaceutical company.

Modeling sweaters in Japan.

Author in the comfort of his workshop, modeling for a stock photography company.

Chara Rodriguera (Calderone) and the author, as Duncan, before a performance of *Macbeth*.

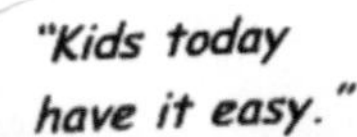

Author playing the traditionalist for a well-known Fortune 500 company.

Author portraying Matthew B. Brady, a 19th century American photographer, best known for documenting the Civil War.

Mon Tresor III getting underway.

View of 9/11 site from *Mon Tresor III* at Liberty Landing Marina, Jersey City, NJ. Taken 9/12/2001.

Memorial atop Mount Suribachi at the flag raising site on Iwo Jima.

US Marine legend from New Jersey, John Basilone, May 1943, Medal of Honor, Navy Cross, and Purple Heart recipient. Killed in action on Iwo Jima.

The author on Iwo Jima with Mount Suribachi in the background.

Standing on Mount Suribachi looking north towards invasion beaches. Basilone Beach is to the forefront, right.

Above and left: The author (above back row, right) and his classmate at the Kings Point 50th reunion.

The author (on right) with his first roommate George Wilson at Kings Point 50th reunion.

Above: The author receiving the Outstanding Professional Achievement Award from Vice Admiral Joseph D. Stewart, USMS, at Kings Point honors dinner, September 27, 2007.

Left: The author and his grandson Nicky IV at the honors dinner in front of an SS United States mural.

Author's static-display, scratch-built, museum-quality model of USS *New Jersey* (BB-62) as she appeared in 1985.

Visit in 1993 to San Costantino, Italy, my mother's home town.

Mom (on right) reunites with a childhood friend.

Above: Mom, at 89 years old, frolicking under the oak tree she loved as a child.

Typical street in San Costantino.

The neighboring village of Noepoli with the Sarmento River in the background.

San Francesco Beach on the island of Ischia, Bay of Naples, Italy

The corpses of Mussolini (2nd from left), his mistress Claretta Petacci (3rd from left), and his henchmen were hanged in Piazzale Loreto in Milan on public display, April 29, 1945 (actually 7 were hanged). Achille Starace, secretary of the Fascist party 1931-9, is on the far right. The fact that Mussolini was hung by two feet suggests the deep level of rage and betrayal felt by the people towards their once beloved "Duce."

Corricella fishing village, island of Procida, Bay of Naples, Italy.

Family picture collage

better. Clearly, my bout with cancer gave me new respect for the sanctity of life.

†

The next tragedy came in 2005. This time it hit my daughter-in-law Suzanne. She was married to my son Michael, and died October 14, 2005 at age forty-one after a two-year bout with cancer, chemotherapy, and all of the rest that goes with trying to survive the dreaded disease. She gave all of us a lesson in strength and courage that would remain an inspiration to her family and ours, and especially to her sons Benjamin and Brian.

Loss of life at any age is tragic. But in Suzanne's case it was especially so because her life was flourishing. Her new executive position at a major publishing company showed ever-increasing promise. Yet, she never lost touch with the demanding needs of her family. We recall her multifaceted talents as mother, wife, professional, friend, and homemaker who did it all so exceptionally well. Artistic too, she helped instill in her sons a deep appreciation for the arts. Brian's achievements in playing the piano and saxophone are examples of artistic endeavors in which he and his brother Benjamin consistently excel.

Michael and the boys picked up the pieces of their lives and moved on, relying very heavily on each other, and on Suzanne's legacy. However, we all shared some dark ruminations. Our fortunes seemed to be in decline for no apparent reason. Were we witnessing events going on in the family that seemed a microcosm of what was going on in our great nation, which was also suffering misfortunes at home and abroad? There are indeed parallels. Perhaps we were overextending our commitments and our finances. Were we in spiritual decline? Were we too focused on material prosperity? Were we committed to the same values that had been a cornerstone of our success to date? More specifically, had old-fashioned values such as discipline, loyalty, obedience, and being responsible been irretrievably lost? Had we forgotten about the power of prayer? Did we care enough about those less fortunate than ourselves? Lastly, had we forgotten our roots; the roots that gave us moral courage and strength that became the foundation on which everything else was based? I grappled with these issues on a national and personal level. Since Nicky's suicide and the ensuing tragedies, I had become sharply cognizant of these questions, and made efforts where I could to do something about them, however humble. I was doing my best to focus on the importance of giving to the people around me—giving time, skill, money, and talent. From it came a new credo, "Life's greatest gift is to give." That will be my epitaph. I began volunteering at the local VA hospital, and also felt that I had become a more compassionate person.

I developed a bond with Gerry Salveson, brought about by sharing what I believe to be life's greatest pain, the loss of a child—mine to suicide, his, to the Harrods bombing. An even stronger bond developed between my sister Anne and I, who had lost her daughter, Ellen. Only a person who has lost a child can truly relate to the never-ending anguish, and Anne had given me love and support at a time when I needed it most. She understood that when you lose a child you never stop grieving, nor do you ever know real joy again.

There are simply too many painful reminders. Nicky's favorite song was Ritchie Valens's "La Bamba." As a toddler, he would laugh and dance around like a jumping bean every time he heard it. Difficult, too, is listening to

Eric Clapton's poignant song "Tears in Heaven," which he wrote after his four-year-old son fell from the fifty-third-story window of an apartment. Every time I hear the lyric wherein he asks his son, "Would you hold my hand if I saw you in heaven?" it brings a lump to my throat. However, the most touching tune was Nicky's own composition, "My Dad." The lyric consisted of just two words—"my dad." Every morning as I walked out the door he would sing it to me over and over again to his own melody. It still rings in my ears. Even writing about it now is painful. With the passage of time the grieving is no less acute; the only difference is I'm now able to at least talk about it. Still, there is this terrible ache every time I see a child who bears the slightest resemblance. The final joy for me is to know there is one more crying hug waiting for me upon entering the Pearly Gates, as I hear the good Lord whisper in my ear, "Your boy is waiting for you."

Oh, but how life sometimes plays out in mysterious ways. In December 2003 my daughter Dorine was blessed with a son whom she named Nicholas IV, after her brother and me. I somehow feel he is a reincarnation of the son we lost. So maybe God doesn't work in such mysterious ways after all—he gave my son back to me. With his birth I am thankful every day for the joy he brings me, joy I thought I could never feel again. "Joy" is the warm feeling I got from something he said to me recently. Curious to know what happens to people when they get old and need to be *fixed*, I told him that sometimes they have to go to the doctor and maybe even go to the hospital. He mused for a bit and then asked what happens if they can't be fixed? "Unfortunately," I said, "They will eventually die." He then said, with the sweetness that only a five-year-old can exhibit, "Granddad, I want to die when you die."

Every night after he goes to bed, I go to his room, and just before he falls asleep I gently kiss his blond head and whisper in his ear, “Goodnight sweetheart, I love you.” In the comfort of his warm bed, with a belly full of his favorite pasta, a slight nod of his head tells me he heard me. It is impossible to explain how much I regret not having done that every night with my Nicky. It is what every parent should do every day of their lives in one form or another—let their children know they are loved.

†

If I consider how I handled the quadruple whammy, I will say I did pretty well. I wasn’t “depressed for months” after these events, nor did I experience “utter despair.” There was distress and tension, yes. But there was still much to live for. I had to get on with my life and face up to the responsibilities around me.

In my lifetime I’ve probably had more than my share of close calls. As I look back on those incidents I rejoice and am thankful that my guardian angel works overtime. There’s a marvelous witticism in an Annie Lennox lyric that so aptly captures the downright frustration many of us feel in dealing with life’s challenges. The great Scottish singer-songwriter in her ballad, “Cold,” tells us, “Dying is easy. It’s living that scares me.” Sometimes I think my life reads like a soap opera—son’s suicide, divorce, cancer survivor, two children involved in near-death car accidents, loss of my daughter-in-law, several near-death experiences, earthquake survivor, numerous surgeries, military death in the family, survivor of terrorism and of hurricanes in the North Atlantic and typhoons in the Pacific Ocean—but I’m certainly not ready to abandon the ship of life. I continue to be an optimist, a sentimental fool, the dreamer who wallows in the prospects of a utopian world void of evil and tyranny.

Sometimes I wake up believing that to "make love, not war" is impossible in the face of human frailties and weaknesses. The world can never be a perfect place, because people are not perfect. We are victims of a vast complex of human prejudices that are difficult to understand, let alone combat. Religious strife continues unabated as a cornerstone of international conflict, as it has for centuries. The human race continuously proves it is capable of heinous crimes. However, when I get too down on myself and the world around me, and need inspiration, I reflect on Mother Teresa, an ethnic Albanian whom I consider to be the greatest person of the twentieth century. Her legendary charitable work was the embodiment of integrity and humility. She dedicated her life to serving "the poorest of the poor," from her base in Calcutta, India. When she died in 1997, her Missionaries of Charity had nearly four thousand nuns and ran nearly six hundred orphanages, soup kitchens, homeless shelters, and clinics around the world. And when critics questioned her Nobel Peace Prize, she replied with the noblest and most divine words that I have ever heard, and which still ring in my ears: "The fruit of service is love, and the fruit of love is peace."

19

NORMANDY, A SEA OF WHITE CROSSES

Never in the field of human conflict was so much owed by so many to so few.

—Sir Winston Churchill, speaking of the RAF in the Battle of Britain in WWII

As I weathered my cancer surgery and segued into the pleasant trauma of retirement, my focus was changing dramatically from that of a working stiff to a man who wanted to do all of the things I had been putting off for so many years. After all, I earned it. I had been working very hard since I was twelve years old. In over thirty years in the corporate workplace I don't think I called in sick more than ten times. Sixty-hour work weeks were commonplace.

Heretofore my responsibilities had always come first—my upbringing, training at Kings Point, and military service all had a common message: *Be responsible.* But now it was my turn. My "to do" list would no longer be directed to home repairs and the like, but to owning a boat, to doing volunteer work, to building more ship models, to getting back into modeling, to writing a book, acting, and traveling. Not fun and sun travel, but the kind that had historical significance. The kind that might help me find and better understand my roots, my identity. The kind of travel that would please the sentimental fool in me, and let him take some wonderful trips down memory lane. The kind that would, for example, open the doors to my two favorite hotels in the world—the stately Connaught in London and the elegant Vier Jahreszeiten in Hamburg. I was on the threshold of all these opportunities and eager to cross over.

My first venture was a trip during the summer of 1994, before retirement, to join a historical tour commemorating the fiftieth anniversary of the June 6, 1944, D-Day invasion at Normandy. After the tour was over, I went off on my own and did a self-tour of Verdun and other notable World War I historic sites in France. I also visited Oradour-sur-Glane, which I will discuss later in this chapter. In 2005, after retirement, I ventured to Iwo Jima as part of a historical tour commemorating the battle's sixtieth anniversary. It was a way of keeping in touch with the family military history. Those war stories I heard and read as a youngster could somehow now become real. Perhaps I could capture the image of Uncle Tony trudging through the Argonne Forest in the Battle of Meuse, or visualize Uncle Pete slugging it out in the jungles of Guadalcanal, or my brother Tony on a destroyer stalking German U-boats in the North Atlantic, or Second Cousin Pete storming ashore into the scalding inferno that was Tarawa. I was never called upon to make those kinds of sacrifices. But I have on many occasions asked myself if I would have measured up if called upon. I ask myself the same thing about my children. Thankfully, at this stage of our lives, we'll never know the answers, but I like to think we would answer the call with honor, dignity and courage.

For well over a century our family thrived in this country, achieving the American dream. Step by step, each generation got closer and closer to the dream's fulfillment, even while the very concept of America was changing at home and abroad. For better or worse much of that change was brought about by its military involvement worldwide. In the case of my family, as with millions of other families, a part of the legacy they leave us comes from the enormous sacrifices made by virtue of their call to arms. My family was one of the ones who made the ultimate sacrifice. But this is also a country that rewards its sons and daughters like no other in the world. There is no better example than the GI Bill. It yielded incredible dividends. More compelling is the realization that the American way of life cannot become reality without continued hard work and sacrifice—sacrifices to give children an education, to enhance their development, and to afford opportunity. And so it is vitally important that we remain vigilant. We must continue to work hard and make sacrifices, lest the dream become a nightmare.

†

As a World War II history buff, my ambition was always to visit *Mecca,* the invasion beaches at Normandy. Living in England for the second time from 1983 to 1985 had given me my first opportunity. It was a quick one-day visit that merely left me thirsting for more. After visiting the Normandy American Cemetery, we arrived home at the house in Kingston-on-Thames. As I recall, we got home around 11:00 p.m., exhausted. What I had seen that day made such a profound impression that I could not erase it from my mind. I had never seen anything like that before; thousands of white crosses stretching out as far as the eye could see. How could a thing like that happen in the twentieth century? I turned on the TV to see the late evening news, and instead tuned in to a variety show. There was music playing—Glen Campbell singing "Galveston." My emotions were running so high that I broke down. It had been welling up in me all day and the sound of his voice, and especially that song, was all it took to pop my emotional cork. All I could feel was a profound sorrow for all those poor souls who never had a chance to live their lives. The only comfort was the certainty that they had not died in vain. They had secured for all of us our freedom and our lifestyle.

I went back again in 1991 and saw different sections of the assault beaches and museums I had not seen before. Here again, however, I came away frustrated by not spending enough time to see all there was to see. And so in 1994, I joined a military historical tour commemorating the fiftieth anniversary of the Normandy invasion. On that terrible day, 153,000 Allied troops and 70,000 Germans engaged in the start of a long campaign to liberate Hitler's fortress, Europe.

The tour group jumped off from London, June 2, 1994. We were driven by bus to the Southwick House, a mansion near Portsmouth, before taking a passenger-car ferry to Normandy. Southwick House has been fully restored to the way it was on June 6 and is a strong prelude to touring the beaches. It is where D-Day began—where General Eisenhower and his command set up their forward headquarters from which Operation Overlord would be orchestrated. D-Day was originally planned for June 5; however, the beginning of June saw severe storms over the English Channel. The weather forecast for June 6 indicated calmer weather, essential for night parachuting and disembarking on the beaches. Consequently, Ike decided to postpone the landings. Finally, on June 5, 1944, Ike made the historic and agonizing decision to launch the D-Day invasion on June 6, with his famous order, "OK. Let's go." That decision launched an armada of five thousand ships and boats of all sorts, with a mass of equipment and vehicles never seen before or since.

Our passenger-car ferry arrived in Normandy on June 4 and we were quickly transferred to our hotel in Deauville. To describe all there is to see and do along the invasion coast and inland is well beyond the scope of this book. My intention is to share with you some of things I found unusual and emotionally moving. I begin, then, with the most moving experience I had during the entire trip. I'm speaking of the Normandy American Cemetery, which is situated on a cliff overlooking Omaha Beach and the English Channel in Colleville-sur-Mer. It covers 172 acres and contains the graves of 9,387 American military dead, including those of the roughly 3,000 killed at "Bloody Omaha." For the second time in my life, I walked through the endless sea of white crosses, embedded in perfectly manicured acres of grass. Even though I was seeing it a second time, I was not prepared for the emotional experience of that cemetery. I wept unashamedly, as did those around me. The view captured in an instant the futility of war. When the mournful "Taps" sounded over the grounds, as it does several times a day, you can't help but get choked up for all the guys who never had a chance at life. I thought to myself, *I'm standing on the very ground that embraces the men who fought their way across France, who bled and died to help give France back to the French, and liberate Europe.* The whole scene harkened back to an oft-quoted comment from a British D-Day veteran who said, "They gave all of their tomorrows for our todays."

The experience resonated with a visit later in the trip to another cemetery. In all my travels in Europe, I had visited concentration camps, but never a German cemetery. However, the tour made a stop at the German Cemetery at La Cambe. As we disembarked from the bus, a local guide took us through the cemetery. The headstones were flat and embedded in the ground such that they barely extended above the ground surface. What took me aback was the sight of German veterans embracing American and British veterans, most of them getting very emotional. I had never seen this sort of camaraderie before, but thought to myself, *This is a good thing*. They say time is a great healer, and surely here it was doing its work. I would see similar scenes throughout the trip, as there were many German veterans attending the ceremonies, as well as Chancellor Helmut Kohl. I believe his presence marked the first time a German head of state attended any of the preceding Normandy ceremonial services.

On June 6 our group was assigned to attend the commemoration service at Pointe du Hoc, located eight miles west of Omaha Beach. There were ceremonies going on at numerous locations throughout the region, and you could only attend one of them. Pointe du Hoc was significant on D-Day because of its one hundred-foot cliffs that commanded a view of the beaches, and had gun and bunker emplacements. This mission was entrusted to the 2nd Rangers Battalion under the command of Lieutenant Colonel James E. Rudder. There was reputed to be six, 155 mm gun emplacements that covered the American beaches, and so it was necessary to destroy them. One gun was demolished in a massive air attack in April 1944. Unbeknownst to the Allies, the Germans relocated the remaining five guns inland. The Ranger force of 225 men shot grappling irons and ropes onto the cliff face under close naval artillery cover. German troops were leaning over the edge of the cliff, machine-gunning the Rangers as they climbed. Nevertheless, the Rangers managed to scale the summit and capture the cliffs. For the remainder of the day and into the next, they successfully repelled German counterattacks. By the end of the second day only ninety of the original 225 were still able to bear arms. Worse, it had been a heroic and futile effort to silence guns that were not there.

When we arrived at Pointe du Hoc for the 11:00 a.m. ceremony we learned that President Clinton was going to be the guest speaker, so you might say we got the top draw. Mrs. Clinton was with him. Coincidentally, the weather was miserable; almost a copy of what it was on that fateful day. He and the First Lady were ferried in by helicopter from a U.S. Navy aircraft carrier standing off the Normandy beaches. His remarks, although cryptic, captured the essence of why we were all there: to pay homage to the fallen heroes. After the speech, the President and Mrs. Clinton moved freely amongst the guests. I'm sure his Secret Service agents were there, but I was nonetheless surprised at how openly the President and Mrs. Clinton mingled with the crowd. It gave visitors a chance to meet and shake hands with them. I even had a chance to meet Hillary, who seemed pleased to be there, the weather notwithstanding. We chatted briefly before she moved on. There were lots of notables in the crowd, too. Former New York Governor Hugh L. Carey, a World War II army veteran himself, was there. So was former Senator Bob Dole, a World War II veteran, and current Vice President Joe Biden. Later we had a chance to meet and have a few drinks at the Hotel Normandy in the chic Normandy beach town of Deauville, where we were all staying. (The elegant hotel boasted the finest gourmet seafood and a panoramic view of Deauville's boardwalk and beaches—once the sort of hot spot that the French Riviera later became. It is still home to the annual American Film Festival.) One of the politicians quipped, "The local food is good, but you can't find a decent hamburger around here." We closed the bar in the wee hours, swapping *sea* stories.

Our tour bus visited Pegasus Bridge, famous for having been the site of the initial D-Day landings. This occurred shortly after midnight on June 6. Located behind enemy lines over the Caen Canal at Benouville, France, British glider pilot regiments were ordered to take the bridge in order to prevent German armor from reaching the area behind Sword Beach and interfering with the landings there. A house near the bridge owned by the Gondree family was the first to be liberated during D-Day. It still exists and now contains a café and a small museum shop. As you might imagine the whole area was swarming with tourists, but five of us managed to get a table in the café and have a drink and a snack. We also met the proprietor. She was a small child living in the home when it was liberated.

In our group was a Battle of the Bulge veteran named Joe, and his wife, Mary. In the closing days of the war, Joe's foxhole took a hit that left him permanently blind. During his recovery at a veteran's hospital in the United States,

Joe met Mary, who helped nurse him back to health. They got married and had five kids. They have been married for nearly fifty years during which time (Saint) Mary raised five kids, ran their home, took care of Joe, and worked outside the home. To be so devoted to someone comes as close as anything I can think of in answering the eternal question, "What is love?" I came away feeling her place in heaven is more than secure.

While in the café another casual meeting took place between Mary and Joe, and an English married couple that was sitting at the next table. The bloke was a D-Day veteran who had been wounded during the subsequent Battle for Caen. He, too, married the nurse who took care of him during his many months in the hospital. She filled a role identical role to Mary's, except they had three children, not five. And like Joe, he would depend heavily on his wife, for he was also blind as a result of war-inflicted wounds. They sat around for an hour and a half, reminiscing about the war and the trials and tribulations of living with blindness. There was no remorse, no bitterness, and no lingering hostility in their voices. They did what they had to do and got on with their lives, which were, as far as I could tell, very productive. The goodbyes were emotional for all of us. The two veterans hugged, cried, and held the hug for ten to fifteen seconds. They separated and hugged again on the other cheek, tighter, for another ten to fifteen seconds. Their wives were a bit more poised. They too hugged, but upon separating, held hands while staring intensely into each other's tearful eyes as if to say, *They fought the good fight, but we gave them life.*

It was touching to see each couple walk away from the café hand-in-hand. The entire experience with these folks reminded me that I had perhaps missed that many-splendored thing.

†

Fortuitously, I crossed paths with my old shipmate, Vice Admiral John D. Bulkeley. We met at The Battle of Normandy Museum in Bayeux, of which he was a director. As I moved away from a display, he and his wife Alice were walking in my direction. When our eyes met we smiled, shook hands vigorously, and hugged. I told him, as I had many years before, how honored I was to have served in his command. We reminisced about the good old days and then had lunch at the museum. We brought each other up to date on the last thirty-five years since we had seen each other, during which I reminded him that he was to thank for my promotion from Damage Control Officer to Engineering Officer with responsibility for ninety-five men in the Engineering Department. He laughed and with his usual wit, said, "Well, we all make mistakes."

He told me about a new book, *Sea Wolf*, a biography of his life written by historian William B. Breuer. In it he talks about his time as skipper of the USS *Tolovana*. Later I would read it and find a passage that summed up his values and what he expected from his officers:

> I want to see discipline, and I want to see professionalism. I will not tolerate incompetence nor will I permit a cancerous, defeatist attitude from any member of this crew. I hold each of you personally responsible for the course this ship takes. I expect you to do whatever is necessary to make *Tolovana* an operating, functional asset that can be called upon to perform her required duties.

> You have my full support. Anyone who does not understand this can pack their sea bag.

What I appreciated about serving under him was that whenever we sat down as a group to critique an operation or exercise, he gave it to us straight and honestly; you knew exactly where you stood and you had better get it right the next time out. These many years later, he was gracious enough to sign my copy of the book, and in it he wrote: *Nick, For my friend, a great shipmate and officer, with great esteem from John Bulkeley, Vice Admiral, USN.* I will always cherish that book and its message from a highly decorated, daring American hero.

†

The village of Sainte-Mère-Église is famous for being the first town in France liberated by U.S. troops. It had to be taken because it stood in the path of roads and railroads that the Germans would most likely use to mount a counterattack on the troops landing at Omaha and Utah beaches. In the early morning (0140 hours) on June 6, units of the 82nd and 101st Airborne Divisions landed directly on the town, a maneuver that resulted in very heavy casualties. As bad luck would have it, some buildings were on fire that night, and they illuminated the sky, making easy targets of the descending paratroopers. Some fell into the fire. Many hanging from trees and utility poles were shot by German defenders on the ground. There was a famous incident involving paratrooper John Steele, whose parachute got caught on the spire of the town church. A German soldier spotted him hanging from the church and fired, hitting him in the foot. Thereafter he played dead until he could be rescued. The incident is portrayed in the movie *The Longest Day*.

There is so much to see and do here that several bus tours spent the entire day in Sainte-Mère-Église and its outlying areas. The townspeople turned out en masse to welcome the veterans *home*. For many of them it was there first time on French soil since 1944. I think most of our guys were stunned by the enthusiasm of the reception they received. Homes were brightly decorated with signs of welcome, and many invited the vets into their homes. They marched in a huge parade, led by the mayor and other dignitaries, through the town streets to the church square. Applause from the locals was virtually non-stop. The church square had a grandstand erected for VIPs and speechmaking. There were food stands everywhere, and the wine flowed freely. There was a huge band playing swing music of the '40s, mostly Glenn Miller—he lost his life when his plane went down over the English Channel for reasons that are still unknown. However, I like to think his spirit was with us that day. If it was, he must have been thrilled by everything he saw and heard; everybody was dancing with everybody else in the square.

The thing that stands out in my mind is how appreciative these veterans were towards the locals. They kept thanking everyone; whereas the response was invariably the same, "No we're the ones who should be thanking you."

The day, however, ended with a rather unfortunate note. The program for that day included a bus trip to the same drop zone that many of the veterans jumped into on June 6, 1944, in the early morning. An actual jump was staged, with approximately six hundred paratroopers jumping out of a variety of aircraft as we watched in awe. Included in this group were veterans who were actually in the original jump. Of course they were in their seventies, and one guy even topped out at eighty years old. All went well until one veteran hit a hard landing in an open field; he broke his leg and injured one hip. He had to be taken to a hospital, and that pretty much brought his trip to an abrupt end. In case you're wondering, he recovered well, and the eighty-year-old vet completed his jump with flying colors.

†

As we drove away from Sainte-Mère-Église en route to the next town, one of the guys in our bus, Matt, started yelling, "STOP THE BUS, STOP THE BUS!" The driver stopped the bus, thinking something was wrong. Mark disembarked, excitedly explaining, "It was here, right here where we had a firefight with a detachment of German troops. They were on the other side of this road (where the bus was) and we were pinned down in and around that house. We exchanged gunfire for approximately two hours before reinforcements came up and we were able to knock out the German positions. We lost a lot of good guys that day."

His wife Marion implored him to get back on the bus, but he wouldn't have it. We soon found out that Matt was with the 101st Airborne Division that had dropped in this area on the early morning of June 6. Now, just the sight of that house made it all come flashing back to him. He even remembered enough to say the house hadn't changed much. He was so excited he could hardly contain himself as he rushed toward the house and frantically knocked on the door. A woman answered. She was very cordial as she listened to him try to describe in English the fighting that had taken place, his fingers pointing and jabbing in different directions.

From what we could determine later, she spoke very little English, but was able to understand what he was trying to say by virtue of his rapid sign language. All of a sudden he disappeared into the house, his wife following close behind. We waited fifteen, maybe twenty minutes before Matt and Marion reappeared at the front door with their French hostess. They exchanged parting words and hugged. As they walked down the path leading away from the house, Matt reached down, picked up a handful of dirt and slipped it into his pocket. This was the first time he had set foot on French soil since his war days, but now he seemed anxious to take a piece of it back with him. As he boarded the bus his eyes were still moist from the tears he had shed. In Marion's hand was a bag of freshly baked cookies the French woman had given them after they finished the coffee she had prepared. He said the richness of this one experience and the woman's genuine gratitude for their efforts made the trip and his earlier sacrifices worthwhile. For me it was a glimpse into the rich rewards of human kindness.

Naive perhaps, but wouldn't it be wonderful if religions, governments, and nations could come together in a similar way. Here was a woman who wasn't even born when Matt was part of the grand war machine that was liberating Europe. Yet in a matter of minutes they bonded by exchanging kindness and sharing common interests. Perhaps the lesson is that in life, we might be better served by putting more emphasis on the things that bring us together, rather than the things that drive us apart.

Today the beaches of Normandy rest under a ghostly stillness, unlike that chilly morning when they shuddered with the sounds of gunfire and the thunder of bombardment. Nowhere is that better captured than in the opening twenty-five minutes of Steven Spielberg's Academy Award-winning *Saving Private Ryan*, which depicts the Omaha beachhead assault. The sights and sounds of men coming out of their landing crafts into bloodied water and onto bloodstained beaches left me spellbound. The savage gunfire of German emplacements welcomed them into an inferno that many would never leave. And through it all, one cannot help but admire the courage, determination, and exemplary values of these men and women of the Greatest Generation.

Largely fictional, the story is loosely based on the real-life case of Sgt. Fred (Fritz) Niland, who lost his brothers Preston and Robert during the Normandy landings. Apart from the opening scene, the film's most powerful scene to me is the one in which the mother of Private Ryan is to be informed of the death of her other three sons. The scene opens with the mother standing in front of the kitchen sink looking out onto the winding road leading up to her house. Her back is to the camera. Through the window over the sink the viewer can see a military car coming up the road to her house. Sensing bad news she stiffens and then moves slowly away from the sink towards the front door, the camera still at her back. Just as she steps out onto the front porch, the vehicle pulls up in front of the house. An army officer and clergyman step out of the vehicle and approach the porch. At that moment she wavers from side to side, and then slowly collapses on the porch deck from the shock of the devastating news she is about to receive. Resting on her haunches she looks out at the two men in anguish. The scene ends at that point.

The remarkable thing about the scene is that not a single word is spoken, yet because the scene is so masterfully crafted it has an incredible impact on the viewer. It struck a chord and harkened me back to the church procession that came through my block in Brooklyn during the Korean War. In recalling Eleanor's grief at the loss of her son Vinnie, I had been witness to a mother's anguish much like that depicted in *Private Ryan*.

†

As if I hadn't seen enough of the ravages of war, I drove to the idyllic French village of Oradour-sur-Glane, after visiting Verdun. On June 10, 1944, the village was completely destroyed by fire, and 642 innocent men, women, and children were massacred by soldiers in Hitler's elite Waffen-Schultzstaffel (SS) army. The ruins of this martyred village have been preserved both as a shrine and a chilling reminder of the horrors and brutality of war. The ruins stand today just as they did on June 10, 1944. The village was never rebuilt. Instead, a new Oradour was built near the old village. I first became interested in the story from watching the British TV documentary *World at War*, which is in my view the finest World War II documentary ever made. In it, there is a segment that describes what happened on that fateful day in June 1944. The story of this ghost town seemed so captivating that I vowed that I would someday visit the village.

As you enter the ruined village there is a sign that implores visitors to be silent and remember the 642 villagers killed there. The small museum is somewhat informative, but the destroyed village speaks for itself. In the public washroom I saw a pile of vomit, presumably thrown up by someone unable to control what he or she was feeling. As you walk through the streets you see burned-out building after building. There are roofless stone structures with broken-down walls. Wires still hang limply from leaning telephone poles. Lying on the streets are the charred remains of cars with their twisted metal frames, tireless wheels and burned-out interiors. The grimmest sight was that of a crumpled bicycle lying in the street just as the child must have left it. I kept gazing at it, numbed by the vision of kids playing around it in the street. There are no restrictions on moving through the village, and so it was possible to look inside the houses. In some of the homes sat gardening tools, kitchen utensils, and burned-out sewing machines. Cooking pots still hang over empty grates. In the local bakery we saw the pans, trays and other implements used by the baker. If you closed your eyes you could hear them rattling. As we walked down one of the streets we could see a sign on each building identifying the type of structure, who lived there, and in some cases, who died there.

We felt like we had just stepped back in time fifty years. We had stepped back into a twilight zone made all the more dramatic by what seemed to be a supernatural silence. The people were gone, but their ghosts were all around us. Walking through the town and looking at the remnants gave us the eeriest feeling we had ever experienced, or would again.

So why Oradour? Our visit and the literature we took away did not tell us much about why this remote village became the object of annihilation. After all, the town had not been in an active war zone, nor had it been an active resistance stronghold. Moreover, it was far removed from the Normandy beaches, where just days earlier (June 6, 1944) the allied landings took place. The more I thought about it, the more I wanted to get some answers.

The first answer that my research uncovered was that the reason for destroying Oradour is still a mystery. However, the most plausible theory suggests that when the German forces in the south of France got word of the Normandy invasion they were ordered north to help repel it. As they moved north, French resistance fighters stepped up their efforts to delay their movement. Bridges and roads were blown up. A few German soldiers were killed. An SS officer was taken prisoner. Although the Germans were anxious to get to Normandy, they paused long enough to retaliate. The most commonly held belief is that Oradour was selected because it was "on the way," so to speak; it was quiet, inoffensive, and there had been no rumors of partisans there.

On the morning of June 10, a company of German half-tracks loaded with troops entered the village. Others surrounded the village. Villagers found this very curious because German troops had seldom been seen in the village. Citizens were told to assemble on the fairground in the center of the village, a spot we saw and noted by virtue of a sign posted there. They were led to believe this was to be a security check. Soldiers entered schools, barns, shops, and homes moving the occupants toward the village center. Soon there were hundreds of people standing in the open fairground. Then the men were herded into barns and garages. The women and children were crowded into the town church.

The slaughter began on signal, a pistol shot. Then all hell broke loose. Within minutes the population of Oradour ceased to exist. The SS troops used machine guns and hand grenades to disable and kill all 642 men, women, and children. Then they closed the buildings and lit fires. One account I read said that after all of the occupants in the church had been killed or wounded, the soldiers piled wood on the bodies, some of whom were still alive and set it on fire. The heat was so intense that the church's brass bell melted in the inferno and flowed to the floor. The burning village became a crematorium. Only a handful escaped the carnage to tell their gruesome tales. Only one person escaped from the church, a Madame Rouffanche. She saw her younger daughter killed by a bullet as they attempted to find shelter in the vestry. She then ran to the altar end of the church where she found a stepladder used to light candles. Placing it against a wall below a window she climbed up and threw herself out the window onto the ground some ten feet below. As she picked herself up, a woman holding her baby tried to follow, but they were seen by SS soldiers at the window and both woman and child were shot. Madame Rouffanche managed to escape and later gave vivid accounts of what happened that day. As you go through the roofless church as it stands today, there is no evidence of the hundreds of women and children who died there. Most poignant is the melted tower bell on the floor.

At the same time that the church was burning, the SS fired their machine guns into the men crowded in the barns and garages. They deliberately fired low, so that many of the men were badly wounded, but not killed. The soldiers then piled wood and straw on the bodies and set them alight. Many of the men thus burned to death, unable to move because of their injuries. Five of the men miraculously managed to escape under cover of darkness and tell their stories. After killing all the townspeople they could find, the soldiers set the whole town on fire and left early the next day, laden with loot.

Upon leaving the town we visited the adjacent cemetery, the real memorial to the victims. The plaques give a ghastly picture of the destruction of entire families, and an entire school class. When it was all over the soldiers journeyed up through France to Normandy to join the rest of the German army in attempting to throw the allied invasion back into the sea. Many of them, including Adolph Diekmann, who led the attack on the village, were killed in the Normandy fighting.

The ending to this story has a lamentable twist. Twenty-one members of the SS who took part in the atrocities at Oradour were tried at Bordeaux in 1953, the same year as the inauguration of the new village of Oradour. None were officers; the highest rank was that of sergeant. Of the twenty-one men, fourteen of them came from the French province of Alsace, which had been taken over by the Germans following the French surrender in 1940. In the eyes of the Germans, these men had been German. In the eyes of the French, they were traitors, and their brutalization of the village had no military necessity. Members of the Resistance said they should have refused to take part in the massacre; they should have helped their fellow countrymen escape and that they were even guiltier than the Germans. The lawyers defending the Alsatians said that with one exception they had been conscripted into the SS and therefore had no choice but to obey. If they refused they would have been executed. The people of the province of Alsace wanted all the men freed while the people living in the Oradour area wanted them all executed. The court pronounced verdicts of either death or hard labor for the accused. Exactly one week later, they were free. Amid a furious national debate on the question of collective guilt and the fate of Alsatian conscripts, the government enacted a general amnesty law, much to the despair and rage of people in Oradour and other French citizens. How's that for justice?

The phrase, "Man's inhumanity to man," was coined by the great Scottish poet and lyricist Robert Burns in his poem, "Man Was Made to Mourn." Like everyone else I had heard the phrase, but had never seen it in full light, until now. At this stage of my life I had felt disappointment, despair, and heartache. The loss of my son had left me with an emptiness, a void of any capacity for joy. I had seen poverty, destruction, violence, and death. However, nothing could compare with the disillusionment I felt for the human race and its capacity for cruelty. But why should I be disillusioned? Humankind has a history of the same behavior since the beginning of recorded time. The hope, however, lies in our compassion, our conscientiousness, and our faith in the human spirit. The world is probably a better place now than ever before, due in part to the men and women from all walks of life who have made a difference. On a smaller scale the world saw much the same kind of progress in eliminating the Nazi scourge thanks to those who answered the call. It caused me to reflect on the contributions of my own family with great pride. Their sacrifices also helped make a difference. Hopefully civilization will continue to grow in wisdom. If it doesn't, Scotland's favorite son, Robert Burns, warns us in the last two lines of his poem:

Man's inhumanity to man
Makes countless thousands mourn!

20

DOWN TO THE WEE IN SHIPS

> *Perfectionists satisfy everyone except themselves.*
>
> —Nicholas F. Starace II

I've seen the world from ship-decks and quaysides. But you could say it took the miniature version—model ships—for me to see my family and the path my life would take.

Years from now when my grandsons read this book I want them to know and understand the path my life took, for that defines my legacy. I wonder if they will have the same feelings about me as I did about my grandfather, and if I will have been the same positive influence on their lives as he was on mine. His was an influence that helped shape my entire life, thanks to what I affectionately call the "anchor gene." I hope my grandsons will grasp the same values that made it possible for our family to thrive, and to live by those values. In this day and age, that may be more of a challenge than it was in his or mine. As a symbolic example, there won't be bicycle rides to the 31st Street pier in Gowanus Canal, because it's fenced in and restricted to "authorized personnel only." They'll have to find their dreams and "belching steam whistles" elsewhere.

The course I steered to achieve my dreams was through Kings Point. I served in the merchant marine, served in the navy and naval reserve, and devoted an entire career to the maritime industry. In business and pleasure it has been about my fascination with ships, boats, and the sea. It was, still is, and will always be at the core of my soul. I have owned boats starting with a sixteen-foot rowboat when I was sixteen years old. Like my grandfather, I have been an avid model shipbuilder virtually all my life, starting with a scratch-built ten-inch model of my father's boat I built when I was twelve years old. The son we lost, Nicky, showed early signs of the same passion—he built a beautifully hand-crafted twenty-one-inch model of an American clipper ship, without any encouragement from me. Its details are exquisite, especially when you consider he was only fifteen years old when he built it. The cherished model stands as a reminder of him and how much he had to offer. Even my three grandsons Benjamin, Brian, and Nicky have dabbled in it a bit, Nicky having started at three years old. On a couple of occasions I have heard Benjamin say, "Granddad, I'm a boat guy." We'll see.

As I progressed in the hobby, I came to realize that serious ship modeling requires a great deal of skill, precision, and of course patience, the latter of which I often lack. It's sort of analogous to what I have been doing on these pages as I rebuild the story of my life.

†

Marine art takes different forms, most notably paintings, drawings, sculpture, and ship models. Ship modeling is probably as old as shipbuilding itself. Some of the oldest models date back to the twelfth century, and have been found mounted in churches, where they were used to bless the ships and those who sailed in them. Ship modelers, however, did not have any reference material to draw upon, since through the earlier centuries, and even into the eighteenth century, virtually all small craft (and many of the larger ships) were built without any formal plans. Shipwrights were apprenticed to their craft at an early age and the art was passed down from father to son. Later, during the wars between France and Britain, prisoners sought relief from boredom by building ship models from scraps of wood and bone. They still remain highly sought-after collectibles. This evolved into the art form as we know it today and the subsequent sale of models to the public. For example, a 42½-inch model of HMS *Prince of Wales,* a ninety-eight-gun British ship of the line, made of ivory, wood, and bone, was sold in 2007 at Christie's, London, for $224,595. It was crafted in intricate detail by French prisoners of war incarcerated in England circa 1800.

Ship modeling got off to a slow start in the United States. Many of the older models from the turn of the nineteenth century onward were built by seamen who modeled the ships on which they served. You'll have to forgive me for being biased, but I feel confident in saying that we have caught up, producing many of the finest models in existence anywhere. To perpetuate the craft there are now an infinite variety of plans and books from which the ship modeler can draw upon to weave his or her magic.

Unfortunately, the talent for rigging ships is practically lost since those types of ships no longer exist, except for some training vessels and full-scale museum pieces such as the *Cutty Sark* at Greenwich, England (and which was ravaged by fire in May 2007). However, this precise art is very much alive thanks to those avid ship modelers of period sailing vessels who devote their time and talent to the rigging of model ships. My grandfather Michael built nothing but period sailing models. It is a pity that of all the models he built there is only one left in our family. The amazing aspect of his craft is that he did all the rigging from memory, right down to the minutest details. He drew on his many years of experience working on large sailing ships as a ship caulker. Then, as now—in the real world as in the ship-modeling world—those who aspire to sail are in my humble opinion the purists of the maritime community.

Although most ship modelers dabble in it as a hobby, there are aspects of ship modeling that play a vital role in shipbuilding and the training of ship operators. In the latter case, manned models are used to train pilots, masters, and officers in the operation of large ships like supertankers and container ships. The models, usually built in 1:25 scale, are designed to behave just like real ships, thereby giving the ship handler the same sensations. For realism, a typical facility uses a man-made lake designed to simulate the full range of harbor and sea conditions a vessel may encounter. While computer simulators are more realistic when it comes to the bridge environment, most operators prefer the manned model for a better understanding of ship behavior. In the case of shipbuilding, models are used in towing tanks to determine primarily how much power will be required to achieve design speed. Typically, a model is towed in a basin fifteen to twenty feet wide and hundreds of feet long, equipped with a towing carriage that runs on rails on either side. Self-propelled models are also used in towing tanks to determine the maneuvering characteristics of a vessel in model scale.

So the hobby is not necessarily all about art. Like any hobby, it's about deriving pleasure from time spent doing or creating something special, regardless of the results and skill level. We're in it because we love it. Few things can match the gratification that goes with standing back admiring something you've created, and sharing it with those closest to you. In my post-retirement years, and the few peaceful years after our family's string of tragedies, I turned my attention to this quiet corner of my life with every intention of being, well, *retired.*

I have been a member of the Ship Model Society of New Jersey (http//www.njshipmodelsociety.org/) for over twenty years, and even served as its president for four years. Its members include professional and non-professional builders, naval artists, authors, and maritime historians. Club interests cover the entire spectrum of maritime subjects, from Viking longboats to nuclear submarines. The models are serious business—both in man-hours and sometimes in money. One of the most gratifying aspects of the club is the willingness of its members to share ideas and knowledge regardless of skill level.

My first venture into ship modeling clubs was in Singapore, after the "ant" incident chased me off from golf for a while. Every Sunday a group of us would meet at a lake and run our ship models. I got the idea of starting a ship model club, so I ran an ad in the local newspaper—and was swamped with calls. The positive response led me to organize and establish the Singapore Ship Model Club. As its founder and first commodore, I was delighted to sign up thirty members before the first wood chips hit the floor. The vice commodore of the club, Derek Scully, had a particular interest in British naval warships. During one of our Sunday afternoon regattas, there were seven of us steaming our radio-controlled models in tight formation in front of quite a large crowd. Without warning, his beautifully crafted four-foot model of a sleek British destroyer suddenly began to sink. GURGLE, GURGLE—within minutes she slipped below the surface taking with it fifteen hundred of his precious man-hours and nearly $2,000 of his money. Dumbfounded, all we could do was console the poor guy who, out of frustration, then flung his radio transmitter into the lake. There went another $550. Ever seen a grown man cry? It's not a pretty sight.

The same thing would have happened to me were it not for the type of construction I used in building the model. We were attending a sailing regatta on a lake at the Jersey Shore. I had my five-foot, radio-controlled, scratch-built model of the USS *New Jersey* cruising gracefully around the lake. Without warning, some guy's forty-pound model tugboat went berserk. I tried to steer clear of the beast, but it rammed me squarely on the starboard side, tearing open a large section of the hull. My model immediately began to take on water. Fortunately though, I used double-hull construction in building the wooden model. The side shell plating was made of a double wall, with a void space in between the walls. Although the outer wall was penetrated, the inner wall was intact. Even with the model listing, I was able to maneuver it to shore and retrieved it. I had thirty-six hundred man-hours in that "Best of Show" model, not to mention the money. After dry-docking and repairs, she was as good as new. AMEN.

Here's another close call with the USS *New Jersey*, which shows you just how intricate these models can be. I was running the model in the lake behind my son Michael's home in West Windsor, New Jersey. Grandsons Benjamin and Brian were enjoying the sight of the great battleship going through her paces. The model is fully animated, having twenty-one radio-controlled operating features such as smoke generation, lights, taped music, flag hoisting, rotating catapults, sirens, horns, rotating radar, and of course motor propulsion and rudder control. Most notable are the three rotating main gun turrets. Each turret has three sixteen-inch miniature guns that fire black gunpowder. I saved the best for last, firing all nine of the sixteen-inch guns—three shots from the number one forward turret, and then did likewise from the second turret with dazzling results. That's usually the showstopper. When I fired the last turret, one of the three guns in the turret back-fired causing a loud mini-explosion. The entire turret blew off its foundation several feet into the air before falling into the water. Little did I know that the blast damn near blew a hole in the bottom of the hull. The propulsion system was still working, so I was able to maneuver the model back to the dock. When I opened the model by lifting off the superstructure I found that the space below the gun pretty much shattered. Moreover, there was indeed leakage from a small crack blown in the hull bottom. However, here again a double-wall construction, this time in the bottom, saved the model. Later, I waded in the lake for about an hour trying to retrieve the turret, but it was lost to the muddy bottom. Lucky for me, that's all I lost that day.

†

Like my grandfather, I take special pleasure in the historical side of modeling. His subjects were always about ships with white sails. Inspired by him, it has always been my philosophy to only build models that reflect a part of America's maritime heritage. Following his legacy, I was soon focused on two of this country's most historical maritime legends—the steamboat sternwheeler, and the American clipper. I had completed a model of one of the latter, the *Flying Fish.* That left me with the challenge of building a sternwheeler. No subject better captures the imagination and spirit of America's maritime heritage than these wonderful old boats belching and churning their river magic. A frequent guest speaker at club functions, I am pleased to see how much interest people have in that heritage.

The result is my most accomplished work as a ship-modeler, the steamboat sternwheeler, *Dorine,* a typical steamboat as found on American Western rivers, circa 1870. It is a generic creation that I designed and built, and named after my daughter. It was inspired in part by the steamboat painting *Night Run to Friar's Point*, and by my favorite marine artist, John Stobart. The print I own of *Night Run* is one of my most treasured possessions, as is a replica of a painting by Montague Dawson, *Racing Home – The Cutty Sark.* It is the majestic image of that British clipper ship that adorns the cover of this book.

In building *Dorine* I placed emphasis on achieving authentic detail throughout. Except for some manufactured items such as chain, cordage, and some of the power plant components, the model is entirely from scratch.

Fully animated, it has nineteen radio-controlled operating features that include Dixie and calliope music, triple rudder control, lighting throughout, horn and whistle sounds, gangway hoisting and running water in one washroom. The model is forty-eight inches long and fitted with a working, miniature steam power plant. The horizontal tandem reciprocating double engines are driven by 35 psi steam generated from a fire-tube boiler. The main throttle valve affords control from "full ahead" to "full astern." Special features include the use of real glass for ports and windows; 1,500 pieces of hand-laid deck planking; several furnished cabins with removable roofs to enable viewing; and a paddlewheel of 1,747 hand-crafted parts that are assembled in the same way as a full-scale paddlewheel. The aft cabin roof is removable to enable viewing of the furnished cabins, one of which has the running water. Other features, such as decorative gingerbread and hand-carved ornamentation, are my own creations.

Completed in 1995, the project, including research and design, took sixty-four hundred hours to complete, spanning eight years. A "Best of Show" winner on several occasions, the most rewarding aspect of the model is to see it operating on the lake with its steam engines puffing, stacks belching, paddlewheel churning, and its bow and wake formations looking just like the real thing.

†

In 1998 I presented a paper at the Nautical Research Guild Conference and the 2000 World Marine Millennial Conference in Salem, Massachusetts. The paper, titled "The Sinking and Modeling of the Ill-fated Sidewheeler Sultana," having to do with steamboats of the America's Western rivers, received national attention and inspired me to start thinking about my next ship model project.

One of the discussions at the conference centered around the concept of Manifest Destiny, i.e., the belief that the United States was destined to expand the Atlantic seaboard to the Pacific Ocean. It was explained as a guiding force in American history; it was the philosophy that created this nation. And come to think of it, it probably was much like the philosophy that drove Christopher Columbus across the Atlantic. On a much smaller scale I might even say it is what drove my grandparents and mother westward from Europe. They must have firmly believed that their destiny was linked to the New World and its promise of expanding fortunes.

The thing that got my juices going was the fact that the movement westward spawned the river steamboat. The success of a philosophy depended on it. I came away from the conference more enthralled by the steamboat than I was from building *Dorine*. I have to admit too that my maritime roots were egging me on. I could hear a voice saying, "Yes, Nick, this is where you belong." That echo helped convince me that there was no better way for me to capture that period of history than with another model of one of its workhorses, but this time a sidewheeler in the image of the legendary *Robert E. Lee*. (I wouldn't build her because she is a subject that has been built very often.) Had my grandfather been alive he would have thought it a great idea. Maybe it was his voice.

But which steamboat? The one that captured my imagination was the one that was associated with an incredible story—one of the greatest maritime tragedies in history, greater even than the *Titanic*, but far less known. On the frontier's rivers, speed was paramount—as revenues depended on how fast steamboat owners could deliver goods and passengers. For the purpose of maximizing speed, unscrupulous operators would often gag boiler safety valves, thereby enabling them to operate the boilers above safe working pressures. When the boiler or boilers exploded, the results were catastrophic. Boat and body parts would be found for miles around. Days later, dead bodies would wash up on the riverbanks.

The most notorious boiler explosion on our western rivers is that of the *Sultana,* a 260-foot sidewheel steamboat built in 1863. At two o'clock on the morning of April 27, 1865, just north of Memphis, Tennessee, three of her four boilers blew. First came the explosion, then the terrible ripping and tearing of wood and metal as the entire superstructure surrounding the boilers shattered, flinging charred bodies and material into the night sky. The intensity of the explosion drove live coal and splintered timber like shrapnel through the upper decks. The massive smoke stacks toppled like felled timber. Worst of all, scalding steam and boiling water burned, killed, and maimed passengers beyond recognition.

There was another dimension to the tragedy. The *Sultana,* which was registered to carry 376 passengers, was crowded with 2,400 Union soldiers, most of whom had been released from the infamous Confederate prison camp at Andersonville, Georgia. There was no room to lie down, or sufficient facilities to take care of bodily functions. Food was in short supply. Men were packed on decks so loaded they sagged in places. One man described it as worse than slave-ship conditions. At about 2:00 a.m. all these home-bound soldiers woke to the thundering noise of what must have seemed like a volcanic fury of exploding boilers. More than 1,700 of them died, making it the worst marine disaster in U.S. history, and one of the worst of all time. The number of deaths on the *Titanic*, forty-seven years later, was 1,522.

Two military boards were commissioned to investigate the loss of *Sultana.* Both reached similar conclusions in that excessive steam pressure, low water level, and poor repair and maintenance procedures were probably all contributing factors. After a farcical trial during which one officer was tried and found guilty, he was then exonerated because the office of the Judge Advocate General viewed his role as wholly subordinate. No one would ever be tried again, and no one would be punished for the loss of life—a whitewash all the way. In effect, the army absolved itself of any wrongdoing in the sacrifice of so many lives. Underlying all of these events was the smell of a cover-up. Everything that I have read suggests concerted efforts on the part of those responsible to obscure the greed, neglect, and sheer stupidity that led to the disaster. There was an attitude of the less said the better. Clearly this was not a proud chapter in American history.

The reasons for *Sultana* passing almost unnoticed into the pages of history can partially be explained by looking at the tumultuous events that rocked America at the time. Newspapers across the nation were still full of the Civil War, which had ended only weeks before the loss of *Sultana.* President Lincoln's death occurred nearly two weeks before it, not to mention John Wilkes Booth who was killed April 26, the day before the *Sultana* disaster. People were desperate for good news, and the *Sultana* and its tragic tale were relegated to the editors' wastebaskets. Moreover, the tragedy occurred in the West, far removed from the large newspapers in the East. The *New York Times* gave scant coverage of the event, and of course, there were no VIPs or generals on board.

The last survivor died in 1931. With his death the *Sultana* and her passengers became a mere footnote in the pages of American history.

With the loss of *Sultana*, and the political fiasco that followed, we were beginning to see in our nation the seeds of greed and corruption that in the following century would usher in an avalanche of political and corporate scandals that echoed through the halls of corporate America and Washington. For example, the Warren Commission would come to be known as a massive whitewash of the events surrounding the JFK assassination. And long before Watergate, there was the Teapot Dome oil reserve scandal. Presided over by the Harding administration, it is considered to be one of the most fascinating scandals of the twentieth century because it was so blatant, and was orchestrated by the highest members of his cabinet. These and many other scandals would rock the nation to its very foundation. They would become a bellwether of things to come in the twenty-first century when names like Madoff, Kozlowski (Tyco), and Blagojevich became household names. Yet, if we look at *Sultana*, and dissect the incident against today's standards, there is less chance of that type incident happening again. We are a more transparent society, quick to acknowledge and analyze our problems; then to find solutions and implement reform to minimize the risk of reoccurrence. There were lessons learned, and *Sultana* was the perfect *model.*

My model of *Sultana* is a work in progress, and remains so primarily because of the time demands in writing this memoir. It would be unforgivable of me not to finish this marvelous example of riverboat architecture on the Western rivers.

21

"HERE'S LOOKING AT YOU KID"

The capacity of Italians to create beauty is unparalleled.

—John Kuhn Bleimaier

It all started in Japan in the early 1970s, but not until many years later did I get back into another kind of modeling (besides my ships), and extend the hobby to include acting. I took classes, and then worked in community theater to gain experience. I was positioned to pursue even more of this work as I approached early retirement in 1997.

However, the prospect of getting out from under the corporate umbrella was a bit intimidating. After all, I had spent a lifetime of labor and purpose. But now I was moving into a new arena. I would still be the gladiator, but in an arena where both the spectators *and* I would be having fun. The stakes were only as high as the price of an admission ticket. And I would still be growing, but in a different direction, and that would add a new found purpose to my retirement. That was critically important, because I knew that when one stops growing, one stops living.

Living in Short Hills, New Jersey, I soon got involved with the Paper Mill Playhouse in nearby Millburn, and was in two of its stage productions, *Follies* and *An Ideal Husband.* In addition, there was background work in *The Departed, The Interpreter*, and ten episodes of the *Sopranos, Law & Order,* and *Rescue Me.* More importantly, I got to be the principal performer in numerous industrial promotional videos, commercials, and infomercials. The area where I had the most success was in print (modeling) work, in what is probably the most competitive market in the world—New York. I was cast mostly as a patient, dad, granddad, or businessman; the profile suggests I'm a rather sickly, fatherly, aging, professional. The best acting advice I ever got was from film director Sydney Pollack. He told several of us during a scene from *The Interpreter,* "Do not act." In other words, be natural. Guess we didn't get the message, because he didn't use the scene. Through it all I have met some fascinating people and been challenged by some of the work. For me, challenge is vitally important in anything I pursue. Otherwise I quickly lose interest.

The work I did was pretty much a mixed bag of challenges, laughs, gratification, and disappointment; mostly the latter. I jumped at the chance to do background work in *Angels in America*, an HBO film starring Al Pacino and Meryl Streep. As this kind of work is dull and certainly not challenging, I was inclined to turn it down. However, I accepted the two-day stint because it was a rare opportunity to see these two great actors, and Mike Nichols directing up close working live. As an added bonus they wanted to display my "Best-of-Show" winner, 1987 Mercedes-Benz 560SL red roadster on location in New York City. I would receive more for the use of my car than for my own work, and on the first day of shooting I found out that Al and Meryl were already finished shooting all their scenes. But I did meet Mike Nichols, an intelligent, plainspoken guy who is as much a gentleman as he is a professional. In later TV, stage, and film work I met such notables as Nicole Kidman, Cameron Diaz, most of *The Sopranos* and *Law & Order* principals, Tony Roberts, Susan Lucci, Ann Miller, Kaye Ballard, tennis star Maria Sharapova, and Stephen Sondheim.

One time, we were on set in a New York downtown restaurant doing a scene for a *Law & Order* episode. I was sitting at a table miming a conversation with my actress wife. Seated at a table next to us were the leads, Sam Waterston and Elisabeth Rohm. After the scene wrapped we all went outside for a break. The area was cordoned off, but a woman somehow got through and came running over to me with a pad and pen asking for an autograph. The only thing I could think was that she had mistaken me for one of the notables. I politely declined telling her that I was a *nobody*, just doing background work. Then she implored me to give her an autograph. Embarrassed, I again politely declined.

After she left, an actor who had heard the conversation came over to me and said, "Heck Nick, you should have given her the autograph. Some people just get their kicks doing that no matter who you are." I then began to feel a bit guilty about the incident. I looked over my shoulder thinking I might spot her, and maybe make amends. Sure enough, there she was standing with a friend behind me outside the cordoned area. I could hear her tell her friend, "You see that actor over there [pointing to me]? I asked him for his autograph and he refused. Imagine that ... And the lousy bum is a nobody."

†

Soon after, things got marginally better when I got another modeling job. This time they were looking for torsos. The description read, THE SHOT WILL MOST LIKELY BE UNRECOGNIZABLE—JUST OF THE TORSO. CLIENT IS LOOKING FOR BOTH AVERAGE AND FIT SENIORS. With my six-pack flab, they must have considered me the average one. I got the job and $300 for two and a half hours' *work.* A far cry from the stuff I was doing in Japan, but in New York everybody starts from the bottom. I needed to learn patience because success does not come easy in this business, if at all. For encouragement I only need to look to my nephew, David Goldman (my sister's son), a singer, songwriter, and producer (www.DavidGoldman.com). He has been toiling at his craft for approximately thirty-five years, and achieved the success that he has only after many years in the business.

In April 1998 I appeared in the production of *Follies,* staged at the Paper Mill Playhouse. It was an elaborate revival of the 1971 musical with a cast of approximately thirty performers. Hollywood tap dancing legend Ann Miller co-starred in the same show performing the role of Carlotta Champion, who like Ann is a movie star well past her heyday. For that reason Ann sounded so sincere when she sang the showstopper "I'm Still Here," the anthem to survival in show business. It was a thrill for us to view a private showing in her hotel suite of the film *Easter Parade* in which she starred with Fred Astaire and Judy Garland.

When the show closed I had the good fortune to get a hug and an autographed photograph from her. Unfortunately Ms. Miller is no longer with us, but her legend certainly is.

I was elated when an agent called and asked me to audition to be Kirk Douglas's stand-in for a forthcoming movie. Finally, he was going to do a long-overdue screen pairing with his son Michael in *It Runs in the Family* (2003). A stand-in occupies an actor's space during rehearsals and acts out scenes while the scene is being blocked. During blocking, movements of the performers and mobile filming equipment are charted. When I asked the agent, "Why me?" she said I had a similar build and could hopefully convey his type of athleticism. I went to the audition during which they took a load of photos from every possible angle using a variety of clothing and shoes. In the end, some other guy got the part.

I got lucky when I landed a modeling job that paid $7,000, less a 20 percent agency fee, for three and a half hours' work. It may sound as though there is a lot of money in this kind of work, but that's true only if you get a lot of work, which only the big names do. For most of us, the big paychecks are few and far between, and if I had to earn a living at it I would starve. But this job had a slight twist to it. The client required that I agree not to do another commercial for another pharmaceutical company for a similar product for two years. If you are a busy model-actor, that could be a drawback, because you are in effect depriving yourself of other potential income. In my case, it was a no-brainer. I took the money and ran. After the two years were up they came back and extended the contract for another year. I received $3,500, less 20 percent, and all I had to do was sign another agreement with the same exclusivity clause. During the three years, I never had to walk away from a job because of it.

It was not until September 2007 that I hit the jackpot. I got my first Screen Actors Guild (SAG) job wherein I would be receiving residuals for as long as the client ran the commercial. In this case the client was a major U.S. bank who would be going national with the ad on TV, websites, and publications. The shoot took two and a half hours, and the commercial could run on and off for months, maybe years, thereby generating thousands of dollars. The real payoff was that, as a principal performer, I was then eligible for SAG membership, the most distinguished performers' union in the world. Most performers consider receipt of a SAG card to be a milestone in their professional careers. In 2008, SAG and the Alliance of Motion Picture and Television Producers became bogged down for nearly a year in negotiations over a new contract. Having joined the American Federation of Television and Radio Artists (AFTRA) six years earlier, I was content to sit on the sidelines waiting for the ramifications of a new SAG contract before joining. A few months after the April 2009 settlement, I happily nestled the SAG feather in my cap, thus becoming a full-fledged, dues paying member.

For a brief period, I thought my screen hobby might become something more—because at the end of 2007, a major cruise ship company was seeking actors to do a commercial that was to be filmed on board one of the luxury passenger vessels. The intersection between my hobby and the love of my life, the maritime world, seemed to be some kind of sign. The lucky actors would be flown to Italy to join the vessel. They would then ride the vessel to England, stopping at ports of call en route. All the filming and print work would be done on board during the passage. Upon arrival in the U.K., the performers would be flown home. This would be a two-week, all-expenses-paid trip, including a nominal per diem. Add to that a fee of $9,500 for each performer, and you have a job to die for. The company was looking to cast two couples, and approximately one hundred guys showed up for the audition. That gives you an idea of the odds against getting the job.

I got a call-back. The producers, et al., were down to the last two, maybe three guys and couldn't quite make a decision. So they had me come in to audition again. I went, and I gave it my best shot, and I came up empty. It took me months to get over that one. I still do a slow burn when I think of it. As is often said in the business, you have to learn to live with rejection—and I do, but it's not easy especially for someone as vain as I am.

All told, I learned you had to expect nothing. I had my family and my health, a rewarding career behind me, and my retirement in front of me. Any successes in show business were just gravy. From that perspective, I could appreciate what was most fascinating about the hobby—the glimpses into lives so different from mine. For instance, I landed a job as Ben Gazarra's stand-in for a short film he did with Lauren Bacall. Working with these two giants of stage, screen, and TV was an amazing experience. The most amazing part was to see the poise demonstrated by Natalie Portman, who was directing the film. At twenty-seven years old, she was directing two stars, who together could boast 120 years of professional acting experience. How intimidating is that? Even so, this talented young actor-director pulled it off beautifully. The job didn't pay much, but if the truth were known I would have done it for nothing. During the shoot I reminded Ms. Bacall that we had met when she came backstage after a *Follies* performance. Not surprisingly, she didn't remember me.

Celebrities weren't the only perk. Community theater and the thousands of people across the country dedicated to its survival make an important contribution to our culture. Many are talented enough to perform at the professional level. However, they are not motivated by money or fame, only passion for the theater, and they give of their talent without any financial gain. I was a part of one such group and saw firsthand the talent not only of actors, but of those unsung heroes behind the scenes—the set designers, stage hands, wardrobe and makeup artists, lighting and sound technicians. Without their talent and effort, performers could not do what they need to do, nor could community theater survive.

†

No discussion about show business would be complete without a word about that dreaded affliction, stage fright. I think most have had it in our lives. I certainly had it at an early age, and the one thing I found that helps more than anything else is to do more and more performing. The more you get up in front of people in any assemblage, the more comfortable you will feel over time. And that's true whether it is on stage in front of an audience, at a business presentation, or in front of a church group. The other thing I find helpful is to do relaxation and breathing exercises before "going on." Clearly, the more relaxed you are, the better will be the performance. Some of the biggest professionals like Barbra Streisand, and Rod Stewart get stage fright. Even Richard Burton, and Laurence Olivier used to get it. And what I am saying about stage fright should not be confused with ordinary pre-performance anxiety, which can actually be a good source of energy as it keeps the adrenalin flowing.

I saw stage fright first hand in a community theater production wherein the male lead, a priest, had to get down on one knee and deliver a monologue. There were five of us on stage at the time. He froze in that position without a word coming out of his mouth. Moments later somebody threw him a line, but still nothing. What heightened his predicament was that he was downstage, center, with footlights in his face, while looking directly into the faces of the audience, who waited, and waited. Then we heard him murmur, "What should I do?" The stage manager then rushed out onto the stage. Just as he reached the actor, the poor guy tossed up his dinner. SPLATTER. It hit the stage and sprayed a few people in the front row. It hit one of the footlights, which exploded, thereby adding unrehearsed fireworks to the show. Poor guy—I thought, *There but for the grace of God go I.*

The next night he went on and knocked them dead. After the show and a few drinks at a nearby eatery, we lifted our glasses on high and said to him jokingly, "Here's Puking at You Kid!"

22

AMERICA STANDS TALL

America will never be destroyed from the outside. If we falter and lose our freedoms, it will be because we destroyed ourselves.

—President Abraham Lincoln

I had fantasized about owning a boat for as long as I can remember. Problem was that for many years I couldn't afford one. Later when I could afford it, I didn't have the time for it, given all the business travel I was doing. Even more inhibiting was the fact that I lived overseas on-and-off for a total of eleven years. Finally, as I approached retirement, I said to myself: *If I don't do it now, I'll never do it.*

I semi-retired in 1997, and in the winter of 1998 purchased my first power boat, a thirty-four-foot cabin cruiser that I named *Mon Tresor*. No, the name is not derived from the protagonist, Montresor, of Edgar Allen Poe's classic horror story, "The Cask of Amontillado." Given my love of the French language I knew I wanted to give my boat a French name, but what? Since my daughter Dorine and my daughter-in-law Suzanne had both studied French in high school, I asked them for ideas. They came up with quite a few, but the one I favored was Suzanne's *tresor*, meaning treasure. How appropriate was that? I added the *mon* to arrive at the name *Mon Tresor*, my treasure. Two boats and thirteen years later I now own a forty-four-foot yacht named *Mon Tresor III* and she's got all those wonderful gadgets I dreamed of as a kid, and then some. My dream had finally come true.

†

With that dream came some humorous incidents. One was a tough docking for my neighbor at the marina, thanks to the prevailing wind and current. As I stood at the dockside waiting to help with his lines, he told his mate to jump ashore as soon as possible to get a line on a cleat. She did exactly as she was told, launching herself like a gazelle when the boat was about eight feet from the dock. The problem was that she was holding five feet of dock line tightly in her hand. When she reached the end of the line (literally), she stopped cartoon-like in midair and dropped straight into the water, which complicated the docking even more. Later she said, "I was infuriated because the SOB didn't even jump in after me—the boat was more important." I can relate!

In another incident, a neighbor moved his yacht forward out of the slip after casting off everything except the shore power cord. As his 25-ton yacht moved out, the cord stretched like a rubber band until it tore out the dockside power terminal, resulting in a brilliant display of fireworks and a cloud of smoke. Sorry to say, that ended their plans for a lovely day of cruising.

†

I did plenty of sailing in my boat. I had plenty of fun times and fun adventures. But there was one day when the boat would be more: I would be willing to put her in service of her country.

Like every American, I will never forget where I was and what I was doing on September 11, 2001. I had just arrived at the field where our softball team was scheduled to play a game. As soon as I got there I was told the Twin Towers had been hit. I immediately used my cell phone to call my daughter-in-law, Suzanne, who was commuting in to New York City. Surprisingly, I was able to get through, at which time she told me she had seen one of the Towers hit just before her train dipped into the tunnel. For the moment she was stranded at Penn Station, as all public transportation had come to a standstill. At least she was safe.

I immediately went home and turned on the TV. By that time both towers were down and we were all beginning to realize the gravity of the situation. It then occurred to me that perhaps I could be of assistance by offering my boat, located in Jersey City directly across from lower Manhattan, to evacuate people. I called the marina's dock master, who was grateful for the offer but assured me that for the moment they had enough commercial boats evacuating people. I drove to the marina and almost gave up because all the major roads were closed. However, I knew enough of the back roads to finally reach the marina, which by now had turned into an armed camp. I called the dock master again to let him know I was in the marina and readily available. The eleven adjacent acres were turned into a triage area to offer assistance to evacuees. The grounds were so thick with emergency vehicles of every sort from every town in New Jersey, that you could barely see a blade of grass. As it turned out, virtually none of the medical equipment was used. For the most part, people either perished or survived without serious injuries. The few survivors who I did see trickle through the marina after disembarking from rescue boats were—judging from their ghost-like faces—in shock. When I asked one woman what it was like over there, she said, "Now I know what hell is like!"

When I boarded my boat I looked across the Hudson River to where the Twin Towers once stood. I was frozen by the sight of the billowing smoke and the fire's red glare. That evening the sound of wailing sirens and the kaleidoscope of twinkling lights blending with the flames made a ghastly and unforgettable sight. I felt a terrible ache in my heart. I thought to myself, *How could this have happened? Is it really happening?* I slept on board *Mon Tresor II* hoping I would awaken from the nightmare. I stepped out on deck the next morning to witness the horrible reality that the towers were indeed gone. I saw it with my own eyes, and I still don't know how it could have happened.

†

The event was to become a symbol of the new millennium. And even though there were terrorist acts in the United States and elsewhere before 9/11, I think for most of us, 9/11 represents the real beginning of the war on terrorism. Down the road it will serve as a test of our great national strength, and hopefully bring us closer together.

I saw evidence of that closeness immediately following the tragedy. It was a delight to see people come together as never before to help one another and to offer that extra measure of kindness. You saw it at the supermarket, on the roads, in the parks ... Virtually everywhere. I marveled at it during trips into New York City. Wouldn't it be wonderful if we could always maintain that kind of spirit?

I also saw evidence, sadly, that there was no going back. I thought of my days on these very same waters as a young lad when we would overnight on my father's boat and anchor off the Jersey City shoreline behind the Statue of Liberty to go crabbing. The catch was typically two or three bushels of New Jersey's finest "blue claws," some measuring six inches tip to tip. I never recall having been stopped by a U.S. Coast Guard vessel. That is a far cry from post-9/11. Nowadays, if you get within three hundred feet of the statue, you'll be warned off by police or USCG boats.

Another time, Suzanne, Benjamin, Brian, and I had spent the night on my boat at the marina. The next morning we decided to cruise up river. No sooner had we gotten underway when a USCG vessel hailed us down and boarded us. Security was so tight they had orders to board and inspect every other pleasure boat. And on another occasion, a few of us sailed up river thinking it would be a great idea to anchor and stay overnight. What better place to be on a hot summer night? No sooner had we fallen asleep when we heard a loud-hailer requesting permission to board us. The inspection was routine, and the Coast Guard boarding team was courteous, but the message was clear and symbolic—best move on. I'm reminded of the symbolism when I reflect on the memorable lyrics from Simon & Garfunkel's "Mrs. Robinson":

Where have you gone, Joe DiMaggio
Our nation turns its lonely eyes to you
What's that you say Mrs. Robinson
Joltin' Joe has left and gone away.

Most of us know people who were personally touched by the disaster either directly or indirectly. A neighbor of mine at the marina worked on the seventy-second floor of one of the towers. On September 10th he had returned from a business trip late that evening. So late in fact that he slept late on the morning of the 11th, something out of character for him. Fate was on his side, for the act saved his life. If he had been in his office the usual time, around 8:00 a.m., he would have perished.

Several years after 9/11, I was reminded of how profoundly terrorism has permeated the world we live in. I read a newspaper article stating that eight men with alleged links to senior al Qaeda terrorists were arrested in Copenhagen. I couldn't believe it—riots in Denmark, which is probably the most peaceful, safest and civilized country on the planet. Studies consistently show their quality of life to be among the highest in the world. For that reason I used to look forward to traveling there on business, which I was doing quite often while living in London. I have never met a Dane I didn't like—warm, personable, honest, unpretentious and professional. Perhaps that makes them even more vulnerable. I asked myself, *What in God's name is the world coming to?* With the arrests, the local authorities claim to have foiled a major terrorist attack. Clearly, something is rotten in Denmark, and it's not in Hamlet's

Kronborg Castle at Elsinore, but it is enough to make you think that perhaps a nuclear Armageddon is coming.

In spite of 9/11 and the terrorist activity since then, I know we shall prevail. Of our American traits, the one I admire the most is our resilience in the face of the most severe adversity. Somehow we always manage to pick ourselves up, reassess, adjust, and do whatever it takes to bounce back even if it means reinventing ourselves. The best examples I can think of are the ways in which the country reacted in the aftermath of the Vietnam War and 9/11. This is a quality not common to all countries.

Another admirable trait is that we firmly believe anything is possible. I believe the “anything is possible” attitude is one of the main reasons my grandparents, as well as millions of others, immigrated to this country. In a social and political sense there is nothing we cannot change or achieve. Consider Barack Obama’s election to the presidency. No matter what one’s politics are, his is a vision for change that has not only captured the American imagination, but the world’s. There is no denying that black-white race relations have improved dramatically in the past two centuries. In addition, I think his being elected has done more to improve those relations than any other single event in American history. Now, let’s hope and pray he succeeds in fulfilling the promise of real change, while shouldering the enormous burden the world has placed on his shoulders. Wouldn’t it be a marvelous twist of fate if President Barack Obama stepped out from the shadow of Abraham Lincoln, to help do for the oppressed of the world what Lincoln did for African Americans?

Lastly, we have an enormous drive to succeed—to be the best, to win, to lead, to invent, and in the process, be respected. Our history proves that. Sometimes, however, we need to temper that drive or it can turn into counterproductive greed. I'm afraid our history proves that too. Who can forget the corporate fraud and moral corruption associated with Enron, Arthur Anderson, AIG? Consider Imclone's stock trading improprieties, too. Let's face it—there's no easier way to make or lose money than in the stock market. We do not need corporate improprieties adding further risk and volatility. The apparent demonization of corporate America continues right up to the present day with the government's near-$800 billion stimulus package passed in 2009. That bailout—sorry, *rescue*—for the country's leading financial institutions, although not a cure-all for all of the long-term economic problems, will help mitigate the impact while helping most families to get near-term tax breaks, especially with regard to home and car buying. Most would agree the need for a bailout and greater fiscal responsibility was brought on by corporate greed and mismanagement. Insofar as moral corruption, do Watergate and Chappaquiddick ring a bell? Ever hear of the *Sultana*?

All told, however, there is such a thing as the American spirit, and a sense of fair play. Justice will be served. And it would be for the European immigrant. I need look no further than the plight of the those immigrants, like my grandparents and mother, who, upon marching onto American soil through the hallowed gates of Ellis Island found social injustice, poverty, and discrimination. Nevertheless, they not only endured, but rose to achieve unparalleled success and make enormous contributions to the American spirit and culture. In peace and war, they gave unselfishly, and upon gaining success, eventually found justice in their cause. The thing I find compelling is that there was rarely a compulsion to extract revenge for their plight. Now, as I look back on the New York where I grew up and compare it to today's New York, I am proud to say that we are the fortunate benefactors of that forlorn journey now so long ago.

23

TIME TO GIVE SOMETHING BACK

> *These 58,226 answered their country's call without asking why. Thinking of their supreme sacrifice always brings a tear to my eye. At The Wall, people stand and cry, paying tribute to their man. I'd like to think he hears them... maybe he can...just maybe he can.*
>
> —Harry E. Gilleland, from "The Wall"

In December 2002, Mom died. She left a void in my life that can never be filled. Other than knowing she is in a better place, the only other consolation in her death was the certainty that I had no regrets about our relationship. Often in life we hear of children who, after a parent passes, regret not having patched up an estranged relationship, or simply not having said, "I love you." After all, hadn't I made that mistake with *my* father? I was cognizant of this while she was alive and made every effort to ensure I would not feel that kind of guilt once she had passed. One of the ways

I did this was to visit her every Wednesday—that was "her day," so to speak. I'd go into Brooklyn, run her errands, do her shopping, take her out for a while, and do all of the things that needed doing around the house. My sister Anne performed a similar function every Monday. (My brother Tony was living in Charlottesville, Virginia, at the time.)

To Mom the most important thing that needed doing was for her to remain in a state of grace. That meant receiving the Body and Blood of Christ on a regular basis. So we made arrangements with her parish for a Minister of Communion to bring her Communion, or, I would bring the consecrated Host to her in a pyx. When I think of her, I will always think of the image of my *Mother Teresa* kneeling, reverently receiving communion in her home.

However, the image I remember most is the last one. The end came shortly after surgery for a broken hip that she sustained from a fall in the bathroom. At the age of ninety-six—yes ninety-six—she had little choice other than to have surgery. The rehabilitation period, which included exhaustive physical therapy, was agonizing for her. For the first time, I saw her lose the will to live. The rehabilitation center called and said she refused to eat. My sister Anne and I visited to try and feed her, but she declined. She actually refused to open her mouth. I was struck by how at ease she seemed to be, the serenity in her face—as if she had made her peace with the Lord. As the three of us wept, kissed, and hugged just before leaving, she nodded slightly as if to say, *It's OK, I'm ready for the Lord.* The next day, she was gone.

†

Soon after she died I decided to do volunteer work, which I had been putting off since retirement. After so much help along the way—from my family during my youth, mentors during my service days, colleagues at work, and from everyone during the time of Nicky's death and my divorce—I had a strong feeling that it was time to give something back. In 2003 I interviewed at several locations, but had no difficulty in deciding to work at the VA Hospital in East Orange, New Jersey. My attitude was pretty straightforward—motivated by simple altruism I would do anything they asked me to do. We talked about working on the floors in support of doctors and nurses; teaching basic computer and math skills; assisting veterans with their paperwork to register for health care; and working as a guide to help veterans get around the hospital, especially those in wheelchairs. And yes, I was even willing to sweep floors if that's where they needed me. However, they gave me the job of curator/docent at the New Jersey Veteran's Museum, which was located at the hospital. The other regular duty I was later asked to do was to serve on the Ethics Committee. Other than that, I would be frequently asked to take on a variety of other projects.

Working at the hospital, I began to notice a phenomenon with regard to the proportion of wounded to dead American soldiers in Iraq. According to one report,

> The thing that really distinguishes this conflict is how many soldiers *don't* die, but suffer appalling injuries. In Vietnam and Korea, about three Americans were wounded for every one who died. The ratio in WWII was nearly 2:1. In Iraq, 16 soldiers are wounded or get sick for

> every one who dies. The increasing ratio marks progress: better body armor and helmets are shielding more soldiers from fatal wounds. And advanced emergency care is keeping more of the wounded alive. The military has done a great job with pushing technology, training and medical personnel so far forward in the battlefield that they are able to save more lives. Soldiers who survive the first few minutes of an explosion and make it to the hospital alive have a 96 percent survival rate.

That's great, but there's a downside to this progress. It is the realization that many of the survivors lead lives of quiet desperation, not only because of their physical injuries, but also because of the social and psychological implications. On one occasion I talked with a doctor at the hospital who told me of a patient who lost three limbs and had brain damage resulting from action in Iraq. His standard of living, as well as that of others who suffer similar massive injuries, has been compromised. In some cases, physical disabilities are complicated by the further realization that nearly one in five veterans who served in Iraq and Afghanistan suffer from post-traumatic stress disorder. Some might consider life intolerable. I have asked myself, W*ould I want to go on living in such a condition? Would my life be productive?* Some believe in the sanctity of life under any circumstance; that where there is life there is hope. It is a dilemma with no easy answers, because we all have different values and expectations. We have different levels of tolerance and vary widely in our faith. What is certain is that medical technology will continue to evolve and improve, as it should. In all probability it will result in a further increase in the wounded-to-dead ratio. The end result will be veterans who become more and more incapacitated, and therefore less able to lead productive lives without assistance from family and health care workers.

While there are no easy answers, each handicapped veteran is left to decide in his or her own way how to best get on with their lives while preserving some measure of dignity. He or she may be thankful for survival, but will have to reconcile that with a lifestyle that requires a great deal of faith, hope, and forbearance.

Notwithstanding the enormous risks of military service, these wonderful young people keep coming forward to serve our nation. They are probably the most dedicated, best-equipped, and best-trained combat units this country has ever put in the field. I talk with them nearly every time I go to the hospital. Their spirit is undeniable. Their dedication is beyond reproach. They serve out of a sense of duty. They are still willing to walk in harm's way to make a difference and to make the sacrifices we ask of them. Will they ever reach a point where they lose faith in our national leadership and refuse to defend our interests? I doubt it.

And that is why it is so important that our government continue to act in good faith to earnestly work for peace in settling international disputes, and that armed conflict be utilized only as a last desperate resort. It is equally important that the government and each of us in our own way create an image of America that will generate friends, not enemies. We need to make more friends who will stand by us, not because of our power or material wealth, but because they respect our values and what we stand for. We need to urgently find a way to win over the angry young men in the Muslim world who seem hell-bent on destroying our way of life, because we owe it to the wellbeing and future of our citizenry and all who serve.

†

My work at the VA Hospital has rekindled a long-standing sore spot with me, especially after having come in contact with many Vietnam veterans. You may recall that in chapter seven, "The Navy of My Youth," I talked about "what might have been," referring to what it might have been like to serve in Vietnam. The post-Vietnam experience would have been disappointing, given the deplorable treatment afforded veterans upon returning home; and the veterans I met in the hospital confirmed my supposition.

I wonder how I would have felt if in passing through an airline terminal in uniform, a woman spat on me yelling out, "You baby-killer." I wonder how I would have reacted to the elderly gent who walked up to me at a train station and said, "You're a disgrace to that uniform." Returning veterans were being told to take their uniforms off when they got stateside, as things weren't going well for anyone who wore it. Unlike their World War II brethren, they were not being hailed as returning heroes.

Such treatment still remains a terrible wound in the psyche of this country. We know the war was an unpopular one—not that any war can be popular. For many Americans it was a war fought for a questionable cause. What aggravates the hell out of me, though, is that the American people took out their frustration on their military. Don't misunderstand me. No one should deny our right to oppose the war—any war. But we do it by demonstrating, by writing to our politicians, by supporting antiwar groups, by voting for antiwar candidates, and if need be, by screaming our fool heads off from the rooftops. We do not do it by abusing the men and women who are sent in harm's way to defend our lifestyle. They are merely doing their jobs. And in so doing, they have every right to be given our full support, especially in the case of Vietnam, where our soldiers bested the Vietnam military on the battlefield every time out. And we certainly don't do it by going to Hanoi in the despicable and treasonous way Jane Fonda did in 1972, giving support to the enemy.

In recent years Jane Fonda has been pushing her autobiography, and on the talk show circuit the subject of Vietnam invariably comes up. She expresses regret with a less-than-convincing argument: poor judgment. The woman should have been tried for treason for giving aid and comfort to the enemy while they were killing our people in the field. Who can ever forget that shot of Hanoi Jane sitting on a North Vietnamese anti-aircraft gun that was used against American aircrews? While in Hanoi she participated in several radio broadcasts on behalf of the Communist regime. That was fitting, I guess, for someone who was quoted as telling a student audience at Michigan State University in 1969, "I would think that if you understood what communism was, you would hope, you would pray on your knees, that we would someday become communist." When cases of torture began to emerge among prisoners of war (POWs) returning to the United States, future U.S. Senator John McCain among them, she called the POWs "hypocrites and liars." Notwithstanding what many of us characterized as treason, the Nixon Administration dismissed calls for legal action against her, probably because the notoriety would have done more damage than good to the national image. To pour salt in the wound, Barbara Walters had the audacity to *honor* Fonda as one of the "100 Women of the Century." In my view that was an affront to the other 99.

It doesn't take a historian to recognize that our withdrawal from Vietnam was a political defeat, not a military one. The war was lost at home due to a lack of public support. A brilliant and highly respected leader of the North Vietnam military, General Giap wrote in his memoirs: "What we still don't understand is why you Americans stopped the bombing of Hanoi. You had us on the ropes. If you had pressed a little harder, just for another day or two, we were ready to surrender! It was the same at the battles of the Tet Offensive. You defeated us! We knew it, and thought you knew it. But we were elated to notice your media was definitely helping us. They were causing more disruption in America than we could in the battlefields. We were ready to surrender. You had won!!" To me, this demonstrates the enormous power of a biased media to cut out the people's heart and will.

†

Judging from our recent involvement in Iraq and Afghanistan, we seemed to have learned a hard and valuable lesson. Again we are involved with a controversial political and military agenda. This time, however, our military personnel are receiving our full support, negative public opinion notwithstanding. But we are still subjected to a biased media, this time criticizing government policy and its miscalculation about the existence of weapons of mass destruction (WMD's). Many feel we should not be there because WMD's have not been found. We keep hearing and reading an extraordinary amount of media hype condemning the Bush administration for telling us there were WMD's, when in fact there were none. While that is a fair criticism, there is very little balance in the news. For example, very little is said about the positive outcomes of the war. After all, the war with Iraq gave freedom to 50 million people and decapitated Saddam Hussein, a murderous, Hitler-like tyrant who murdered millions of his own people and gave every indication of killing millions more. That is a very worthwhile achievement. Sure, the causes of the wars in Iraq and Afghanistan are many and controversial—oil, big business, sectarian strife, and the capture of Osama bin Laden, to mention a few. But even now, as fighting escalates into Afghanistan, our main goal in maintaining a military presence in the region is, first and foremost, to combat terrorism. In so doing, I believe it is imperative to continue that fight on their home turf now, be it Afghanistan, Iraq or any other rogue state, like Iran. Otherwise there is the risk of having to fight it on our home turf, later. Nobody wants another 9/11.

I feel deeply for the Vietnam veterans, salute them, and regret they did not get the full measure of support they so justly deserved. When we stand at The Wall, that cold black granite memorial, and touch it—we feel your pain. We see your tears. We sense your spirit crying out for praise and recognition. We feel your anguish, as that of a child unjustly punished who cries out, "Why?" And so in this small and humble way we offer a belated "thank you" for serving. The heroic sacrifices you made were not in vain and shall never be forgotten. May God bless each and every one of you, and may your 58,226 brothers and sisters who never came home rejoice in God's kingdom.

While my initial hopes at the hospital were met, I find myself welcoming more responsibility. I spent an entire career working worldwide in the maritime field. Yet, nowhere have I met a more dedicated, courteous, and professional group of people than I have at the hospital—the well from which these veterans can draw optimism, healing, and hope for the future.

My work was—and still is—humble. Outside of my family it is the most important thing I do with my life these days. The gratification is immeasurable. The biggest return is the satisfaction that goes with giving. I feel it every time I complete a job at the VA hospital. I feel it every time I shake the hand of a veteran who is near the end of his life, because it shows me that people out of the public eye still need compassion. I feel it whenever I give a talk to a group of visiting youngsters at the hospital about the sacrifices veterans have made, and the importance of never forgetting those sacrifices. I feel it every time I thank a veteran for sticking his neck out to save mine. I feel it every time the people I work with give me a smile, my annual U.S. flag lapel pin, and say, "Thanks, Nick, for being here. Thanks for making a difference." The feeling is something eternal, something enduring I can hold on to.

24

BACK TO THE SANDS OF IWO JIMA

In the shadows of Mount Suribachi,
Where crosses mark our dead,
We read the names of our buddies,
And stand with bended head.

—Harry Claassen, from "From a Foxhole on Iwo"

On March 12, 2005, we mustered in the lobby of our hotel in Guam at 4:00 a.m. for our flight and one-day visit to Iwo Jima (Sulfur Island). Finally, after years of anticipation I was to retrace the steps of those heroes, who sixty years ago were engaged in the most savage battle in Marine Corps history. It would also be a way for me to retrace some of the steps of Uncle Pete, who for three years fought his way through the jungle islands of the South Pacific. It would also give me a glimpse of the wretched jungles where our cousin Pete contracted the malaria that would eventually take his life.

For Marines it is a visit to *Mecca*. It is where all Marines aspire to visit once in their lives. This was not to be a victory celebration of the battle, but a dignified memorial to honor the men, Japanese as well as American, who fought and died here. This would be a time for healing, for remembrance and for brotherhood. The order of the day was to treat the island, presently inhabited by approximately four hundred Japanese troops, as hallowed ground. Our group was made up of roughly 450 people including approximately seventy-five veterans who fought in the battle. In addition, there was a contingent from Washington, D.C., including the Marine Corps Commandant, politicians, and other VIPs.

Surprising how different the island looked from the sulfuric smelling chunk of craggy, volcanic terrain I had read about and seen in photos. Surprising too was the tranquility of the sulfuric mists that still spiraled out of the earth. Its interior is thick with thorny foliage and mostly covered with vegetation—a result of having been seeded by U.S. Air Force drops on the island shortly after World War II. Shrapnel still litters the ground, and we were informed that unexploded shells remain a hazard.

I found it hard to imagine the carnage here sixty years ago. The Marines landed February 19, 1945. The Americans who went to Iwo Jima knew it would be a tough fight, but they always believed they'd win. The Japanese were told they wouldn't come home; they were being sent to die for the Emperor. The standing order from their commanding officer was for each man to take ten American lives. After thirty-six days of battle, American casualties were 25,851. Of those, 6,825 were killed in action. More Marines (27) earned the Medal of Honor here than during any other battle. More Marines (110,000) were sent to Iwo Jima, barely ten square miles in size, than to any other battle in Corps history. Nearly all of the 22,000 Japanese on the island fought to their deaths.

Once on the island we were free to move about on foot or by making use of the military vehicles put at our disposal by a contingent of Marines who were sent down from Okinawa to look after our group. We were able to visit the airfields, landing beaches, memorial sites, Mount Suribachi, naval gun emplacements, Japanese bunkers, General Kuribayashi's HQ, numerous caves, and more. At noon we attended the memorial service (Reunion of Honor) and wreath-laying ceremony at the joint memorial that overlooks the main landing beach. The service was attended by a contingent of approximately one hundred Japanese including a handful of veterans from the battle, former Prime Minister Yoshiro Mori, and Mr. Yoshitaka Shinda, the grandson of General Tadamichi Kuribayashi. The service was solemn and dignified, and as the then-Commandant, General Michael W. Hagee, closed his remarks I heard a familiar refrain. It was from President Lincoln's Gettysburg Address: "The world will little note, nor long remember, what we say here, but it can never forget what they did here." It was remarkable to see former adversaries, on the site of such a bitter struggle, jointly hold a commemoration ceremony and genuinely wish for everlasting friendship and eternal peace together.

There were so many memorable moments for me during this trip. I will never forget the sight of those Marine veterans eagerly searching for the exact spot where they landed, or fought, or got hit, or where their buddy got hit. Some wept. Others earnestly hugged each other as the images of sixty years ago came flooding back so vividly. For most, this was their first trip back.

Sometimes we don't realize what these men did—these skinny kids out of the Depression who joined the service. The average age of enlistees was nineteen. Among the group was Pfc. Jack H. Lucas whom I had the privilege of meeting. Jack had defied all odds. A big kid for his age at fourteen, he begged his mother to enlist in the Marines after Pearl Harbor. She collaborated in lying about his age in return for his promise to someday finish school. He turned seventeen when he hit the beach, and a day later, February 20, was fighting in a Japanese trench when a grenade landed at his feet. He had just mashed it into the sand with his rifle when another grenade rolled in near his comrades. He then threw himself onto the grenades and absorbed the explosions to protect those around him. It's what Marines do. He was blown into the air by the two explosions. Everyone assumed he was dead and moved forward. Later a medic, assuming he was dead, was about to take his dog tag when he saw Jack's finger twitch. Eventually, he underwent twenty-two operations, lost a lung and lived with more than twenty pieces of shrapnel in his body. After months of rehabilitation, he returned to school as he'd promised his mother, a ninth-grader wearing a Medal of Honor around his neck. He had become the youngest Medal of Honor recipient of World War II. At seventy-seven, Jack was the youngest Iwo veteran in our group.

I talked with another Iwo vet who told me a similar story. He too had pounced on a grenade to save his buddies. He lived to tell about it simply because the grenade was a dud. Many of us have seen these kinds of heroic acts in movies, but thought it nothing more than Hollywood fantasy. It took this experience for me to realize it really did and does happen.

I was reminded of this while listening to President Bush's speech during a ceremony marking the opening of the National Museum of the Marine Corps on November 10, 2006. He described how Marine Cpl. Jason Dunham died from wounds suffered in Iraq after using his body and helmet to save two fellow Marines from an insurgent's grenade. He went on to announce to an audience of about 10,000, including Dunham's parents, that Cpl. Dunham would be awarded the nation's highest decoration, the Medal of Honor, to be presented to his parents at the White House. This account reminded me too that the Marine spirit lives on and always will as long as there is a Corps. A Marine is expected not only to give his life for his country if called to do so, but also be willing to lay down his life for the Marine next to him. It is the code by which they live.

†

It is very hard to describe the sensation one feels standing atop Mount Suribachi looking out over the island. It is even more difficult to describe standing on the very spots where the first and second flag raisings took place. I let my imagination run wild with visions of the landing and subsequent struggle. From here I could see all the way to the pristine black-sand beaches embraced by the blue Pacific Ocean. The scene filled me with awe.

This was sacred ground and a fraught site for the Marines who had been on the island when those flags went up. As the Japanese had honeycombed the mountain with gun positions, observation sites, and tunnels the capture of Mount Suribachi was a formidable mission. From all accounts I have read, that task was left to a forty-man patrol that on February 23 successfully fought their way to the summit under the most deplorable conditions. Part of the enduring drama of the Suribachi flag-raising was the fact that so many people observed it. Marines all over the island could see the patrol during its ascent. Likewise, hundreds of binoculars from the nearly five hundred ships offshore watched the Marines climbing ever upward.

Finally they reached the top and raised a 28 by 54 inch flag for all to see. Suddenly the Stars and Stripes fluttered bravely. Lusty cheers rang out from all over the island. The ships sounded their sirens and whistles. From one account, wounded men propped themselves up on their litters to glimpse the sight. Strong men wept unashamedly. As the flag was thought to be too small to be seen throughout the island, a second larger flag was raised to more cheers three hours later by another patrol. Another account suggests the second flag-raising was done because the Secretary of the Navy demanded to have the first flag as a souvenir. Whatever the reason, it is that second photo of the flag-raising that became the most famous picture ever taken in any war. It came to immortalize the bitter battle and symbolize the Marine fighting spirit. It is still the single-most recognizable icon of Marine Corps valor. Its image high atop Mount Suribachi was as inspirational to the American cause on Iwo as it was demoralizing to the Japanese, who were infuriated by it.

The actual flag is on display at the National Museum of the Marine Corps in Quantico, Virginia. The Marine Corps War Memorial located near the Arlington National Cemetery bears an inscription in the granite base "Uncommon Valor was a Common Virtue," a tribute by Admiral Chester Nimitz to the Iwo Jima veterans.

Our Marine guide made a special point of showing us Basilone Beach. Here, the legendary John Basilone from

New Jersey fell mortally wounded by a Japanese mortar shell. He didn't have to be here. At Guadalcanal on October 25, 1942, Gunnery Sgt. Basilone was ordered to help hold off a regiment of 3,000 Japanese troops attempting to capture Henderson airfield. According to one account, with only 15 men (12 subsequently killed) he held the line for 72 battle-filled hours and was able to steady his terrified men. With a .45 pistol and two machine guns—one cradled in his arms after the other was knocked out—he stopped a screaming banzai attack and held out until dawn when reinforcements came up. Nearly a hundred sprawled enemy dead were found around his cut-off position. The fact that he managed to do all that is a testament to his extraordinary bravery, skill and determination. After the battle, a Marine who lost a hand in the battle was surprised to see Basilone next to his bed a little after dawn.

> He was barefooted and his eyes were as red as fire. His face was dirty black from gunfire and lack of sleep. His shirtsleeves were rolled up to his shoulders. He had a .45 tucked into the waistband of his trousers. He'd just dropped by to see how I was making out, me and the others in the section. I'll never forget him. He'll never be dead in my mind.

John, at 26 years old, became the first Marine in World War II to be awarded the Congressional Medal of Honor. When he received the nation's highest decoration, he replied modestly, "Only part of this medal belongs to me. Pieces of it belong to the boys who are still on Guadalcanal."

He was then ordered home to sell war bonds. He could have sat out the rest of the war, but demanded to be returned to his unit in the Pacific. It's what Marines do. When he returned it would be on the black sands of Iwo Jima, February 19, 1945. At the head of another machine gun squad, he would drive hundreds of frightened raw troops off the beaches toward their assigned objectives. In those early invasion hours of Iwo Jima, after destroying a Japanese gun emplacement, he was killed on the beach leading his men. A Marine who saw the action was quoted as saying, "It's Medal of Honor time again for John Basilone." In addition to the Medal of Honor, he was awarded the Navy Cross (the Marine Corps' second highest decoration for valor) and the Purple Heart, making him the only Marine to be awarded all three medals. These were to go along with the other six medals and citations he had received. When they recovered his body, a medic noticed that on his outstretched left arm was a tattoo: "Death before Dishonor!"

It was amazing to go through some of the caves occupied by Japanese troops leading up to and during the invasion. They were cramped and lacked all creature comforts. During the invasion there was a severe shortage of food and water. The stench must have been unbearable. Under these deplorable conditions, and considering the Japanese honor-in-death psyche, dying probably seemed preferable to living. One cave had just been opened by the Japanese authorities as part of an ongoing project to recover Japanese remains. In it we discovered a rusted bayonet, sake bottles, and a decaying shoe. Nearby we observed what appeared to be a religious station with religious ornaments and candles left undisturbed since the battle. This was one of many caves open to visitors. There were, however, strict rules prohibiting the removal of any articles from the island with the exception of sand. Before the trip we were advised of this and encouraged to bring bottles if we wanted to take any sand from Iwo Jima back with us. I did just that in a bottle thoughtfully provided to us by our chartered air carrier.

Decades after the battle, several hundred letters were unearthed from the island's soils. The letters give faces and voices to the Japanese men who fought there, as well as their extraordinary general who turned what was predicted to be quick defeat into 36 days of heroic and resourceful combat. I was impressed with the notion that war surely is not just a clash of arms but of cultures. It showed me that no matter what uniform you wear, we are all driven by the same emotions and aspirations.

†

As I wandered about the island, somewhat dazed by this time at what I had seen, I asked myself what my grandfather would have thought if he could have seen this place. After I spoke with some of the veterans, I realized the price his sons and grandsons paid to inch a step closer to his notion of the American dream. Would he have thought it was worth it? Would he and his wife have made that historic journey to the New World over a century ago? Could they have possibly imagined what would have been expected of them in defense of their new homeland?

I think not. I also think that when they considered what they had achieved in the face of tough challenges, their answer to those questions would have been a resounding yes. These were people of selfless humility, without formal education, whose only dream was to carve out honest, productive lives, and to contribute to American culture.

Events like the war effort gave their lives purpose to that end. They stood with a generation of their peers who would rise up to resist and put down tyranny. To them it was a just cause, and the sacrifices they made were worth it because the world was now a safer, better place. That was reward enough.

I hasten to add, however, that my grandfather did not live long enough to see some of the emotional scars left behind from that effort. I saw some of those scars later, in Uncle Pete. There were others as well. Having been to places like Iwo, Normandy, Verdun, and Oradour-sur-Glane I could understand their torment in a way I could not have from the family stories. At least the places were real for me now, if not the events that took place on them. Fittingly though, before the emotional scars were cut, the soldiers would be welcomed home as heroes by throngs of crying and cheering fellow Americans. There were block parties everywhere. This "greatest generation" of warriors, unlike their Vietnam brethren, would relish in well-deserved adulation for a job well done. They had saved the world. They, and the rest of American citizenry, would go on to give this country its greatest period of prosperity.

†

When we checked through security at the airport upon leaving Iwo, the security and inspections were the tightest I have seen anywhere, and I had been just about everywhere. They opened every piece of baggage and thoroughly searched it. The return trip to Guam was subdued and reflective. We would not soon forget what we had just witnessed or those warriors that were lost sixty years ago.

In what could be a testament for all those who did come home, one veteran said to a friend who asked him what it was like on the island, "I've served my time in hell."

Given my keen historical interest I had signed up for this trip to visit the remnants of one of our country's bloodiest and most fabled battlefields. However, to witness it alongside veterans who actually were there sixty years ago added a measure of realism and made it more emotional than I could have ever imagined. I came away from it with an even stronger reverence for the U.S. Marine Corps than I had previously. It also gave me a greater sense of appreciation for the sacrifices made by the many veterans I worked with during my weekly volunteer work. Yet any mention of these valiant men must also acknowledge the airman they saved. I discovered that after the first B-29 landing on March 4, even before the island was secure, there were 852 similar forced landings over the next three months. The Army Air Force estimated that in the course of its strategic bombing campaign on Japan, more than nine thousand pilots and crew members were saved because the Marines, who with the support of the navy, took Iwo Jima at great cost. It's what Marines do. The following year I attended the opening and dedication ceremony of the new National Museum of the Marine Corps at Quantico, Virginia. This day also marked the 231st anniversary of the founding of the Marine Corps. The Corps finally had a museum of its own. During his heart-warming paean to the Marine Corps, President Bush pointed out another first. He mentioned that Brooklyn-born General Peter Pace, who I was privileged to meet, was the first Marine to ever be appointed Chairman of the Joint Chiefs of Staff.

The ceremony was followed the next day by a tour of the museum. Located adjacent to Quantico Marine Corps base off I-95, the museum is visible to all travelers as the 210-foot steel-tilted mast that replicates the flag raising over Iwo Jima, clears the skyline. It is designed to portray the Marine experience and to evoke the raising of the flag at Mount Suribachi. The 118,000-square-foot facility also includes a memorial park, parade grounds, museum gift shop, classrooms, and a conference center. It was fascinating to see some artifacts and exhibits that go as far back as mock-ups of the crow's nest on the USS *Constitution*; others are as contemporary as today's fighter jets and Persian Gulf tanks. The flag from Iwo Jima is here. A guide was quick to mention how the museum exemplifies the extra measure of dedication, courage and commitment it takes to become a Marine.

†

I cannot conclude a chapter about the Marine Corps without being reminded of Lenny Catanzaro, one of my best friends from high school. He is a part of that sacred brotherhood. He belongs here too because he helped shape my values and goals for the future. Lenny and I had much in common, most notably that we were from immigrant families who shared aspirations for the American way of life.

We were pretty thick in high school. We belonged to the same fraternity, played varsity football together, got in and out of scrapes together, and did some double-dating. In fact, both of us even ended up marrying our high school sweethearts. When Ronnie and I had our first child, Dorine, Lenny and his wife, Millie, visited us and gave her a teddy-doll. It became her favorite, the kind of toy a kid will simply not part with. Year after year Ronnie would stitch and re-stitch it even though it was threadbare.

Lenny knew he wanted to be a Marine at an early age. And so not long after graduation, off he went to the recruiting office to sign up, starting his career from the bottom as a private first class. His leadership qualities rapidly shone through and led him to the Marine Corps Officer Candidates School whereupon graduation he was commissioned a second lieutenant. Several years later Vietnam was heating up and Lenny got his first one-year tour in Vietnam. He was flying F-4 Phantom fighter jets out of Da Nang Air Base, which was being used by U.S. forces as a major base during the Vietnam War. Lenny being Lenny, he volunteered to serve a second one-year tour. He came away from those experiences battle-fatigued, disillusioned with government policy, but still in one piece. He was decorated with twenty-nine—yes, twenty-nine—combat mission air medals. It's what Marines do. By now he was a major, a career man all the way who exemplified the best the Marine Corps stands for. He would not, however, get to be a twenty-year man.

In 1975, during a training exercise, the cockpit canopy of his F-4 Phantom fighter jet accidentally separated from the aircraft. He was ejected from their jet and killed instantly. When I learned of his death I was devastated. I pondered to myself, *Isn't it dreadfully unfair that after twenty-nine combat missions and two tours in Vietnam, he should die in a training accident?*

When I resumed contact with Millie decades later, I was touched by the tranquility with which she faces life, taking joy in the daughter and two grandchildren Lenny left behind. She seemed grateful, too, for the life they had together, and the cherished memories.

Outside of my family, Lenny was one of the people whose ideals and values made a difference in my life. He exemplified the kind of officer I wanted to be. My mother used to say, "Show me your friends and I will show you who you are." In his case, I truly hoped she was right. Today my daughter is a mature woman who has kept that doll. I will never forget my dear friend, because of what he stood for, and because of that cherished keepsake that has come to symbolize our friendship. *Semper Fi*, Lenny—your spirit is always with me.

25

NOSTALGIA

In the sports arena, true greatness is as much about behavior and achievements off the field as it is on the field.

—Nicholas F. Starace II

My return to Japan in 2007 was like a breath of fresh air. It didn't take long for me to realize that my affinity for the culture had not diminished. (Uncle Pete, please forgive me, wherever you are.) I say that because of the wonderful qualities that remain staples of Japanese culture such as politeness, orderliness, cleanliness, punctuality and *service*, the latter being a word that, sorry to say, has greatly diminished in American society. Let me illustrate—our dentist in Japan would invariably sit down with his patients at the appointed time for ten to fifteen minutes of small talk and a cup of coffee. Then, and only then, was it time for the chair.

I lived in Europe and Asia for eleven years, including nearly four years in Japan. I had been traveling to Japan for almost fifty years, and still I marveled at its tranquil beauty. I marvel too, at how deferential the Japanese still are in dealing with each other and foreigners. Albert Einstein said it a lot better than I ever could: "It was wonderful in Japan—genteel manners, a lively interest in everything, an artistic sense, intellectual honesty together with common sense—a wonderful people in a picturesque land."

The trains, planes, and buses still run on time, nearly all of the time. The taxis are still large, comfortable, and pristine. The drivers still wear white gloves, neatly pressed white or colored shirts, shined shoes. There are no mad dashes, no weaving in and out, no speeding, no shouting or middle finger thrusts at other drivers. The opening and closing of doors is done by the driver's remote control. As the taxi drives off you almost feel that you dare not move in your seat for fear of upsetting the lovely balance around you.

It was during one of my taxi rides that I got up enough courage to clumsily test some of my long-lost "knowledge" of the Japanese language. I actually found myself capable of giving the driver directions such as turning left or right, or to go straight or stop. I was pleasantly surprised that he understood me and that we got to where I wanted to go. I think I was as thrilled as he was surprised. That built up enough courage for me to take it a step further by trying it during a brief shopping spree. The results were not as good because I foolishly tried to put together sentences of more than three words.

One of the first places I visited was a favorite restaurant in the city, which was still there although under a different name and management. I couldn't resist going in to have a bite to eat. But it was a lonely meal, for as I sat there eating, all around me were long-gone co-workers from one particular meal decades ago. We had finished dinner and then proceeded to the bar to top it off with an after-dinner drink. Our Japanese hosts suggested that we try a unique drink, and it was that night that I took my first and only drink of Mamushi Sake. This concoction, indigenous to Okinawa, is typically served in a one-gallon clear jug similar to a pickle jar. It contains sake and a dead viper snake coiled up in the bottom of the jug. One of the guys explained that poison from the snake seeps into the wine and acts like an aphrodisiac. I did not want to seem like a stuffed shirt. The Japanese businessmen entertaining us further explained that the juices from the snake give the sake a unique flavor and its yellow color. The color also gave my imagination a hint as to what it probably tasted like. All it took was a sip. I suddenly straightened up as my head rocked back and the taste confirmed what my senses had imagined. All around me, my colleagues laughed and slapped me on the back.

I returned to what is probably the finest steak house in the world, Aragawa, a small, intimate restaurant that serves what else—Kobe beef. It is still an absolutely unforgettable dining experience that is nearly matched by the service. Select your favorite cut, top it off with a bottle of my favorite red wine, Saint-Émilion, (Chateau Simard), a French Bordeaux, and you are in for one of the most gastronomical treats on the planet. But in the 37 years I have been dining there, the astronomical prices haven't changed either. Would you believe $275 *per person,* for a 3-course dinner plus coffee and a cocktail? In 2007 Forbes did an article titled, *World's Most Expensive Restaurants 2006.* In it they state, "For the second year in a row, the top restaurant on our list of the world's most expensive restaurants is Aragawa, (the original one) a little steak house in Tokyo's Shinbashi district. Reservations are excruciatingly hard to come by, and the tab starts at $370 per person. But the platters of Kobe beef, which is sourced from only one local farm and served simply with pepper and mustard, make the expense worthwhile." I guess at $275 I got a bargain.

Almost everywhere I went I was reminded of the past. I visited a small place called the North Pole where you could sit and have a drink, listen to soft music, and socialize with some of the locals—sort of like an English pub. It was situated close to the train station I used to use on my way home. In the North Pole, like many of these small bars, you could leave your own private stock in a cubicle that was all your own. Even your name was posted on it.

Long ago I had introduced the owner and his wife to my own concoction, which I call a Cognac Manhattan. It consists of one part red vermouth, two parts of my favorite cognac, Remy Martin XO, and a teaspoon of maraschino cherry juice, garnished with a cherry, and mixed with ice (but served without). I suggest using cognac only instead of other brandies, as it is considered to be the brandy of all brandies and comes from the Cognac region of France. In the beginning I had to show them how to make the drink, but after a short while they had it down to perfection. I'd nip in after work and have a drink or two, and all these years later, I really didn't expect the same people to be there, but had hopes of enjoying a Cognac Manhattan. To my disappointment, the North Pole was gone forever. In its place stood a fragrance boutique.

One aspect of Japanese culture that I was happy to see still evident has to do with personal security. The Japanese have always believed that the country's homogenous population and values contribute to its low crime rate and economic strength. When we lived there, we marveled at how safe it was. Break-ins were rare. Parents would let their young children use public transportation unaccompanied. Our daughter Dorine who was twelve years old at the time frequently used public transportation and we were not uneasy about it. In talking with a few of the expatriates living there today I sensed a similar degree of comfort.

Unfortunately, there is an aspect of Japanese life that has not changed and that is their proclivity for suicide. During this visit I read an article that stated, "Japan's suicide rate is still among the highest in the industrialized world. Data shows that the number of people who took their own lives in Japan topped 30,000 for a ninth straight year in 2007. Alarmingly, among the victims was a record 886 students, up by 25 from the previous year and the highest figure since the authorities started taking statistics in 1978." There is a general consensus that a lack of flexibility in Japanese schools and corporations contributes to the high suicide rate by ostracizing nonconformists. A strong sense of losing face and roots in the samurai custom of taking one's own life, have also been cited as reasons. New measures by the government to reduce the suicide rate try to reduce unemployment, boost workplace counseling and filter Internet sites that promote the taking of one's own life. I think the flexibility issue has also been detrimental to Japan's military effectiveness during World War II. Everything I have read on the subject suggests that the Japanese military was able to execute a plan flawlessly, but lacked imagination and decisiveness if a situation called for improvisation.

Undoubtedly the biggest change in Kobe has to do with the rebuilding of the city since the 1995 earthquake. The earthquake had a seismic intensity of 7.3, with tremors that lasted approximately twenty seconds. Land moved seven inches horizontally and five inches vertically. Approximately 6,400 people were killed. Many of the city planners thought the rebuilding would take at least twenty years. The results are nothing short of stunning and a tribute to the industriousness of the Japanese people. It also underscores an indelible strength in Japanese society and that is their ability to work as a team. The reconstruction was completed in approximately ten years and has resulted in an ultra-modern city with an amazing network of new roads and bridges. In the one-hour ride into the city from the Kansai International Airport I counted thirty-four bridges. The twenty-seven-story office building where I used to work was undamaged. I even went up to the seventeenth floor to see my old office, where I managed to get a few inquisitive looks.

I think it is safe to say most cities ravaged by such a disaster spend years trying to rebuild what they once had. During my visit, however, I discovered that Kobe took a different approach. Rather than waiting for its mainstay steel industry and port facilities to get up to speed, Kobe decided to reinvent itself as Japan's premiere biomedical center. To their credit, all of this was accomplished while the country was going through a period of economic stagnancy.

To commemorate those lost in the 1995 earthquake the city built the Port of Kobe Earthquake Memorial Park. Simple and dignified in its design it gives a dramatic chronology of the events that took place on that fateful day. Part of the park encompasses an area that was heavily damaged, and has been preserved in its damaged state as a stark reminder of the devastation. In addition, there are many photographs on display showing the terrible extent of damage, most of which focused on the waterfront.

†

I had visited Kobe several times on business since we left in 1974. This time, overall, I was not surprised to see how much has changed and how much has stayed the same. Despite its heroic efforts to rebuild, it managed to retain its old small-town-city feel.

The trip was nostalgic, as this was a place and culture for which I had enjoyed, and had so many pleasant memories of Ronnie, Dorine, Nicky, and Michael. On the other hand, there were bittersweet moments as well. This time I did not have my family with me. Nor was I here on business, making contact with old business associates over a round of golf. This time I was alone. As elsewhere, many of the old shops and haunts were gone. The school my kids attended on the mountain had been torn down and relocated. Even the house we lived in was abandoned.

As the taxi trudged its way up the side of the mountain, my first glimpse of the house revealed that it was empty. It almost looked haunted, with broken windows, rear door hanging off its hinges, overgrown brush, and floor-to-ceiling cobwebs. It was not, however, damage from the earthquake, but from the ravages of time. In retrospect, it was almost as if the fall of this once fine home was a metaphor of what happened to our marriage. Yes, we had lived here; there was the proof. As I walked up the steps I could see, "The Staraces 1973" engraved in what used to be a newly paved set of steps. I went in and visualized the life and laughter we once knew here. But instead of my kids running around the place, there was a spooky cold silence as the wind blew through the place. Another reminder was the old basketball hoop Nicky used to play on. I couldn't believe it, but it was still there after all these years. For a moment I could even visualize him shooting baskets as he did hundreds of times. It brought tears to my eyes, and I lingered only as long as I could stand it.

In leaving Japan again, I knew that there was one *gaijin* who felt a strong need to give thanks to the Japanese people for some of the most memorable and fascinating years of his life—from cherry blossoms to ryokans, from Kabuki theater to Sumo wrestling, from raw fish to obentos, and from Imari porcelain to supertankers—and then some.

†

I continued my trip down memory lane going from Japan to Taiwan and two other places I had lived and worked, Singapore and Hong Kong. This was the final leg.

My first visit to Taiwan was nearly fifty years earlier as a young naval officer, and my most recent one had been in 1982. This time, however, I was on vacation, and I could focus on seeing more of the country and its culture. What hit me almost immediately was the marked improvement in the quality of life. The signs were all around—progress in education, technology, and infrastructure, not to mention advancement in cars, office buildings, and housing. It was almost as if I had never been here before. Even the terrible pollution had changed, and the constant dust plumes I remembered were virtually gone.

In the past twenty-five years Kaohsiung had grown dramatically. When I was last there, the tallest building had been a forty-story hotel. Today it is the eighty-five-story Splendor Kaohsiung Department Store and Hotel complex. It has a spectacular view of Kaohsiung Harbor. In Taipei, in 2005, the Taipei 101, the world's tallest building at the time, opened its doors. Those were marvelous achievements for this small country of approximately 23 million people.

Here, as in China, I saw evidence of why and how the United States was being challenged for world market dominance. Labor was and still is cheap, working conditions are poor, labor relations barely exist, quality control standards are marginal, and workmanship is sometimes shoddy. You don't have to visit these countries to see that; we were seeing it in many of the products the United States imported. China in particular has been flooding the world with a variety of poorly designed and manufactured products. But make no mistake—I vividly remembered a time when Japanese products were considered inferior. Looking at that success story, I thought that Taiwan and China might be headed toward the same improvement, too. Or, are they mere images of Japan destined to ignite and then flame out? Whatever the answers, China will have to do more than copy technology and products to gain lasting market leadership. In recent years the Chinese have demonstrated that they can also be innovative. Ah, but to be creative, that's another story—you be the judge.

I'm happy to say that a few things hadn't changed. My first meal during this trip reminded me of just how good the food is. I was all but drooling in anticipation of my first meal, which I knew was going to be my favorite Chinese dish, Hainanese Chicken Rice. I guess it's the combination of ginger and sesame oil that give it its distinctive and spicy flavor. My favorite restaurant was near the Ambassador Kaohsiung Hotel, where I usually stay, and to my delight it was still there and the food still delectable. I had dinner there a second time, so I could order my other favorite, Peking Duck. The thin crispy skin of this delicacy is to die for. My ordering it was an exception—I usually stayed away from it because of the cruel manner in which the ducks are raised, being forced-fed several times a day to make them extra plump. Nevertheless, the whole experience reinforced my opinion that the Chinese food in Taiwan is the best in the world, better than anything I have tasted in any Chinese restaurant or home, despite decades of dining throughout Asia including China. Then too, I have always been amazed at the incredible variety in Chinese cuisine; no people do more with food.

The other side of that coin is a "delicacy" called Bird's Nest Soup. It is usually made using the nests of the swiftlet, a tiny bird found throughout Southeast Asia. Not to put you off, but the swiftlet makes its nest not from twigs and straw, but chiefly from interwoven strands of its own gummy saliva, which hardens when exposed to air. After the nests are harvested, usually from caves, they are soaked in water, and then stewed in a pot for several hours. Like so many foods used in Chinese cooking, bird nest is claimed to have numerous health benefits. It is even claimed to be an aphrodisiac. (I swear, if all of the foods claimed to be an aphrodisiac were in fact an aphrodisiac, nearly all men would be in a perpetual state of arousal. And ladies, I heard that remark.) Anyway, I tried it again in Hong Kong and still found it to taste like a chicken soup that's been left standing a few days. Worse yet, no arousal.

Upon returning to Kaohsiung I was happy to also find that the friendliness of the people had not changed. In spite of sweeping modernization and industrialization, the trait has endured. So has the courtesy and generosity with which they treat visitors. The surprise "welcome back" dinner party given to me by a few old friends after all these years was great comfort.

†

I went in search of that snake shop, the one I had happened upon in 1981, where I watched the serpent being hung, "dressed," bled, and fried. I found it—the very same one—but it had lost some of its life. There were no more shows or demos out front. You could still go in and pick out a snake for your dining pleasure, but there were fewer to choose from. Perhaps it's the 7-Eleven just three doors down that had taken its toll on business. Such was the dichotomy of Taiwanese culture, and it never ceased to amaze me.

Sorry to say the political impasse between Taiwan and China is as real today as it was during my previous visits, with no solution in sight. The threat of invasion persists as it has since Chiang Kai-shek moved his forces there in 1949. China's efforts to subjugate Taiwan are stronger than ever. Both sides are struggling with new diplomatic initiatives and strategies in an effort to reach some sort of peaceful settlement, and that's a vast improvement over the shooting and bombardment that was going on when David and Goliath duked it out during the navy of my youth. In spite of China's military, economic, and political muscle, Taiwan is still a free and independent country and determined to remain that way. And to my mind, a comparison is inevitable: Does Taiwan's spunk and courage remind us of another budding nation, one that only 233 years ago lived under the shadow of a nation-giant?

At this juncture, my trip down memory lane was nearly over, and the nostalgia-thirst satisfied. For me, memory lane is often more like memory lake. I can look into it and see reflections of who I am, and how I may have changed. So it was each time I returned to Taiwan, which was an especially good mirror because I was looking into a lake at fifty years of my life. In a strange sort of way, some of those changes were a reflection of Taiwan itself. Hadn't we both become tempered by a world caught up in changes that we didn't fully understand, but tried to accommodate? Taiwan increased its efforts to achieve political (if not military and economic) parity with China, whereas I too had developed a greater sense of compromise. That is to say, I was a little less headstrong if the objective mattered.

And hadn't we both developed as international players? Clearly, Taiwan had become one of the Four Asian Tigers and had the industrial might to show for it, just as I had touched every continent except Antarctica, and certainly had the experience to show for it.

And hadn't we both matured emotionally? Taiwan from a fledgling nation after its liberation from Japan in 1945 to a vibrant democracy. Me, from a green young naval officer on my very first tour, to that of a family patriarch, business executive, and volunteer worker.

Lastly and most notably, I found another parallel in charitable giving. Taiwan is typically one of the first to participate in disaster relief efforts and international medical aid teams. There are collaborative efforts to combat AIDS. Recent efforts assisting earthquake and tsunami victims also has a Taiwanese footprint. For a small country it does very well for its size. More important, as its wealth increased, it has taken on a greater share of its relief responsibility. For my part, I still believe that life's greatest gift is to give. I like to think that when I hold out my hand to share my time, skill, money, or talent, I am indeed doing

God's work, as humble as it might be. The loss of my son Nicky served a purpose I could never have imagined. It made me focus on the importance and spirit of giving more than I had previously thought I should.

†

In closing, I want to share a tender moment that I experienced while walking along the street where I used to live. The weather changed suddenly, and it started to rain heavily. Caught without an umbrella, I started to walk quickly to get back to the hotel. (As in any city in the world, try to find a taxi when it rains.) As I walked past a school, a girl—she was maybe thirteen years old—came up alongside me and lifted up her umbrella, signaling for me to get under it with her. There wasn't a parent or guardian in sight. We smiled at each other and walked together for about ten minutes. We chatted for a bit, but I do not think she understood a word I was saying. But the warmth in her eyes told me she understood my feelings. Finally, as we approached an intersection, she peeled off and went about her business. She smiled and waved to me as she departed. I did likewise. I was touched by that child, that she should do such a kind thing for a total stranger, and a foreigner no less. It gave me such a warm feeling.

No, I was not surprised by it for it was what I had come to expect from the locals when I lived here. How gratifying, I thought, that some things had not changed. I came away feeling Taiwan is in good hands.

26

HEAVE HO MY LADS, HEAVE HO!

I must go down to the seas again,
to the lonely sea and sky,
And all I ask is a tall ship and
a star to steer her by,
And the wheel's kick and the wind's
song and the white sail's shaking,
And a gray mist on the sea's face
and a gray dawn breaking.

—John Masefield, from "Sea-Fever"

In September 2007 we gathered at Kings Point for our fiftieth reunion, to celebrate our lineage and legacy. We were a bit wiser, a bit grayer, and a bit slower. Well, not *that* slow. Several of us even ran the 5K race, which I completed in around thirty-eight minutes, coming in third in a field of six. Not bad for a fossil.

It was interesting to compare notes on the different paths our lives had taken. And I'm proud to say that without exception, they are lives that have been productive and responsible—both personally and professionally—thanks in large measure to the wonderful women with whom we had chosen to share our lives.

During these kinds of gatherings the discussion invariably gravitates to the world scene, politics ... All of it. The world had changed many times over since we walked our hallowed halls. America's role at home and abroad changed so dramatically for good and ill that we agreed it was sometimes hard to believe we were living in the same country as fifty years ago. However, my sense of the general attitude was one of hope and optimism for the future; there was no querulousness. Happily, there seemed to be a continuing dependence on faith to lead us through the hard times. Unhappily, I sensed skepticism about the lack of confidence in our leadership.

Kings Point graduates employed in the maritime industry at sea and ashore are still playing a vital role in the support the nation's military efforts and installations worldwide. The purpose of the Academy is ultimately to provide the nation with shipboard officers and leaders in the transportation field, who will meet future challenges. In fulfillment of that mission the Battle Standard of the Academy bears honored testimony to the 142 cadet midshipmen who paid the ultimate price during World War II. Kings Point is the only federal academy to have a battle standard, as it is the only academy to have lost cadets while serving on duty during wartime.

Today, Kings Point graduates are still the mainstay of a merchant fleet that delivers the equipment and material our forces need as they are deployed throughout the world. Moreover, many graduates are serving on naval vessels who serve an equally vital role in keeping the sea-lanes open for commercial and military shipping. There is no better or more current example than the support our military forces have relied upon during the Iraq and Afghanistan wars.

During the homecoming festivities I was indeed honored to receive one of two Outstanding Professional Achievement Awards. Receiving this recognition at the alumni awards banquet during the homecoming weekend made it one of the proudest moments in my life, one that I was able to share with my daughter Dorine, son Michael, his fiancée Jessica, and grandson Nicholas. I was especially grateful because everything that I have been able to achieve and every opportunity I have had, I owe to "my school." However, I am not the brightest light on the tree. I could point to many of the guys in my class who have achieved more than I have. My guess is that the Alumni Awards Committee probably chose me because I came as close as anyone to fulfilling the mission of the Academy: "To educate and graduate professional officers and leaders of honor and integrity, who are dedicated to serving the economic and defense interests of the United States in our Armed Forces and merchant marine, and who contribute to an intermodal transportation system that effectively ties America together."

By now, I had spent an entire career dedicated to the maritime industry afloat and ashore. Even today I continue to work with and support U.S. maritime causes such as the SS United States Conservancy and SS United States Foundation, whose missions are to preserve and revitalize the SS *United States,* the largest and fastest ocean liner ever built in this country. My memberships, past and present, in the United States Power squadrons, Nautical Research Guild, United States Naval Reserve, American

Bureau of Shipping Engineering Committee, National Maritime Historical Society, Marine Engineers' Beneficial Association, Silverton Yacht Owner's Association, Society of Naval Architects and Marine Engineers, Ship Model Society of New Jersey, Singapore Ship Model Club, Garden State Model Boaters, and Battleship New Jersey Historical Society are further testaments to my dedication. Regarding the latter, I was asked by the Battleship New Jersey Home Port Alliance to build a museum-quality static-display model of the USS *New Jersey* (BB-62). That model is on display and is the centerpiece of exhibits in the museum on board the USS *New Jersey* at Camden, New Jersey.

I had also supplemented my Kings Point education by obtaining a Master's Degree in Engineering. And in June 2005, I received a U.S. Coast Guard 100 ton Master's License, which is pending upgrade to 200 tons. This came nearly fifty years after receiving my first USCG license as Third Assistant Engineer. I'm tooting my own horn, which I have been known to do—but my point is that these kinds of activities, while certainly not earth-shattering, together seemed to demonstrate a strong allegiance to the academy's mission to the awards committee.

The highlight of the week was something that flashed me back to the January 20, 1957, inaugural parade for President Dwight D. Eisenhower, in which the entire Kings Point regiment marched, including yours truly. It was the rousing performance of the regimental band during the Ceremony of Beating Retreat. I love marching bands, especially those that can actually march as well as play music. Under fluttering banners and flags, the band was in constant motion from the time they stepped into the gym until the time they stepped out. The uniforms were immaculate. Their formation and maneuvers were breathtaking because they were executed within a very tight framework of ranks and files necessitated by the confines of the gym. The walls amplified the sound—and the louder, the better. I was so moved I wanted to jump out and hug each and every one of them. The band played a wide variety of military and patriotic marches, but when they played the Colonel Bogey March, I damn near collapsed because it transported me back fifty years to a hot Saturday afternoon. I was in my stifling formal "monkey suit," rifle on shoulder, marching onto Tomb Field for a regimental review thinking of one thing—going on liberty that afternoon. When the National Anthem played I was reminded that some things do not change—every note resonated through my body while standing at rigid attention.

The then-Superintendent, Vice Admiral Joseph D. Stewart, USMS, gave the closing remarks. In them, and in fact all week, I kept hearing words like dedication, service, courage, sacrifice, and duty to describe graduates, midshipmen and their deeds. The vibrant marching music and his stirring remarks not only gave me goose bumps, but made me feel proud of the Kings Point family and its accomplishments. He was caught up in it as much as anyone—and, he got emotional, which showed me just how genuine the guy really was. His remarks reminded me of another Stewart, TV host and political satirist Jon Stewart—both have that rare quality to be simultaneously eloquent and humorous. All of the pomp and ceremony reminded me, too, of a French phrase the Marine Corps uses to describe why it is so special: *Esprit de Corps*. It means team spirit, and is at the very core of any successful endeavor or unit. It is in fact what I have always seen at Kings Point, in its students, in its faculty, and especially in its graduates. It is that sense of belonging to something special that motivates all of us to excel. May it always prevail at my beloved alma mater. ACTA NON VERBA!

†

During the entire homecoming week I had my forty-four-foot motor-yacht *Mon Tresor III* docked at the Academy. My world had come together—Kings Point, my classmates, fond memories, and my boat. Many of us enjoyed the same pastime we had enjoyed for the last fifty years: swapping old sea stories. Each time they are told, they got a bit more risqué and much bolder. To make the time even more complete my longtime friend Kathy joined me for the final two days. After my divorce in 1991 we enjoyed a long relationship, but over the years our bond had been tempered and cooled into what was essentially an important and treasured friendship.

That night, as talk and laughter spilled across the water, I sat in my favorite spot, the open foredeck, enraptured by the moonlight, my dear friends, and the joy of being on my boat. The sights and sounds I knew from my youth were still there—the twinkling lights, the squawking sea gulls, the belching whistles and the buoy gongs. It seemed so little had changed. I couldn't help but reflect on the events of the last fifty years, and in particular, my divorce. I asked myself, as I had done so often, if I had found closure. Was the divorce grieving process complete? After all, when it comes to divorce, getting past the past is never easy, especially after a thirty-four-year marriage; moving on is easier said than done.

There were times when I had rationalized staying in the marriage for the kids' sake. I hid behind that attitude, despite evidence suggesting that raising children in a dysfunctional home was more damaging than a *stable* single-parent home. In any event, we stayed the course, and divorced long after our children were emancipated.

I think knowing what you did wrong in a marriage helps achieve closure. Perhaps Ronnie and I missed an opportunity by never sitting down after the divorce to liberate the demons that had stalked the marriage; perhaps it might have helped if we could have let our feelings out just one more time—but the prevailing hostility got in the way. What made the grieving process even more difficult was that we initiated divorce proceedings a mere two years after we lost Nicky. I was already in a grieving mode, and sometimes it was hard to distinguish which loss I was grieving for. That's a double whammy, fraught with deep feelings of emotional turmoil, failure, and disappointment. In a religious sense, the broken marriage vows probably captured those feelings the best.

But now, having been divorced for eighteen years I could say with some confidence I was pleased with my life: I have lived with a positive attitude, and more important, with a vigorous new life. I had not found living alone to be as difficult an adjustment as I thought it would be. I guess that was the loner in me, and maybe why I ultimately stayed single. I had risen up out of the ashes once again and moved on, full of hope for the future; with vastly new interests, and new people around me. I guess that's as much closure as anyone can ask for.

There are many wonderful women who stood out in the lives of my classmates and me, but one of my classmates, Bob Carney, has a story that leaves all of us in awe. He got married about a year after we graduated. He and his wife Eileen had gotten quite busy and had seven kids in just under twelve years. We'll never know why, but the good Lord saw fit to take Eileen from Bob and their kids when their youngest child was just eleven days old. Bob had to raise seven kids, and did, thanks to a special woman named Arline.

Bob's sixty-five-year-old mother, a saint in her own right, was taking care of the seven kids—three were in diapers and three were off to school, with one toddler in between. Three months after Eileen passed, he met Arline, started dating her, and soon afterward he popped the question.

In his book *Lost At Sea,* which I highly recommend, Bob tells us during a tender moment, "Arline ... Look I'm falling for you so much I'm already thinking of asking you to marry me. I can't get you out of my mind. When I'm not with you, I'm scared to death that the next time you'll have changed your mind. Forgive me. I went and fell in love with you. Now, I need you or I'll die all over again. I wish I could stay carefree about you and just enjoy the ride, but I'm sorry, I'm thinking of you in terms of marriage." At this point his eyes were full of tears and he didn't know why. He goes on, "If I asked you to marry me, would you?"

Arline replies, "I feel the same way about you. What do you think, I throw myself at every jerk that comes along? I think you should know there is something special about you. If you asked me to marry you, I might not say no."

Finally, Bob works up enough courage and says, "Arline, will you marry me?"

She started grinning and said, "YES, *God*-damn-it, I'll marry you."

He asks, "Arline, are you sure about what you're saying?" She smiled and nodded yes. He went on in disbelief, "I guess that means we're engaged. Oh, wait a minute! Oh crap—what about the kids?"

Arline calmly replied, "Don't worry about them. I'm marrying you. I'll learn to take care of the kids. They're good kids. I won't replace their mother, but I can learn to take care of them. That'll be my job." He gave her one more chance to get off the hook, but she then took his face in her hands and said, "Bobby, I love you. We'll make love and everything else will work out. Stop worrying about me, "*It's no big deal*!"

And so it came to pass. In the ensuing years they carved out a remarkable life of achievement together, raising seven wonderful children.

To cap off the final evening we opened a bottle of champagne to celebrate the fiftieth wedding anniversary of our dear friends Maureen and George Wilson. As we were tipping our glasses, Frank Apicella and his fiancée Deborah surprised us with the announcement that they were going to be married—for the second time.

"Heck, why wait?" I said. "I have a bible on board and as a licensed captain I could tie the knot for you right now." Frank knew I was bluffing, and he declined. I thought the lad was getting cold feet, but a few weeks later they did re-marry, commenting that love is indeed better the second time around.

As I looked around the cabin, which was a beehive of laughter and chatter, it made me sad to think of the day when we would no longer be able to share this camaraderie.

Recalling that we shared so special a time and place long ago gave all of us an emotional high. As we watched the lights glitter around the boat that night, we reflected on the homage paid earlier that day to the classmates who are "finished with engines." Come midnight my old friends began to make their way back ashore, and as I waved at them from *Mon Tresor III*, I thought of the day when it will be time for my engine to quit. When that time comes, I had decided, I wanted to be cremated and the ashes sent to my sepulcher there in the sea. My children and grandchildren could visit me anytime. They would simply need to go out on any river, lake, or ocean and talk to me—and there I'll be.

27

THE BEGINNING

Everywhere around the world
They're coming to America
Every time the flag's unfurled
They're coming to America.
—Neil Diamond, from "America"

I'm going to end this journey by going back to the beginning of my family's life in America. What better place to start than with the family name, *Starace*? According to one book on last names, ours is commonly found in Southern Italy in the provinces of Foggia, Lecce, and Naples. As it is documented in the twelfth and thirteenth centuries, the name has roots in the names *Stavrakes* and *Starakes*, medieval derivatives of the Greek name, *Stravros*. It means a crossed vertical torture pole. As best as I can determine, that means a crucifix. Another literary source gives the meaning of the name as a "little cross." The Greek diminutive *-akes* was taken into Italian as *-ace*, giving good closure to the name and its meaning. I have probably lived up to the name, because there have been people in my life for who I have indeed been a cross to bear, most notably my mother and Ronnie.

In bringing our name to America we did not tamper with its spelling, as did many immigrants of my grandparent's generation. Many deliberately modified their names to *fit in* with their new culture and environment. For others, it was the non-Italians who made Italian names conform to English language pronunciation, spelling, or names with which they already happen to be acquainted.

Ah, but the pronunciation—that's a different story. Starace in Italian is pronounced stah-RAH-che. My family usually uses the pronunciation sta-RACE. If you follow the rules of phonics, our name couldn't be easier to pronounce. Nevertheless, I got so tired of people mispronouncing it that I came up with an anglicized, phonetic version—star-ace—pronounced just as it is spelled. While that version is not as lyrical as stah-RAH-che, it's a lot easier for most people to handle. In recent years I have been feeling a bit guilty about tampering with the pronunciation at all. Perhaps I'm overreacting, but it's making me feel as if I'm denying my heritage.

†

My surname once got me into trouble—in Italy. During the 1990s I traveled to Europe often on business. On one occasion I had to go to Italy to meet with executives of a shipping company, whose tankers my employer was considering for charter. The company was located in a seaside town near Livorno, and so they booked a room for me in a charming hotel in the town. I checked in late one afternoon and was later joined for dinner by two of the company's staff. The next morning they picked me up bright and early for what would be an all-day meeting. At the end of the day I returned to the hotel.

Meanwhile, my secretary had called the hotel on two occasions and was told there was no one by my name staying at the hotel. She had my complete itinerary, and since I hadn't called her with any changes, she had every reason to believe I was still following the original itinerary. If that was so, then where was I? My boss, the one who initiated the call, began to worry, thinking perhaps I had an accident and was lying in a hospital somewhere. He called our office in Rome and asked them to call the hotel, which they did, and the hotel acknowledged that I was in fact staying there. They took the message and gave it to me the next morning whereupon I called my office. Mission accomplished. Perhaps it was nothing more than a communications glitch.

Upon returning to my office a week later, however, I got curious about what had transpired. So I called our Rome office and spoke with the Italian guy that made the call. I knew him for many years and trusted him to be candid. He gave me the story, and I knew it was true, but still had a hard time believing it.

Achille Starace was one of the founders and secretary of the Fascist Party (1931-1939), and later served as the interior minister. As such, he was considered to be Mussolini's right-hand man. Those of you familiar with World War II history may recall seeing the famous and grisly photograph of Mussolini, his mistress Claretta Petacci, and three others hanging by their heels from an Esso gas station overhead-girder in Milan near the end of the war. They were hanged there after being executed outside the city by partisans on April 29, 1945, just a day before Hitler committed suicide. Achille Starace was one of those hanged with Mussolini—a regrettable ending for a man who earlier in his life was acclaimed for his political achievements and highly decorated for his exploits in World War I.

During the immediate post-war era, Livorno was *the* bastion of the Communist Party in Italy and therefore very anti-Fascist, or for that matter, anti-anything not communistic. Fast forward to my situation approximately forty-five years later, staying at a charming little hotel on the outskirts of Livorno. As explained to me by our guy in Rome, "The hotel management simply did not want to recognize that anyone with the name Starace was staying at their hotel." Even forty-five years later there were enough old-timers around who apparently harbored bitter memories of the war and anybody associated with the Fascist movement.

I asked, "Well why did they book me in the hotel in the first place?" His guess was that a desk clerk who couldn't care less about World War II politics booked the reservation.

So, is there in fact any relationship between my family and Achille Starace? I don't know, but our cousin Constance recalls her father, John Starace, telling her when she was a little girl that one of his cousins was hanged with Mussolini. There is no evidence of it, however, as far as I know—but knowing the history does explain the many double-takes I had gotten from some of Italy's immigration and customs officials.

Currently there's another famous Starace in the news, and for good reason. Italy's number one tennis player is Polito Starace. He is now among the best ten Italian tennis players ever. In October 2007 his world ranking for singles in the Association of Tennis Professionals was 30. His career highest ranking is 27. I haven't a clue if he is related to our clan, but I know for certain that I have none of his talent for tennis.

†

Poppie was from Procida a small island near the well-known idyllic islands of Capri and Ischia in the Tyrrhenian Sea, southwest of Naples, Italy. You have probably never heard of Procida, as it has always shied away from the tourism that attracts people to its neighbors. However, I found the same old-world charm in its narrow crisscrossing cobbled streets, colorful pastel houses, pristine beaches, and fleet of battered fishing boats. Modern civilization has not diminished the natural beauty of this authentic Italian Isle. Daily life is slow and laid back—time almost seems to stand still. The food is marvelous, especially the seafood. You can actually sit at a seafood restaurant on the harbor's edge and watch the fresh fish you are about to order come off the boat it was caught on. How fresh is it? So fresh, you half-expected it to jump off the plate into your mouth. If in doubt about where to eat, you simply follow the smell of the fresh bread baking.

In my mind I had been to Procida many times, trying to visualize where my grandfather grew up. I could visualize him almost as though he were sitting next to me as he did when he told stories of his past. The actual visit was emotional for me. I even thought I could sense his spirit, but in reality I knew I was merely being swept up by the emotion of the moment.

I did see the fisherman scurrying around their boats, though—that was no mirage. I saw the women weaving fishing nets. I saw the boat-builders toiling at their craft as he once did, and as they have done for centuries. I began to realize, yes, this is surely the place of my ancestors. I had found my genetic origins, my roots. I felt like an orphan who had finally discovered his biological parents. The thought that kept buzzing through my head was that if they hadn't made that move over a century ago, this is where my lot would have been cast. My life would have taken a completely different path. Would I have been the happier for it? I'll never know, but it was so gratifying to go back and see what might have been.

Having been to Ischia, Procida, and Capri, I have often wondered why my grandparents ever left the region's sun-kissed serenity and majestic beauty. I was not old enough or mature enough to get into that kind of discussion with my grandfather. I think the answer is probably that the life they knew and left over a century ago was very different from the life I witnessed as a visitor. In his days, most people had a meager existence, living off the land or the sea. The economy was tied in great part to the boatbuilding and fishing industries. Like most of the immigrants of that period their motivation was economic opportunity and a better life in the Promised Land. Today, thanks to flourishing tourism and light industry, the locals probably don't have same kind of incentive to leave. Life is better now, and that's probably one of the reasons the population has slowly increased over the past few decades. Even the film industry has discovered this charming island, as it served as the background for the films *Il Postino* and *The Talented Mr. Ripley*. I still dream of going back, perhaps renting a villa and spending some time with my grandfather. I still think of him a lot.

†

I never knew my paternal grandmother, Concetta Massa, because she died long before I was born. From everything I have been told about her, she was a loving, strong-willed woman whose grit, determination, and devotion to the family helped make the American way of life a reality for future generations of Staraces and their families. I wish I could say more about her, but unfortunately none of her history has survived among her descendents now living in the United States. However, we do know a great deal about her birthplace, Ischia, an island of 58,000. Make no mistake; it's not the sleepy little labyrinth that is Procida. It's a heath resort caught up in the twenty-first century tourism industry, with the traffic jams to prove it.

Dorine accompanied me on one of my two visits. We rented a car and took the ferry from Naples to the island. In that way we were able to see as much of the island as possible, from its world-renowned spas and natural sulfur springs, to the houses piled up the hillside, to its pristine beaches, to its quaint old fishing villages, right down to its rocky slopes falling away into the sea.

Later that year, on another island an ocean away, in tribute to both of my grandparents' sacrifices and courage, I registered their names on Ellis Island's American Immigration Wall of Honor.

†

The maternal side of my family also emigrated from Italy, but a generation later, arriving in the United States in the early part of the twentieth century. My mother was born Doranna (Dolores) Scutari in the small Italian-Albanian village of San Costantino Albanese. It is located on a hilltop in the province of Potenza, which is located in Basilicata, a region in the south of Italy. Some Italian-Albanians from this region refer to themselves as "Arberesh." The term also refers to the language they speak, which is an Albanian dialect.

What are Albanians doing in Italy? Well, I was curious too. It all began in 1448 when the King of Naples enlisted the help of the Albanian army to help him defeat a rebellious uprising in Naples. After successfully putting down the revolt, most of the Albanian mercenaries requested that they be granted land and be allowed to stay in Italy so they would not have to face the ongoing conflicts with Turkey in their homeland. Their petition granted, the Albanians sent for their families and proceeded to settle twelve villages. In 1459, a second wave of Albanians entered Italy when Naples once again needed military assistance to put down a French-supported insurrection. The warrior-like Albanian soldiers effectively saved Naples and were rewarded with sufficient land in southern Italy to settle fifteen more villages, one of them being my mother's village. A generation later, Albania became subject to Turkish invaders. Many fled to Italy and settled even more villages. Since then, the Albanians have survived as a distinct ethnic group in Italy and have lived peacefully there for over five hundred years. Until recently, San Costantino Albanese and other Albanian villages remained quite insulated from Italian culture. It was not until after World War II that Italian-Albanians began to slowly downplay their heritage and assimilate into Italian culture, while still retaining some Albanian traits.

We still have family in San Costantino and keep in touch. I had the good fortune of visiting the village twice during the 1990s, the last time with my mother and daughter. Today the assimilation I mentioned is in full swing, facilitated by rapid travel and communications. Intermingling and even intermarriage are commonplace. That trend will continue, as it has in my mother's family. For example, her deceased sister, three of her nieces, and three of her grandnieces married Italian men.

Assimilation notwithstanding, I marvel at how after all these years, the Albanians in Italy have managed to preserve their culture, and remain fairly insulated from the more influential Italian way of life. This is evident in their schools, language, food, housing, religious traditions, and dress. Normally their dress is rather plain, but during our second visit we saw women dressed in highly decorated colorful clothing, usually reserved for festive occasions. As they gaily pranced by us, we were told that it was in honor of our visit. As the distinctive dress of the Albanians is not as common as it was in the past, we felt privileged at this lovely display of Albanian gaiety and culture. We received more special treatment during the celebration of Sunday mass; for holidays, the housewives bake special pastries for eating after the mass, and sure enough, there was a tray of cookies left out in the back of the church for us even though it was not a holiday. Here again, the hospitality and friendship of the villagers was generous and deeply appreciated.

Another Albanian tradition in some of the towns is called "carrying the water." After the Easter procession to a hilltop shrine, the people go to the village fountain or spring and take a mouthful of water. Then they try to reach the church without spilling a drop of it. This becomes quite humorous, because those who are going to the fountain for their mouthful of water attempt to make those who have their mouths full laugh, and cause them to spit out the water. If you do spill it, then you have to go back to the fountain for more and repeat the journey. The origin of this custom is traced back to the first Albanian settlers, but its meaning is unexplained.

If the paternal side of my family were mariners, then Mom's side were the farmers—with one exception. Our cousin Nick Scutari reminds me that my mother's father Nicola worked as a seaman in the Italian merchant marine. Agriculture still plays a role in their lives and in the local economy. I always admired my mother's green thumb and that of her brother, Frank Scutari, and his wife Mary—they could grow orchids in the desert. Take my word for it, though: none of the "farmer instinct" rubbed off on me. I'd go mad living on or even near a farm. However, the Sarmento River that borders the town could probably satisfy those of my mother's family with an affinity for the water.

The trip's highlight for me was the visit to my mother's old oak tree. On a hilltop just above the village of San Costantino sits a huge old oak tree that she played in and around as a young girl. She often talked of that tree, and to her it embodied her village and her childhood. Every time she returned to the village for a visit she would go to *her* tree. And so it was during her last visit with us. One bright morning we climbed up the hill with her and her nieces who still have summer homes there; and together we turned back the calendar seventy-five years to relive some of her most cherished memories. We had heard about this old tree for years, and to see her frolicking around it like the child she used to be was deeply moving. She told us, "The only thing that was missing was the swing." After we all had a bit of a cry, took photos, and picked figs, we headed back to the family house to feast on the figs, some local cheeses, homemade bread, and local wine. Our host-families graciously shared their homes, food, music, and love, for which we say *grazie mille.*

I never knew my maternal grandparents, because my mother came to America with only her older brother Frank when she was sixteen. She probably had more influence on me than anyone else. She instilled family values in me that persist to this day, and a strong belief that the good you do for others will come back to you, sometimes in ways that are not recognizable. I guess it was her way of telling me that any good karma I accumulated in this life would assist me in this or the next life. Mom was always there for me, giving the love, support, and understanding that kids so often need during life's difficult times. She believed in my goals and in me, and never stopped telling me so, sometimes with just a smile, or with her family-famous giggle.

In time, she would become my friend. That was never the case with my father; he was always just my father. And now, although she's no longer with us, I'm sure her prayers are still helping me get over the bumps in the road.

When I was a youngster now so many years ago, she gave me two poems that have stayed with me all my life as guiding lights, as a kind of mantra. They were an introduction to the world of poetry, which would later be a source of inspiration in my life and help instill a love of poetry. The poems were not hers, but she felt that the writer expressed her feelings, and so they became her *personal letters* to me. I have not always lived up to her expectations as expressed in those poems, but I have never stopped reaching out to touch the edge. I offer the poems here hoping they can be as inspirational to some of you as they have been for me.

SON

You're here to play a part my son,
Upon this grim old earth,
And here where your lot is cast
Do credit to your birth;
Put not your faith in friends nor luck
But play your part alone;
Be not ashamed before God or man
To call your deeds your own;
Take pleasure in your duties,
And make your work your play,
And touch not toys that gamble
Your time and life away;
In all things that you undertake
Ever do the best you can,
And the world will be the better
For you'll grow to be *a man.*

—(Author unknown)

MY SON

God bless you my son and help you
To do what is always right.
Every day may he be near you
And watch over you each night.
Remember always what I have told you.
Always do the best you can,
Then I know that you will one day
Be a great and noble man.
If at time you feel discouraged,
Nothing seems to be just right,
When you feel that you are forsaken

And no longer want to fight
For the things that are good and honest
Things I taught you long ago,
Raise your head and think of Mother.
Son you know I love you so.
Take this little poem and place it
Somewhere near where you can see.
Think my son as you look on it
How I'd like my son to be.
Always help your fellow brother,
Never from your duty run,
That is all I have to say dear,
God bless you, my darling son.

MOTHER

—(Author unknown)

As much as those poems have been an inspiration to me, so has her life been an inspiration to others. Here is what my nephew (my brother's son) Christopher Camuto, an accomplished author and college professor, had to say about his grandmother.

ARBERESH

The hills of Basilicata have been waiting,
patient as time, biding your restlessness
all these years, home and not home
to a head-strong girl who wouldn't stay.

The Sarmento chatters like a gossip,
gathers weather in its rocky bed

biding your absence these long years
still conceding nothing to your dreams.

In Brooklyn, the last great old-world village,
a priest intones the high mass you wanted,
gathered generations of your loved ones
more lost in stony stares than tears.

After they have buried you, go home
to the rocky fields, the larks and falcons,
the fig trees and beech groves, lean sheep
and leaner wolves, dusty roads and stone alleys,
the creaking carts and creaking wells that
embarrassed your young heart's high hopes
so many years ago.

Your soul belongs where you were born.
You will be less lonely there, less sad.
The cuirassed pine waits on the mountain;
the white houses are sturdy and clean-swept.
In May, red scarves flutter in the dance.

—Christopher Camuto
For Dolores Scutari (1905–2002)

What I found most enchanting is the way Chris is able to capture the essence of Mom's village and surrounding area without having visited the region. That left me thirsting for more, and sure enough he comes through by telling us about the conflict between her restlessness to leave "her village" with her hidden desire to stay. I can remember her telling me many times how heart-wrenching it was to leave family and friends, knowing she might never see them again. He goes on to tell us of the mourners, not given to tears as much as the realization that someone who was a part of their lives for so many years, has now left such a void in their lives. In the end he tells us of her return to the village that has never stopped beckoning her home, where she belongs.

Although she is no longer with us, Mom's spirit is ever present. Chris's poem is one reason for that. Another is Dorine, who adored her so much that she gave her only son Nicholas the middle name of Costantino in tribute to her grandmother and the village of her youth. As further tribute, I registered Mom on The American Immigrant Wall of Honor at Ellis Island.

†

Mom, Chris's poem made me realize that, yes, you did make it back after all. For years now I have promised myself I would return to your village one more time. When I do, I will go to that hilltop and look for you at the old oak tree. Together perhaps we can even find that swing. More importantly, I hope we can sit together, reminisce, and enjoy eating figs as we so often did. I miss you.

THE END

ABOUT THE AUTHOR

Nicholas F. Starace II was born in Brooklyn, NY, and now lives in Short Hills, NJ, with his daughter Dorine and her son Nicholas IV. He graduated from the U.S. Merchant Marine Academy with a BS degree, USCG license as Third Assistant Engineer, and commission as ensign in the U.S. Navy. That was just the beginning of a career and lifestyle that would eventually take him to the four corners of the earth, visiting over eighty countries. He received a master's degree in mechanical engineering from Stevens Institute of Technology. In 2005 he earned a USCG 100 ton Captain's License, which is pending upgrade to 200 tons. In 2007 he received an Outstanding Professional Achievement Award from the U.S. Merchant Marine Academy.

A freelance writer, Starace published articles for *Sea History*, *Model Shipwright*, U.K., and the Nautical Research Guild's *Nautical Research Journal*. He has written numerous articles for ship modeling magazines, and his ship modeling awards and activities have been the subject of several newspaper articles. His paper on the sinking in 1865 of the ill-fated sidewheeler *Sultana* gained national attention. He has written book reviews for the NRG Journal. He was fortunate enough to be interviewed by

National Geographic for an article about the U.S. Merchant Marine Academy.

As an authority on ship modeling, this "Best-of-Show" craftsman has given talks on a wide variety of maritime and ship modeling subjects. His modeling philosophy has always been to build models that capture a part of America's maritime heritage. He has given ship modeling courses. A frequent speaker at club functions, he was a guest speaker at the 2000 World Marine Millennial Conference in Salem, MA, the 1989 and 1998 Nautical Research Guild Conferences, and at other exhibits and conferences. In 1985 he was interviewed on Singapore TV for an arts and crafts documentary, as founder and Commodore of the Ship Model Society of Singapore.

A turning point in his life occurred in 1982 when the first terrorist air-bomb exploded on a flight he and his wife were on from Tokyo to Hawaii. Starace had traveled far and wide and seen the world many times over. From his travels and readings he was well aware of how military conflict has changed since the founding of this country and the role his family played during half its history. But as the plane made its death-like plunge toward the sea, little did he realize that he was staring in the face of a new enemy: terrorism. Later, he would lay witness to IRA terrorist bombings in London and 9/11 in NY.

Readers interested in Asian cultures will be intrigued by his many exotic excursions. Some may find solace reading about family battles with cancer and schizophrenia, won and lost. Others may be inspired by Starace's efforts at acting and screen modeling hobbies, which led to memberships in the Screen Actors Guild and American Federation of Television & Radio Artists. Some will get a sense of the gratification that comes with doing volunteer work at a

VA hospital. Another segment of the book chronicles the gradual failure of a thirty-four-year marriage and ponders how—or if—divorced couples ever find closure. Military enthusiasts will marvel at the emotional drama experienced during visits to Normandy and Iwo Jima commemorating the fiftieth and sixtieth anniversaries of the battles. That is a mere glimpse of his emotional rollercoaster ride through a life of adventure, heartache, and achievement. There is so much diversity here that it has the kind of appeal that only a modern-day renaissance man like Starace can foster.

Starace received the Badge of Honor from the Minister of Defense, Taiwan, for his U.S. naval service when Communist China bombarded Taiwan's offshore islands of Quemoy and Matsu during the 1958 Taiwan Straits Crisis. That medal complements others he received: National Defense Medal, Naval Reserve Medal, Outstanding Volunteer Service Medal, as well as five military service ribbons. Of his military service, Starace relates the lessons learned while serving under Medal-of-Honor winner Captain John D. Bulkeley of World War II PT Boat fame. It was his PT boat squadron that evacuated General Douglas MacArthur from the Philippines.

The Staraces had come to this country after it finally emerged from the shadows of a dreadful civil war, and saw it segue from a strong nation into an international superpower. Meanwhile, they labored in its shipyards, learned in its classrooms, toiled in its shops, prayed in its churches, sailed under its flag, and fought and died in its wars. For that, Nick Starace owes it everything, and *White Sails Became Me* is both a tribute to their seafaring heritage and a microcosm of the vast evolution that America underwent since they first set foot on its docks.